W9-BZH-786

WHALE WATCHING

Discovery Communications, Inc.
John S. Hendricks, *Founder, Chairman, and Chief Executive Officer*
Judith A. McHale, *President and Chief Operating Officer*
Michela English, *President, Discovery Enterprises Worldwide*
Raymond Cooper, *Senior Vice President, Discovery Enterprises Worldwide*

Discovery Publishing
Natalie Chapman, *Publishing Director*
Rita Thievon Mullin, *Editorial Director*
Mary Kalamaras, *Senior Editor*
Maria Mihalik Higgins, *Editor*
Kimberly Small, *Senior Marketing Manager*
Chris Alvarez, *Business Development*

Discovery Channel Retail
Tracy Fortini, *Product Development*
Steve Manning, *Naturalist*

Insight Guides
Jeremy Westwood, *Managing Director*
Brian Bell, *Editorial Director*
John Gattuso, *Series Editor*
Siu-Li Low, *General Manager, Books*

Distribution
United States
Langenscheidt Publishers, Inc.
46-35 54th Road, Maspeth, NY 11378
Fax: 718-784-0640

Worldwide
APA Publications GmbH & Co.
Verlag KG Singapore Branch, Singapore
38 Joo Koon Road, Singapore 628990
Tel: 65-865-1600. Fax: 65-861-6438

Printed by Insight Print Services (Pte) Ltd., 38 Joo Koon Road, Singapore 628990.

Whale watching / Nicky Leach, editor.
    p. cm. -- (Discovery travel adventures)
      (Insight guides)
    Includes index.
    ISBN 1-56331-836-9 (alk. paper)
    1. Cetacea. 2. Whale watching Guidebooks. I.
Leach, Nicky J. II. Series. III. Series: Insight guides
(Bethesda, Md.)
  QL737.C4W433 1999
  599.5--dc21   99-36005
                                        CIP

*T*his book combines the interests and enthusiasm of two of the world's best-known information providers: **Insight Guides**, whose titles have set the standard for visual travel guides since 1970, and **Discovery Communications**, the world's premier source of nonfiction television programming. The editors of Insight Guides provide both practical advice and general understanding about a destination's history, culture, institutions, and people. Discovery Communications and its website, www.discovery.com, help millions of viewers explore their world from the comfort of their home and encourage them to explore it firsthand.

About This Book

Whale Watching reflects the work of a dedicated team of editors and writers who have in-depth knowledge of the best whale watching in North America. Series editor **John Gattuso**, of Stone Creek Publications in New Jersey, worked with Insight Guides and Discovery Communications to conceive and direct the series. Gattuso turned to Seattle writer and editor **Nicky Leach** to manage the project. Author of many books and articles on travel and nature, and a veteran of other titles in this series, Leach says the subject matter immediately attracted her. "I live in an area where whales are close enough to feel like kin. This project has deepened my understanding and appreciation of cetaceans and made me care passionately about their future."

All of the writers in this book are similarly drawn to whales. Alaska writer **Kieran Mulvaney** wrote his introductory chapters on cetaceans from a Greenpeace ship in the Bering Sea. A co-founder of the Whale and Dolphin Conservation Society, Kieran covers marine issues for discovery.com and *E!* magazine, among other publications, and is the author of several books. He vividly recalls paddling among a hundred minke whales in the Antarctic one night at 3 A.M. "They were feeding on a krill swarm and were completely uninterested in us," he says.

Lisa Busch and **Robert Woolsey** are writers and radio producers in Southeast Alaska, where they watch wintering humpbacks from their office window. "Living in Sitka, it's difficult not to think about whales; they're always in the back of your mind somewhere," Woolsey says. Their documentary, *Songs of the Humpback Whale*, led to a fascination with these creatures evident in their chapters on whale song, cetacean society, and preparing for a whale-watching trip.

Travel and science writer **Beth Livermore** covered Stellwagen Bank, a popular whale-watching spot off the Massachusetts coast. Livermore visits the area frequently to stay with family and observe whales. Her work has been recognized with journalism fellowships at MIT and the Marine Biological Laboratory at Woods Hole, Massachusetts. **Wayne Curtis** didn't have to travel far from his home on the Maine coast to find whales. Author of guidebooks on New England and maritime Canada, Curtis wrote about beluga whales in the St. Lawrence River, endangered northern right whales off the Atlantic Provinces, and a variety of species in the Gulf of Maine. Yankee whaling history is a favorite subject of New Jersey writer and editor **Ed Jardim**, who traces much of his fascination with the ocean to his Portuguese ancestry.

Alaska author, photographer, and biologist **Tom Walker** covered whale watching on the Last Frontier. For more than seven years, Walker has devoted part of the summer to observing humpbacks and orcas in

Southeast Alaska. "One of the highlights of my career was watching a pod of orcas pass through a group of feeding humpbacks, causing one animal from each species to breach," he recalls. Canadian writer **Bruce Obee** has specialized in wildlife and environmental issues since the mid-1970s and co-authored *Guardians of the Whales* with researcher Graeme Ellis. For this book, he covered the orca-rich waters around his home on Vancouver Island. "Once you've seen wild whales, you'll invariably search the horizon for spouts whenever you're near the ocean," he says. Farther south, Oregon travel writer and editor **Bonnie Henderson** explored whale-watching trips off the wild coast of Washington and Oregon.

A **stylized killer whale** (above), or orca, adorns a wall mural in Juneau, Alaska.

The **16-foot-long flippers** of the humpback whale (opposite) led New England biologists to name it *megaptera novaeangliae*, or "great winged New Englander."

Orcas (below) are toothed whales in the same family as dolphins.

The **sperm whale** (following pages), wrote Herman Melville, "lives not complete in any literature. Far above all other hunted whales, his is an unwritten life."

Journalist **Glen Martin**, who covered whale watching along the California coast, contributes to *Discover, Audubon,* and other magazines and has written a guide to wildlife refuges in North America. He fondly recalls spouting fin whales keeping him awake on a kayak trip to Baja California. "We just stretched out, looked at the stars, and listened to the whales," he laughs. Boston writer **Dick Russell**'s close encounters with gray whales in Baja were "among the most inspiring of my life," he says. He contributes often to *E!* and *Amicus Journal* and recently wrote about the Makah Indian whale hunt. He has published two books and is at work on a new volume about gray whales.

Oregon author **Beth Hege Piatote** is a member of the Nez Percé Nation and first learned of indigenous relationships with whales from Inuit poet Fred Bigjim. In 1998, she traveled to the Makah Indian Reservation to learn and write about the complex issues surrounding indigenous whaling today. The Makah aren't far from the Port Townsend, Washington, home of natural-history writer **David Gordon**, whose chapter on whale lore spans the ages, from ancient Greek to contemporary stories.

"We have a lot to learn from whales and dolphins and should do it on their terms," says poet and environmental activist **Janisse Ray**, who traveled to the Bahamas for her chapter on dolphin watching around the Bimini Islands. She is a former editor of *Florida Wildlife* magazine, and her latest book is *Ecology of a Cracker Childhood*. Massachusetts marine biologist **Nathalie Ward** covers whale watching around the Caribbean island of Dominica. She directs the Eastern Caribbean Cetacean Network and has written five children's books about cetaceans and a guide to Stellwagen Bank. Award-winning Hawaii writer **Rita Ariyoshi** contributes to *Omni, National Geographic Traveler*, and other magazines, and she wrote the best-selling book *Maui on My Mind*. Humpback whales are also often on her mind. "I went whale watching on my birthday once," she tells us, "and God sent me a dozen whales."

Our thanks to the Whale and Dolphin Conservation Society for reviewing the manuscript. The organization, based in the United Kingdom, has helped to fund research and conservation, educate the public, and lobby on behalf of cetaceans since 1987. For contact information, see the Resource Directory at the back of this book. Thanks also to Stone Creek's editorial team: Judith Dunham, Michael Castagna, Nicole Buchenholz, Bruce Hopkins, and Edward A. Jardim.

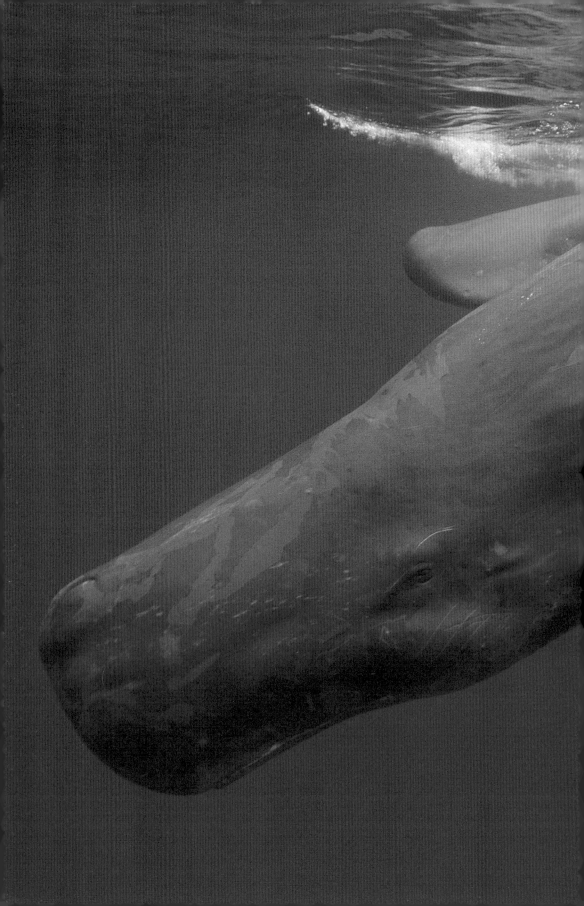

Table of Contents

INTRODUCTION

Making Contact 18
by Nicky Leach

SECTION ONE: BETWEEN TWO WORLDS

1   **Myths and Monsters** 24
     by David George Gordon

2   **Yankee Whalers** 28
     by Edward A. Jardim

3   **A Question of Survival** 34
     by Kieran Mulvaney

4   **Going on a Whale Watch** 40
     by Lisa Busch and Robert Woolsey

SECTION TWO: SECRET LIFE OF WHALES

5   **What Is a Whale?** 50
     by Kieran Mulvaney

6   **How Smart Are They?** 54
     by Kieran Mulvaney

7   **Cetacean Society** 60
     by Lisa Busch and Robert Woolsey

8   **Whale Song** 68
     by Lisa Busch and Robert Woolsey

9   **Who's Watching Whom?** 74
     by Kieran Mulvaney

SECTION THREE: WHALE-WATCHING DESTINATIONS

10   St. Lawrence River, Québec 82
          by Wayne Curtis

11   Atlantic Provinces, Canada 90
          by Wayne Curtis

12   Gulf of Maine 98
          by Wayne Curtis

13   Stellwagen Bank National Marine Sanctuary,
          Massachusetts 108
          by Beth Livermore

14   Bimini Islands, Bahamas 118
          by Janisse Ray

15   Dominica, Lesser Antilles 128
          by Nathalie Ward

16   San Ignacio Lagoon, Baja California, Mexico 136
          by Dick Russell

17   Santa Barbara and the Channel Islands, California 144
          by Glen Martin

18   Monterey Bay National Marine Sanctuary, California . . . 154
          by Glen Martin

19   Oregon and Washington Coast 164
          by Bonnie Henderson

20   British Columbia and Northern Washington 174
          by Bruce Obee

21   Southeast Alaska 186
          by Tom Walker

22   Maui, Hawaii 196
          by Rita Ariyoshi

          Resource Directory 206

          Index 219

MAPS

St. Lawrence River, Québec   **84**

Atlantic Provinces, Canada   **92**

Gulf of Maine   **100**

Stellwagen Bank, Massachusetts   **110**

Bimini Islands, Bahamas   **120**

Dominica, Lesser Antilles   **130**

Baja California, Mexico   **139**

Channel Islands, California   **147**

Monterey Bay, California   **157**

Oregon and Washington Coast   **167**

British Columbia and Northern   **177**
Washington

Southeast Alaska   **189**

Maui, Hawaii   **198**

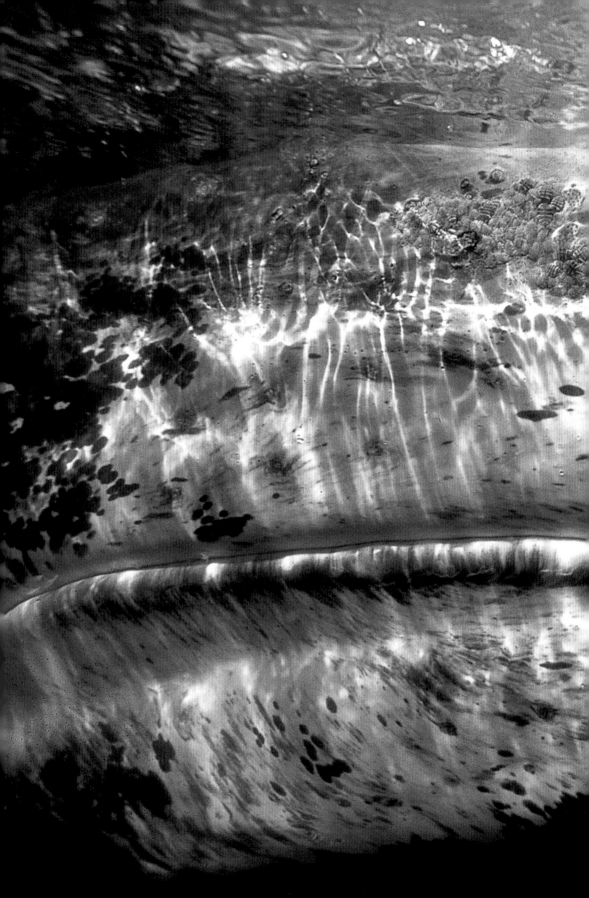

They come in an array of sizes and colors, straight out of the Outsize Department. Large, larger, and Brobdingnagian. Chubby and massive. Slow and speedy. With teeth and without. Their shiny skin glistens black, gray, white, beige, spotted, two-tone. Their heads, dorsal fins, flippers, and tails carry the marks of lives spent negotiating the world's oceans. They chatter, sing, click, clang, whistle, huff, snore, and snuffle. They are whales and dolphins, the group known as cetaceans, sovereigns of the deep and playful pranksters of the waves.   ◆   There's no doubt that we're completely smitten with cetaceans. In one recent year, 5.4 million people in 65 countries took to the seas and rivers to experience the thrill of watching whales and dolphins in the wild, and the number keeps on growing. After years of worshiping them, demonizing them, and using them for our own gain, we are beginning to see cetaceans as important co-habitants on the Earth instead of merely commodities for our own

Whales and dolphins have much to teach us about our own place in the web of life.

survival. And survive they must. The ability of these fellow mammals to overcome toxic pollution and other manmade environmental dangers, not to mention the continued warfare of commercial hunting, is tied to our own future on this planet.   ◆   And there is something more. Naturalist and writer Diane Ackerman suggests: "Human beings possess such immense powers that few animals cause us to feel truly humble. A whale does, swimming beside you, as big as a reclining building, its eye carefully observing you. It could easily devastate you with a twitch, yet it doesn't." When we experience large and powerful creatures exhibiting such gentle behavior toward humans, we are changed somehow, moved beyond the

Diver and dolphin. "Only … in rare and hidden moments of communion with nature," wrote naturalist Loren Eiseley, "does man briefly escape his solitary destiny."

Preceding pages: Humpback cow and calf; gray-whale encounter, Mexico; swimming with wild dolphins, Bahamas; breaching humpback, Alaska.

A mural of humpbacks (left) enlivens a wall at an Oahu yacht harbor.

Petroglyphs of killer whales (below) in Washington were carved centuries ago by Makah Indians.

Gray whales (right) seem to enjoy human company in the lagoons of Baja California.

rational into the mysterious realms of the heart. In the end, dolphin researcher Toni Frohoff says: " ... being in the presence of another species I have learned how to be more human."

To be more human. To take our place in the community of creatures. What an enormous responsibility that is. The technological advances of the 20th century brought exciting gains but cannot tell us the right way to live as embrace the challenges of the 21st. We are beginning to realize just how much we can learn from other cultures, even other species. If whales, once land-based mammals related to ungulates, returned to the oceans and obtained mastery there, perhaps humans will one day cross other boundaries, too. What can we learn from whales? And how will we put this precious knowledge to use?

Fortunately, there are innumerable opportunities to find out. With an increasing number of tour operators offering regular and reasonably priced access, it is easier than ever to follow the seasonal travels of whales along the North American coast. We can float close to grays in tranquil Baja California lagoons and watch them from land as they make their way north along the West Coast to summer feeding grounds in Alaska. We can revel in the acrobatics of humpbacks in the Eastern Caribbean and accompany them north to Cape Cod and beyond. We can kayak among orcas off the Northwest coast, play with wild dolphins in the Bahamas, and boat among ice-white belugas in the St. Lawrence River. We can pray for a glimpse of the world's largest creature, the blue whale, off California, or even of the northern right whale, the world's most endangered whale, from a New England shore.

This book is just the beginning. Go explore the possibilities. The ocean – the Whale Road of the Anglo-Saxons – beckons.

♦

Between Two Worlds

♦

Dangerous devilfish? Undersea gods?
Intelligent kin? The complex relationship
between whales and people goes back to the
dawn of time and reveals an evolving human
engagement with the natural world.

CHAPTER 1

Don't fret if your friends call you a whale hugger. Instead, draw strength from the knowledge that our current affection for all things cetacean can be traced to the very dawn of Western civilization, some 7,000 to 10,000 years ago. ◆ In one of the earliest recorded creation myths, the heavens, earth, and all humankind are born from the body of the whale woman Omorka, slain by Marduk, the supreme being of the Mesopotamian pantheon. This ancient Babylonian story was later enfolded into the mythology of the Greeks, who pitted the sun god Apollo against the monster Delphyne in a similar fight to the death. After this struggle, Apollo assumed the title Delphinios, or Dolphin God. He built the famous shrine at Delphi, or Dolphin Town, and instituted a festival called – what else? – Delphina, to celebrate his triumph. ◆ Whales and dolphins played more positive roles in other myths and legends from

From Greek mythology to New Age literature, whales and dolphins have played on our imaginations for centuries.

Greek antiquity. In the most famous of these, the poet Arion is said to have been sailing from southern Italy when his Corinthian shipmates threatened to rob and murder him on the spot. Arion was granted one final request: to sing a short verse before voluntarily tossing himself and his lyre overboard. So beautiful was his song that it attracted a dolphin, which plucked the lucky lad from the sea and, bearing him on its back, carried him to safety on the shore of Taenarum. ◆ Contained in the texts of early Greek and Roman historians is a roster of equally fortunate folk. In his *Natural History*, Pliny the Elder reported four separate instances from the first century A.D. of dolphins ferrying young boys and girls around the Mediterranean.

Sea monsters resembling whales have an appetite for ships and sailors in this medieval engraving.

Preceding pages: A migrating gray whale in a kelp bed off the California coast.

Aeolian, a contemporary of the scholar Aristotle, contributed three more of these tales in his essay *On Animals*. According to Aeolian, residents of one Greek village even recruited wild dolphins to herd fish into their nets.

Other chroniclers wrote of wild dolphins escorting lost seafarers to safe harbors, or of dolphins wrapping their bodies around ships' anchors and augmenting these holdfasts during fierce storms. This latter image – of a dolphin-entwined anchor – was a common emblem of Roman emperors and popes, signifying intelligence, speed, and steadfastness.

"Such unexpected benevolence," notes the scholar Charles Dorias in an essay from *Mind in the Waters*, "bespeaks a time when enough mutuality existed between people and the animate world that neither was afraid to entrust whole-heartedly and cooperatively, even lovingly, their bodies and souls to each other." Not only humans but the gods themselves were frequently portrayed astride dolphins on pottery, statues, and coins from this blissful period, Dorias points out.

Whale Tales

Just as dolphins were revered in some cultures, whales were feared in others. Representing the dark side of early cetacean-human interactions is the story of Jonah and the Whale. This biblical theme of involuntary engulfment is echoed in numerous works, including *Gargantua and Pantagruel*, *Baron Munchausen*, and *The Adventures of Pinocchio*. Not surprisingly, the malevolence of the whale becomes multiplied in each retelling: While Jonah's giant-sized swallower is described as "a great fish," Pinocchio's is branded a "sea monster," one whose alleged rampages had earned it the nickname "Attila of fish and fishermen."

The colorful stories of 18th- and 19th-century seafarers did little to restore the tarnished reputation of what by now had been dubbed the devilfish – a formidable adversary capable, with one swipe of its fluke, of smashing whalers' longboats and maiming or killing their crews. "I am touched by a certain sadness when I leaf through the volumes of ancient folklore," confessed the late Jacques Cousteau.

Meemf·Inue

Totemic animals like this killer whale (opposite, top) are often depicted in the art of Northwest coastal tribes.

A stranded whale (opposite, bottom) dwarfs curious onlookers in an Esaias van den Velde painting from the early 17th century.

Jonah (left) is released by the whale in this 16th-century engraving.

Saint Brendan (below), a sixth-century Irish monk, erects an altar on the back of a sleeping whale.

"Rising from the pages are images of monsters from the deep, overturning ships and attacking men. I know that it has been the other way around in real life."

New Age Gurus

In more recent years, with the collapse of large-scale commercial whaling operations and the establishment of marine parks and dolphinariums, cetaceans have regained much of their ancestral status as figures of worship. They've re-entered our daily lives, not just on coins and pottery but as inspirational images on everything from jewelry and T-shirts to posters, refrigerator magnets, and wall-sized murals.

Many of these contemporary depictions are remarkably similar to those of ancient Greece and Rome. Such is the case with Flipper, the friendly bottlenose dolphin and star of a popular TV series in the late 1960s. Still alive in the land of afternoon reruns, this helpful cetacean continues to rescue the poets and peasants of his native southern Florida on a regular basis.

Far less of today's adoration, however, is focused on the good deeds of whales and dolphins toward humankind. Largely through the work of scientists like John Lilly, who first popularized the idea of cetacean intelligence and human-dolphin communication, and through a variety of environmental groups, who have established the value of whales in ecological terms, we've come to appreciate these sleek, graceful, and highly intelligent beings on their own terms. Along with this appreciation has come renewed reverence – and the recognition that these icons are indeed our warm-blooded kin.

Yankee Whalers

The nation's true "founding fathers," said historian Fernand Braudel, were her sailors, the ubiquitous Jack Tars and courageous captains whose maritime endeavors transformed a colonial outpost into a world power. The stars of the show were the Yankee whalers, part of the New England fishing fleet that had first gained fame for the colonies. Perhaps when the Massachusetts legislators ordered a replica of the "sacred cod" hung on the State House wall, they would have done well to have considered the whale, too. ◆ American whaling had its start on Long Island, Cape Cod, and other coastal points in the Northeast. Early settlers had watched Native Americans corralling and killing whales that had strayed too close to shore or become beached. Using more efficient tools and techniques, the colonials organized their own lookout systems for coastal whaling, then raised their pursuits up a few notches by venturing far out into the ocean. ◆ At the forefront of the fledgling industry was Nantucket, which recorded its first catch in 1672. Forty years later, a whaling ship blown far out to sea captured a sperm whale and accidentally uncovered spermaceti, the waxy substance that became invaluable in making dripless candles. Soon ships were pushing out ever farther, and by the 1770s the colonies had 360 vessels and nearly 5,000 sailors engaged in whaling. ◆ Even the seaworthy English, long aware of the potential of whaling, were impressed. Addressing fellow parliamentarians in his famous tribute to Yankee enterprise in 1774, Edmund Burke tried to heal the widening British-American rift by commending the colonists to his countrymen: "Look at the manner in which the New England people

New England whalers sailed the globe in search of wealth and adventure.

Death throes. Harpooned and gunshot, a sperm whale turns belly up in its final moments of life in this mid-19th-century painting by Robert Walker Weir, Jr., at Massachusetts' Kendall Whaling Museum.

carry on the whale fishers. No sea, but what is vexed with their fisheries – no climate that is not witness to their toils."

But for the Yankee whalers, the best was yet to come. By the time George Washington took up his presidential duties, they were rounding Cape Horn intent on tapping the lode of the vast Pacific. And tap it they did, decimating sperm whales in the South Seas, then turning north to chase huge bowheads off Canada and Alaska into the Bering Strait and the Japanese fishing grounds. Fortunes were being made through the sacrifice of whales, and other ports along the Atlantic coast got

into the act, places such as Edgartown, New London, and Sag Harbor. Whaling reached a crescendo in 1846, with 735 vessels and a business worth $21 million.

Motley Mariners

The deeper-hulled ships had difficulty crossing the sandbar in Nantucket harbor, and that struck the death knell for the island's whaling industry. Nantucket was soon surpassed by New Bedford, which, with its more accessible mainland bay, was able to dis- patch hundreds of vessels a year. The ships carried thousands of seamen, as well as the

occasional captain's wife. On land, thousands more were involved in auxiliary services: caulkers, coopers, chandlers, sailmakers, har- poon-makers, and all sorts of specialists.

"We were a town of tars," the *New York Tribune*'s Charles Congdon wrote in 1880, as he reminisced about the New Bedford of his youth a half-century earlier. "We had often walking about swarthy Portuguese sailors, and mariners of the true broad-bottomed Dutch type, puffing their long pipes mildly." The mariners were an increasingly motley crew. There were landlubber farmhands and urban drifters, African Americans and American Indians, Englishmen and Irishmen, western Azoreans and multihued Cape Verdeans. Also present were South Sea Islanders, known as "Kanakas," who would become the models for Queequeg in Herman Melville's literary classic *Moby Dick*.

It was an adventur- ous but often grisly and tedious life (Dr. Johnson wondered why men go to sea when there are jails on shore).

Whaling was dirty work – small wonder that proper naval types and merchant mariners held their noses as the stinking masses of blubber were boiled down in nightlong infernos. Exploita- tion was rife. Voyages were excessively long: about 36 months on average. Life in the forecastle was foul and cramped, the food notoriously unsatisfying. Ordinary seamen and other lesser types were assigned minuscule "lays," or shares, then charged exorbitantly for "slop chest" items like tools and tobacco. Some captains who were pious churchgoers at home turned crotchety, if not demonic, at sea.

Mutiny and Mayhem

Desertion was common – sometimes actually encouraged to cut down on expenses – and so was death. Sailors fell from masts, contracted malaria, went down with ships that foundered in fierce gales, or were torn apart on treacherous shoals. Natives attacked on land and sea, and mutinies could turn ugly indeed, as in the rebellion aboard the *Globe* in Hawaii in 1823 when an ax-wielding Samuel Comstock and other rebels bludgeoned

the captain and two officers to death. Before the *Globe* returned to Nantucket, most of the mutineers, including Comstock, had done each other in or been dispatched by the Mulgrave Islanders they had maltreated.

Then there was the whale itself, a clear and present

danger if ever there was one. The moment of truth came with the lookout's signal from above: "Thar she blows!" – sometimes transmuted as "Thar blows" or "A-a-a-a blows." To which came the captain's quick response: "Where away?" and his call to action.

A whaleman (opposite, top) aboard the *Gaspe* in 1922 demonstrates the size of a sperm whale's flukes.

Iron harpoons (left) were often bent by struggling whales.

Moby Dick (below) is depicted with "harpoons all twisted and wrenched within him" in this Richard Ellis mural. Melville (top, right) based much of his tale on his own experiences aboard a whaler.

Herman Melville and the Great White Whale

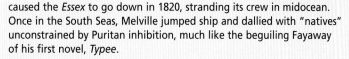

Call him wanderer. In the closing days of 1840, a young and vaguely disenchanted Herman Melville found himself in bustling New Bedford seeking adventure aboard a whaler. The *Acushnet* was a drab ship, its captain crotchety. Nonetheless, Melville became fascinated with stories of enraged whales ramming ships, such as the whale that caused the *Essex* to go down in 1820, stranding its crew in midocean. Once in the South Seas, Melville jumped ship and dallied with "natives" unconstrained by Puritan inhibition, much like the beguiling Fayaway of his first novel, *Typee*.

When it was time to move on again, more adventures followed, and eventually Melville sailed home on a U.S. Navy man-of-war. He was horrified by the captain's practice of flogging and succeeded, through his vivid recounting in *White-Jacket*, in persuading Congress to outlaw such cruel and barbarous treatment.

Mining his experiences, the seaman-turned-author produced a series of works that secured him a place in a literary pantheon that includes such contemporaries as Nathaniel Hawthorne and Walt Whitman. In Melville's masterly *Moby Dick*, the *Acushnet* becomes the *Pequod* and the skipper is transformed into the brooding, peg-legged Captain Ahab, obsessed with taking revenge against the monster white whale of Mocha-Dick legend that caused his deformity. The mad pursuit pulls down all but Ishmael, who, of course, is patterned after Melville himself.

Alas, Melville's own reputation also plummeted. He lived out his days as a customs functionary, brooded over the suicide of his son, and died in 1891 with no inkling of the artistic resurrection that would cause hordes of literary scholars (and countless term papers) to plumb Melvillean themes of good versus evil and feckless man opposing primordial nature.

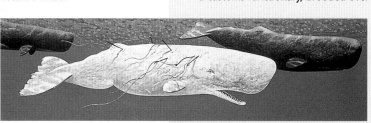

Ambergris

It's an "ugh-ahh" paradox: a foul-smelling substance emanating, it seems, from a sperm whale's intestine (ugh) that lets fine perfumes stay as sweet as they are (ahh).

Ambergris, soft and black in its original shape, is thought to form from feces that collect around the whale's undigested seafood particles. Its rare nature makes it precious, but sometimes large pieces are found. In the latter years of the 19th century, the *Charles W. Morgan* reeled in a whale that produced a mind-boggling 800 pounds of the stuff, enriching Capt. James A. M. Earle and all concerned to the tune of nearly $150,000.

The name comes from its color – amber gray – and the product has been used since antiquity to keep the floral essence of perfumes from dissipating. It is, therefore, a fixative, although Asian chefs have been known to use it as a seasoning in some of their more exotic dishes, and it's used in some countries as a drug.

Ambergris (left) was used as an aphrodisiac, a fixative in perfume, and a treatment for indigestion and convulsions.

A sperm whale (bottom) demolishes a whale boat in *The Other End of the Whale* by Charles S. Raleigh, 1877, at the Kendall Whaling Museum.

Whale oil was used in the making of soap (opposite, top) and candles.

Harpooners deliver the coup de grace in *A Tough Old Bull* (opposite, bottom) by 19th-century artist W. H. Overend.

Into the boats they went for a duel that could take hours. And what a foolhardy enterprise it was! Six men in a puny whaleboat taking on the lord of the ocean thousands of miles from nowhere. The mate coaxed on the oarsmen in a whiny singsong: "Oh, will ye pull, laddies!" to go at the whale from front, side, or rear. The harpooner struck, and the oarsmen backed off fast.

One thrash of those powerful flukes could make splinters of boat and boatsmen alike. Harpooned whales might carry men off to eternity, or the rope that whizzed from coils could prove fatally entangling, as the *Directory of Whaling Masters* attests: "Capt. Charles Dyer taken out of boat by foul line, Aug. 29, 1828." "Capt. John Browne died, fast to a whale." "Capt. Silas Cottle

taken down by whale, Feb. 19, 1856." "Capt. Abraham T. Eddy died from injuries inflicted by whale, July 1835." "Capt. Jesse Luce killed by whale, Mar. 1848." "Capt. John M. Russell lost overboard."

Most dreadful of all disasters was the sinking of the *Essex*, a whaler out of Nantucket that had been rammed twice by an enraged whale in 1820, its crew hopelessly stranded in three boats in the mid-Pacific. Three months later, five emaciated survivors somehow made it to the South American coast. They told a chilling tale of aching hunger, death, and cannibalism. Nantucketers heard with shock that lots had been drawn to decide who would be sacrificed – as it turned out, pathetically, the captain's own nephew. The story of the *Essex* cast a pall for a long time to come and fired Melville's imagination.

But such disasters didn't slow the killing. Yankee

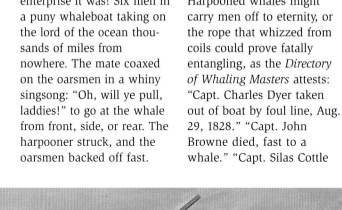

whalers were brutally efficient as they decimated whale populations in every corner of the world. Some species, such as the northern right whale, were so severely diminished that they still haven't recovered. By the 1840s, however, the heyday of whaling was almost over. A devastating fire on Nantucket in 1846 finished the industry there for good, and New Bedford's days were numbered, too. America's future now lay out West, where a new frontier seemed a whole lot more attractive than the dangerous life at sea. Horace Greeley's famous admonition, "Go west, young man," was answered by a loud cry of "Eureka!" in California. The helter-skelter gold rush of 1849 siphoned off entire crews at San Francisco, at a time when shipping agents – more properly dubbed "sharks" – were beating the bushes for seamen.

Dodging Death

Other dangers confronted whalers still taking to the seas. During the Civil War, Confederate raiders sank Yankee whalers by the dozens. Then in 1871, more than 30 ships were trapped in Arctic ice, with huge financial consequences, and there was a similar loss five years later. Most damaging of all was the discovery of petroleum in 1859, rendering whale oil an outdated commodity. Nor did it help when fashion dictated that ladies shed their whalebone corsets. New England investors, ever perspicacious, shifted their interest from whaling to textiles.

Yankee whaling began to ebb around 1850 and the

industry sputtered into near oblivion early in the 20th century. It was the end of the line. Spotting one another in later years, it is said, former comrades were apt to greet one another in the spirit of the old days. Cupping hands to mouth, the greeter would initiate the following exchange:

"Thar she blows!"

"Where away?"

"Two points on the lee bow, sir!"

"Haul up the mainsail! Prepare to lower all boats!"

A Question of Survival

They came slowly at first, one or two appearing on the beach. They generated some local interest, an element of concern, but they weren't obviously a harbinger of anything more serious. Swiftly, however, the floodgates opened. Over the summer of 1987, several hundred bottlenose dolphins washed up dead along the mid-Atlantic coast from New Jersey to Florida. Every day, it seemed, brought fresh reports of new carcasses. By early 1988, the total had reached 750. Even more remarkable than the numbers was the dolphins' condition. Their skin was peeling off, and their bodies were covered with sores and lesions. In the words of one scientist, they looked as if they had been "dipped in acid." ◆ The scale of the disaster was unprecedented in American history. Subsequently, however, a series of similar events occurred around the world:

Whales and dolphins are at risk in an increasingly human-dominated world. Is it too late to save them?

striped dolphins in the Mediterranean between 1990 and 1992; bottlenose dolphins in the Gulf of Mexico in 1990, 1992, and 1994; and various dolphins and whales in the Gulf of California in 1997. The causes are complex and varied, but they demonstrate that despite our love of whales and dolphins and our pleasure in seeing them in their natural habitat, cetaceans and their environment are being critically stressed by human activities. ◆ Chief among these activities is whale hunting, which has been outlawed with only a few exceptions. And those exceptions continue to take to the seas. The *Nisshin Maru* is typical. Drifting on the stormy Southern Ocean, the whaler is a black and imposing 7,000-ton steel hulk. Blood spills through the scuppers as, up on deck, the crew dismembers and packages a minke whale just brought aboard by a

A rescuer attempts to save a long-beaked dolphin stranded on a beach in San Diego, California.

catcher vessel, the sleek, gray, battleship-like *Kyo Maru No.1.*

The *Nisshin Maru* and its accompanying three catchers are the last vestiges of a whaling fleet that once swarmed across the world's oceans. At its peak, in 1937–38, the whaling industry killed 55,000 whales in the Southern Ocean alone. Now, commercial whaling limps on in only three geographic regions – the Antarctic, a small patch of the North Pacific, and an area off the coast of Norway – accounting for a kill of a little over 1,000 whales annually.

But, over the centuries, the damage has been done. The right whale disappeared from the Bay of Biscay, probably during the 16th century, as a result of predation by Basque whalers. The Atlantic gray whale was exterminated by the end of the 17th century. Today, other populations still struggle for survival. The North Atlantic right whale numbers about 300. A generous estimate puts the Western Pacific gray-whale population at 200. The blue whale, the Earth's largest creature, has been reduced to a fraction of its pre-exploitation numbers in the Southern Hemisphere.

In 1982, the International Whaling Commission (IWC) voted for an indefinite global moratorium on commercial whaling. Japan, however, continues its operations in Antarctica and the North Pacific by calling them "scientific research," and Norway received an exemption because it lodged an official objection to the moratorium decision. Today, the number of whales killed by whaling fleets is far lower than it used to be, but with whaling nations continuing to press the IWC for full-scale resumption of commercial whaling, the future of whales still lies in the pendulum swing of science and public opinion.

Smaller Kills

Even if commercial whaling were to resume, the kill numbers would not compare with those of smaller whales, dolphins, and porpoises that

Cetaceans in Captivity

It's a sunny, summer day. The crowd is abuzz as a killer whale swims round the pool. Suddenly, reacting to a subtle signal from its trainer, the orca leaps through a hoop and flops back into the water with a giant splash. There is a collective gasp, then thunderous applause.

Many people regard this sort of performance as entertaining and educational. Others think it's demeaning and cruel. Whatever your point of view, there's no denying that the keeping of cetaceans in captivity is a controversial topic.

Proponents argue that whale and dolphin shows are an opportunity to teach audiences about cetacean behavior and the importance of conservation. Critics claim that such performances put the animals under physical and psychological stress and lead the public to view cetaceans as little more than a circus act.

One flash point in the controversy is the story of Keiko, the orca that starred in the 1993 film *Free Willy*. While audiences thrilled at the dramatic liberation of celluloid "Willy," his real-life counterpart, Keiko, was languishing in a cramped and overheated pool in Mexico City. Widespread public concern led to his removal in January 1996 to the Oregon Coast Aquarium, where he was gradually nursed back to health. Keiko was later shipped to an isolated pen in an Icelandic bay near the spot where he had been captured. It remains to be seen whether he can survive in the wild. His fans remain hopeful that someday he will swim with his own kind.

Keiko (above), the orca featured in the film *Free Willy*, was popular with visitors to the Oregon Coast Aquarium.

A fishing net (opposite, top) entangles a humpback off Nova Scotia. A unique partnership between conservationists and fishers now helps free them.

A researcher (right) rescues a harbor porpoise from a herring weir in Canada's Bay of Fundy.

continue to be hunted worldwide. In Peru, at least 10,000 dolphins are killed annually. Sixteen of the 21 small cetacean species known to occur in Japanese waters are hunted regularly. Catches of Dall's porpoises alone exceed 10,000, sometimes as much as 17,000. Even though catches of striped dolphins have declined in recent years, the IWC Scientific Committee has nevertheless expressed "its great concern about the status of the striped dolphin stock."

Many environmentalists have campaigned for the IWC to accept responsibility for managing the hunts of these so-called small cetaceans, as it does commercial whaling of larger whale species. Other observers point out that,

although cetaceans are involved in both, commercial whaling and hunting of small cetaceans have little in common. They argue that the latter would be ill served by what is essentially a fisheries convention. With a few exceptions, they say, many hunts of small cetaceans occur in poorer, less developed nations against a backdrop of social, political, environmental, and economic problems. Cetacean hunting, therefore, takes place because of the lack of alternatives to overexploited traditional food sources; because dolphin meat provides a free alternative to fish, which might otherwise be expensive to catch or buy; and because of perceived conflicts with local fisheries.

Such conflicts are regularly

a source of human hostility toward cetaceans. Fishermen sometimes kill dolphins because they believe the cetaceans are eating "their" fish. This problem reached its nadir in Japan between 1976 and 1982, when fishermen on Iki Island killed more than 6,000 cetaceans in an apparent attempt to protect local yellowtail. Millions of

other dolphins and whales have died as "incidental takes" in fisheries around the world.

Watchdogs at Sea

To document how often these incidental takes are occurring, environmental watchdog organizations such as Greenpeace monitor fishing practices, often at considerable risk. Researchers were in an inflatable vessel in the North Atlantic monitoring a nearby French drift-netter catching albacore tuna when they were pelted with chunks of dead fish. The fishermen were hoping to prevent the documentation of a swordfish that had become entangled and drowned in the ship's nets. Covered with blood and smelling of fish, the researchers refused to yield until the drift-net was pulled in and its catch observed.

Long, almost invisible, monofilament drift nets up to 25 miles in length are deployed primarily to catch tuna and squid but become "walls of death" for all the ocean creatures unlucky enough to get in their way. During their peak use in the North Atlantic and North and South Pacific, in the 1980s and early 1990s, tens of thousands of dolphins and other marine wildlife became tangled and died in these nets. In 1989 alone, the North Pacific squid drift-net fishery caught an estimated 19,000 northern right whale dolphins, along with almost 2.5 million blue sharks and a wide variety of other marine wildlife. The 1992 United Nations ban on drift-net fishing has drastically reduced the problem, but concerns about illegal use linger.

International measures have also helped greatly in limiting the number of dolphins killed by the yellowfin tuna fishery in the Eastern Pacific, an eight-million-square-mile stretch of water between Mexico and Chile. For reasons that are still unclear, schools of yellowfin often swim beneath herds of dolphins. Since the 1950s, fishermen have taken advantage of this association by deploying nylon purse-seine nets more than 3,000 feet long that surround both dolphins and tuna, then trap them inside by drawing, or "pursing," the net shut at the bottom and hauling aboard the catch. More than six million dolphins have been killed since 1959, and the toll on certain dolphin populations has been dramatic. The eastern stock of spinner dolphins, for example, is believed to have crashed by at least 80 percent. Domestic legislation, consumer pressure, and international agreements have drastically reduced such dolphin kills. Environmentalists and others hope the figure will ultimately drop to zero.

Invisible Threats

Even as steps have been taken to address these direct threats to cetaceans, a less visible, more insidious, threat is emerging. Approximately 70,000 commercial chemicals are available in the United States alone, and another 1,000 new chemicals are produced each year. The toxic effect of most of these compounds is unknown. What is known, however, is that some of the chemicals are severely impacting marine life. Fish and shellfish

Getting Involved in Whale Conservation

Public support is the most important element in the protection of cetaceans. Want to get involved? Here are a few ways to lend a helping hand:

● Choose a group whose work interests you and support it. Become a member, read its newsletter, and follow action alerts. Consider joining an adopt-a-whale program; the fees are spent on research and the Marine Mammal Stranding Network.

● Support federal programs such as national marine sanctuaries. Visiting, volunteering at, or contributing financially to the upkeep of such sanctuaries sends Congress a clear message that the public is concerned about the future of the marine environment.

● Make your voice heard. Call or write your representatives and express support for the international whaling ban and other conservation measures.

● You don't need to be an expert to get involved. Rescue groups depend on committed volunteers to report strandings and assist in the rehabilitation and return of injured animals. Consider joining a research expedition sponsored by such organizations as Earthwatch and the Oceanic Society. Participants work side by side with field biologists identifying whales and dolphins, conducting censuses, and monitoring the health of the marine environment.

For more information, see the list of organizations in the Resource Directory at the back of this book. – *Lisa Busch and Robert Woolsey*

Long-finned pilot whales like this pod on a New Zealand beach (above) become stranded more often than any other cetaceans.

Toxic runoff from various industries (opposite) may compromise the immune systems of whales, dolphins, and other marine animals.

have been shown to suffer from disorders such as reduced birth rates and even "imposex," a condition in which females develop male sex organs and vice versa. Because many of the compounds build up through the food chain, they reach their highest concentrations in marine mammals. Striped dolphins in the western North Pacific, for example, have levels of PCBs and DDT 10 million times higher than the water in which they swim. Documented effects on marine mammals include cancer, increased mortality, lowered reproduction rates, and depressed immune systems.

Many observers have noted that the dolphins who died off the East Coast in 1987 contained extremely high loads of PCBs. One of the difficulties in establishing the effects of these chemicals is figuring out how they react to other pollutants.

The official government investigation into the U.S. dolphin die-off concluded that the dolphins had, in fact, been poisoned by a bloom of toxic algae – an entirely natural event. But it may well have been that the PCBs lowered the dolphins' resistance to algal toxins they normally encountered. Such algae blooms are themselves increasing and becoming more virulent around the world as they are fed by nutrient pollution from cars, factories, and agriculture, and possibly a changing climate, which may be making the water

warmer and more comfortable for toxic algae species.

It remains to be seen exactly what kind of long-term impact these pollutants are likely to have on cetacean populations. As industrialization increases, its impact on marine wildlife will undoubtedly become more pervasive. Twenty years ago, the threats seemed obvious and the solutions simple: stop whaling, save the whales. Now, the situation seems much more complex, and the future of cetaceans – like our own – less certain than ever.

CHAPTER 4

T he more you look, the more you see" is the deceptively sublime motto of one whale-watching guide in Alaska. As obvious as it sounds, the most important equipment you bring along on any whale-watching trip is your eyes. Continually looking at the horizon can be tiring, but distant spouts are often your first indication that whales are present. Wear polarized sunglasses, even in cloudy weather. They help to cut down on the glare from the water so you can observe whales beneath the surface if they approach your boat.   ◆   A second prerequisite is a good pair of binoculars. Though many whales are among the largest animals on Earth, they can look like black specks from a couple of miles away. Powerful binoculars allow you to identify whales and observe their behavior from a distance. Make sure the binoculars **A few practical steps** have a strong neck strap so you always have **will ensure a comfortable** them close at hand and won't drop **and rewarding day on the water.** them into the water in the heat of the moment. What kind of binoculars to buy is a highly subjective choice. Most mariners prefer 7x50. The first number refers to the power of magnification; a whale viewed through these binoculars will look seven times larger than what you see with the naked eye. The second number indicates the field of vision, or light-gathering power, of the optics. The relatively low-magnification 7x50s are easier than more powerful binoculars to keep steady in a rocking boat. Binoculars that may be suitable on land – for birding, say – go up to 10x magnification. In general, fixed lenses are sharper than zoom, and straight barrels have better optics (and are usually more expensive) than barrels with prisms or mirrors.   ◆   If you are buying new bincoulars, try several pairs.

Whale watchers in North America are prohibited from approaching within 100 yards of whales, but at San Ignacio Lagoon in Baja California gray whales often come to you.

spout that tends to billow out like a balloon.

A field guide should also offer line-drawing profiles of the different species, especially the portion of the dorsal fin or fluke that breaks the surface. Since whales are rarely seen entirely out of the water, positive identification depends on piecing together physical and behavioral clues, which a good field guide should describe.

Calming Your Stomach

Few people find the transition from dry land to open ocean easy. Though some whale-watching trips may take place entirely on quiet waters, seas that are calm upon departure can later turn rough. Even people who wouldn't ordinarily get seasick can fall victim when standing on a moving boat trying to focus through binoculars.

The first remedy is pre-vention. Though you may want to celebrate your impending trip, decline that alcoholic beverage with dinner the night before and go to bed early. The next morning, have a nongreasy, high-protein breakfast. Along with your other supplies for the day, tuck some crackers and a carbonated beverage (in a nonbreakable container) into your daypack. Sipping on club soda and nibbling on saltines will help settle your stomach. You'll also find a variety of over-the-counter medications available in doses that last from a few

Focus on objects at varying distances, through the store window or, if you can, outside the store. Base your decision on how well you can see through the binoculars, as well as on other factors such as weight, comfort, and price.

Bring Along a Book

To make your trip more enjoyable, take along a good field guide. Whale watching is more fun when you know something about the species you are watching.

While there are plenty of guides to choose from, look for one that depicts the shapes of various whale spouts. This is often the first thing spotted and, because each species has a distinctive spout, is the best way to make a prelimi-nary identification of species. Orcas, for instance, have only one blowhole, which produces a relatively low, single plume. Humpbacks, on the other hand, with their paired blowholes, emit a tall, dual

hours to all day. Check with your doctor or a pharmacist about the most effective and least sedating motion sickness drugs. Many veteran whale watchers feel that it is better to be a little drowsy than seasick. Follow directions carefully: Many of these medications need to be taken prior to boarding a boat and are useless after you are seasick.

If, despite precautions, you become queasy, try to stay outside on deck (a lower deck, if possible), move to the forward part of the boat, stare ahead at the horizon, and imagine yourself at the helm. Studies have shown that people susceptible to motion sickness in cars do not suffer symptoms while they're behind the wheel and concentrating on

the road. Some people may find relief at the stern of the boat, where there can be less physical motion.

Dress for Success

Weather on whale-watching excursions varies enormously, from frigid rain in Alaska to tropical heat in Baja. As with any extended outdoor adventure, layered clothing is a good idea. Cotton is infamous for losing its insulation value when wet, so wear cotton for comfort, if you must, but don't depend on it for warmth. Over a cotton T-shirt, layer a polypropylene or wool shirt, and a sweater over that. Since even land-based whale watching can be windy, bring a wind- and

Dolphins (opposite) like this one in the Bahamas love to swim in front of ships, a behavior known as bow riding.

A reliable 35-mm camera (above) with several lenses and a 7x50-magnitude pair of binoculars (top, right) are essential for spotting cetaceans and capturing them on film.

Picture This

Photographing a moving whale from a moving vessel is challenging. To get successful shots, you'll need to bear a few things in mind before you point and click.

- Use a 35-mm single-lens-reflex (SLR) camera rather than an automatic camera. SLRs allow you to adjust light exposure (f stop) and shutter speed. They also accommodate zoom or telephoto lenses, which are essential for photographing distant subjects.

- Choose a high-speed film – ASA 400 or higher for color prints or slides – which will result in sharp images. You can also shoot with black-and-white film (ASA 800 to 1600), used by researchers when photographing primarily black, gray, or white whales.

- Know the distinctive features and behaviors of the cetaceans you expect to see. For instance, wait to photograph an orca after it is out of the water and its saddle patch is visible, not as the whale first begins to surface. Humpbacks making a deep dive first show their "hump," then their flukes invariably break the surface. Remember that you don't want to miss the magnificent tail. Breaching, lobtailing, and other behaviors may be performed repeatedly, giving you a second or third chance at a good photograph.

- Try to keep the horizon level in your camera's viewfinder and steady yourself against the boat when it's time to photograph. Tripods are ineffective – and unsafe – on a moving vessel; many tour operators prohibit them onboard.

- Bring a sturdy plastic bag or kayaker's dry bag for protecting your camera if seas get rough, the weather turns inclement, or you'd rather look than photograph. Just one splash of saltwater spray can ruin a camera. If yours is anointed, immediately submerge it in freshwater and promptly deliver it for repairs.

weather-resistant shell for the top layer. And be sure to bring rain gear, because many boats do not have covered decks. Several companies make excellent fabric rain gear that stuffs into its own pocket – a godsend when space is tight in a suitcase or daypack. Toss in wool or fleece gloves and a hat for colder whale watches. In warmer climates, a cap can help keep the sun off your face and the hair out of your eyes.

Remember, too, that the wind and ocean glare can contribute to a mean sunburn. Apply a sunblock of at least SPF 15 before heading out, and reapply it if you are out for more than a few hours or go swimming.

Ride in Style or Paddle a Kayak

Now that you're geared up, what kind of trip, exactly, are you prepared for? Since there is never a guarantee that you will see whales, you should select a trip based on the type of tour and environment you want to experience. Tropical or arctic? Offshore or inshore? Guided or unguided? Whale-watching trips are available in all kinds of vessels, and range from a half day to a couple of weeks or longer. Look for a tour that appeals to you and suits your budget, even if you don't see any whales.

Large boats with viewing platforms elevated some distance above the water usually offer comfortable and dry whale watching. These observation decks are common in places like Alaska and Cape Cod. In tropical locales such as Baja California, the Bahamas, and Dominica, boats have covered decks that shield

Watching from a Kayak

Kayakers are more likely than other watchers to have a profound experience among whales. You'll never feel like such a small fry than when you are sitting in a kayak in proximity to whales. With preparation and care on the water, seeing whales from a kayak is not dangerous. There are no documented occurrences of a whale deliberately harming kayakers, which is a comforting thought to dwell on as you paddle among orcas.

Remember that kayakers are subject to the 100-yard rule that applies to other vessels. It's a good idea to keep whales aware of your presence by tapping the kayak occasionally with the paddle. If a whale chooses to approach you, enjoy the experience while watching quietly and keeping your legs and arms inside the craft.

Above all, be aware of your limits. If you are a novice and an expert discourages you from paddling out on your own to view whales, take a guided trip or a boat excursion instead. Kayaks move easily and gracefully through the water, but propelling one can be exhausting for even the fittest people. The time you spend in a gym preparing to paddle will more than pay you back in pleasure once you're on the water. Make sure you wear a personal-flotation device (supplied by outfitters if you are renting equipment) and know how to right and re-enter a capsized boat.

When exploring by kayak, count on getting wet. In the frigid waters of Alaska, wet clothing can lead to hypothermia, while the calm waters of Hawaii pose little risk. Always dress with the worst possible situation in mind and take extra layers, including rain gear. Your hands will stay warm and be less likely to chafe and blister if you wear gloves made of insulating neoprene.

Kayaks (above) are a good way to get close to whales, as bowhead researcher Kerry Finley found paddling around Canada's Baffin Island.

Research trips (opposite, top) offer the chance to work with cetologists monitoring whales and their behavior.

Whales can be identified by their spouts. These sperm whales (opposite, bottom) blow a little to the left and forward.

you from the hot sun.

Tours with knowledgeable, trained naturalists on board are a considerable step up from, say, a charter fishing captain who is willing to run you out to look at whales in lieu of fishing. Smaller boats with a "naturalist-captain" are potentially your best option for a really exceptional boat-based whale-watching trip. But "naturalist" can be interpreted rather loosely by some boat operators. A few inquiries at a local outfitter or bookshop should help you sort the true naturalists from the amateurs. A number of nonprofit educational organizations, such as the Pacific Whale Foundation, offer whale-watching tours with onboard naturalists

and are probably the best bet for a quality experience.

All operators should prominently display a master's license; if they can't produce one, look elsewhere for a tour. And avoid any operator who suggests pursuing whales on your behalf. Whale-watching boats are required

by law to stay 100 yards from whales, even farther away in sensitive areas such as whale feeding, mating, or calving grounds.

For a more intimate view of whales, paddling your own kayak may be a good choice. Particularly fruitful destinations for kayaking are Alaska's Inside Passage, the

Puget Sound region of Washington and British Columbia, the St. Lawrence River and its tributaries in Quebec, and Mexico's Sea of Cortez – places that generally have calm waters and abundant beaches, coves, inlets, and bays. Outfitters offer a variety of options: guided tours, transport to and from sites with your own kayak or rented equipment, kayaking instruction, and trip-planning advice.

If kayaking among whales doesn't interest you, a good alternative for a close encounter may be a glass-bottomed boat. Most common in the clear waters of the Caribbean, glass-bottomed boats can add a fascinating dimension to the viewing experience. Some words of caution: Captains of such boats often drive through and over groups of cetaceans as they try to get close enough for a good view. This can lead to boat handling that disturbs or injures cetaceans. Make sure that your trip is with an experienced and reputable operator.

Depending on how much time, energy, and interest you have in whale watching, you may consider mixing pleasure with volunteer service. Research organizations such as Earthwatch offer opportunities to participate in whale research. While you may view whales just as you would on any other tour, having some responsibilities as a research assistant can enhance the experience considerably. Some researchers need volunteers to steer the boat while they photograph whales; others ask for help recording notes on the location and activities of whales.

Enhancing Your Memory

Whether you are assisting a

A sailboarder (opposite, top) cruises past orcas off British Columbia.

Inquisitive creatures, whales like this friendly humpback (opposite, bottom) are often as curious about humans as we are about them.

Spinner dolphins (left) are famous for their twirling leaps. They are often seen bow riding in Hawaiian and Mexican waters.

Some whale-watching operators feed gulls (below), hoping that whales will be attracted to the ship.

researcher or just going along for the ride, keeping a log can be a productive exercise. Taking notes or making sketches of what you see can strengthen the memory of your experience and hone your observational skills. Biology in Charles Darwin's time was not much more than this: patient, detailed observation. Your journal should be sized to fit into a daypack and, if possible, be waterproof. Either during a trip or immediately afterward, record the details of every whale sighting – the weather conditions, the time, the presence of other animals and vessels. Write down the size of the animal, what part of the animal's body was exposed, and the type of behavior it was exhibiting. If you take a photograph, note the roll and frame number.

Laptop computers are also handy in recording your trip. Some software programs are designed specifically for maintaining a wildlife database. Keep in mind, however, that your computer will not like salt spray, and it may not be too happy among the airborne chlorides in salt air. Take one along only if you can accept these hazards. Otherwise, use it to record your observations after you're back on dry land.

Likewise, video recorders can be a boon or a curse and are easily damaged by sea spray. If you have a penchant for narrating while you record your video, you can exploit this aptitude on a whale-watching excursion, but stick to the important observational details. Any commentary outside disciplined note-taking will prove distracting should you need to transcribe your observations on paper. Above all, try to use discretion when recording oral notes with a video camera. Your diligent descriptions may disturb other observers, particularly if they're hoping to experience, however briefly, the quiet serenity that accompanies these majestic creatures.

Secret Life of Whales

Although whales, dolphins, and porpoises are difficult to study in the wild, we know that they are highly intelligent creatures and that many exhibit complex social relations and a fascinating repertoire of adaptive behaviors.

What Is a Whale?

CHAPTER 5

"A whale," opined Herman Melville, author of *Moby Dick*, is "a spouting fish with a horizontal tail." *Bzzzzt*. Thanks for playing, Herman, but that's the wrong answer.   ◆   Okay, it's probably a little unfair to single out Melville, normally among the most astute and descriptive observers of cetaceans. And he was right on two counts: Whales do spout, and they do have horizontal tails. But they are most definitely not fish.   ◆   The ancient Greeks knew this; as far back as the fourth century B.C., Aristotle had dismissed the idea out of hand. But, as with so many things in the world of science, the reason and observation of the Greeks were lost in the mists of the Middle Ages. Whales, medieval scholars noted, had body shapes that were roughly like fish; they had no apparent hair, like fish; and they lived underwater, as did fish. Therefore, they were fish.   ◆   But whales also are warm-blooded, give birth

Whales, dolphins, and porpoises belong to an order of mammals known as cetaceans and are exquisitely adapted to aquatic life.

to live young, and suckle them. Most important, they breathe air, coming to the surface and, as Melville observed, "spouting" with a blast of sound and a cloud of water vapor before disappearing once more beneath the waves. Indeed, whales are "conscious breathers," unlike humans and other land animals that do not have to think about breathing. Each breath a cetacean takes is a deliberate act. For that reason, even when a whale is sleeping, part of its brain must always remain "awake" so that the breathing doesn't stop.   ◆   It was the Swedish naturalist Carl Linnaeus, the inventor of the modern system for classifying organisms, who first formally pronounced whales, dolphins, and porpoises to be mammals like us.

A humpback whale and calf off Tonga. Mothers and calves stay close for the first year and are often joined by male "escorts" on mating grounds.

Preceding pages: Belugas live in the icy waters of the north, one of only a few cetacean species able to survive the extreme cold.

Cetacean Evolution

Watching a whale swim effortlessly through the sea, it's hard to imagine that cetaceans and humans are part of the same biological family. We know they're mammals. They breathe air and suckle their young just as we do. And yet, they seem so ... different.

But take a look at a picture of a cetacean embryo. Familiar, isn't it? There are "hands" with five digits, and a head tucked into the chest; some even have phantom hind legs, which are uselessly adrift beneath blubber and muscle.

Although they returned to the sea some 50 million years ago, cetaceans are indeed descended from land mammals, probably hoofed creatures known as mesochynids, forerunners of modern-day antelopes, horses, and cattle. The fossil record suggests a gradual evolution toward an aquatic way of life: The earliest cetaceans, the Archaeoceti, had webbed hind limbs and probably lived in shallow coastal areas.

Between 25 and 38 million years ago, the Archaeoceti diverged into the ancestors of baleen whales and early toothed whales. Both branches continued to adapt to aquatic life. Nostrils matured into blowholes; bodies became more streamlined; limbs developed into fins and flukes. An early whale, *Mammalodon*, may have possessed sieve-like fringes in its mouth that later developed into baleen.

The first modern whale species – the sperm whale and perhaps some beaked whales – appeared about 23 million years ago. Dolphins and porpoises followed about 10 million years later. The last major wave of modern cetaceans appeared about four million years ago, about the same time that our own ancestors began to walk upright.

A killer whale skull (above) displays the razor-sharp teeth of the flesh-eating Odontoceti group, which also includes dolphins, belugas, and sperm whales.

Baleen whales, or Mysticeti, use large, fringed plates of bristly baleen (right) to filter plankton, krill, and other tiny organisms.

Blowholes (opposite, bottom) serve the same purpose as nostrils in land mammals, although whales must consciously come to the surface to breathe.

Linnaeus placed them together in the order *Cetacea* in the same way that humans, the great apes, monkeys, and lemurs are all members of the order *Primata*, or primates.

There are approximately 80 species of cetaceans in the world today. They are found in all the world's oceans, in both coastal waters and open seas, as well as in some of the planet's major rivers – the Amazon, Orinoco, Indus, Ganges, Yangtze, and Irrawaddy. They are divided into two groups: the Mysticeti, or baleen whales, and the Odontoceti, or toothed whales.

Filter Feeders

There are 11 species of baleen whales, so named for the large, fringed plates of baleen that hang from their upper jaw. In the past, baleen was often referred to as "whalebone" and was the material used to make corsets; in fact, baleen is made of keratin, like our fingernails. It functions essentially as a sieve, filtering out mouthfuls of seawater and trapping the plankton, krill, and other tiny organisms on which these giants of the sea feed in huge quantities. Some of the Mysticeti – the blue, fin, sei, Bryde's, minke, and humpback – are known as "rorquals." These whales have large grooves in their throats, enabling them to expand so that the whales can gulp even larger amounts of water than their less well-equipped cousins.

With the exception of pygmy right whales – the largest specimen of which was only 20.5 feet long – baleen whales are known as "great whales," a distinction

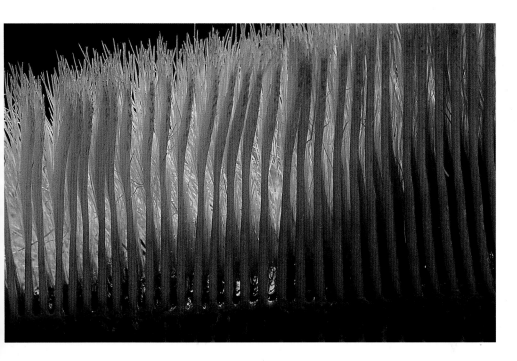

shared by the largest of the Odontoceti, sperm whales. The International Whaling Commission (IWC), the body responsible for regulating commercial whaling, refers to almost all the other species of whales, dolphins, and porpoises as "small cetaceans." This is something of a misnomer, however, for some of these so-called small cetaceans – northern bottlenose whales, Baird's beaked whales, and orcas, or killer whales – can be larger than the smallest of the "great" whales, minkes.

Toothed Whales

It's equally confusing trying to determine, among the toothed cetaceans, what exactly is a dolphin, a whale, or a porpoise. In countries like the United States, just about any kind of dolphin has traditionally been referred

to as a "porpoise." Scientists, however, use the term "porpoise" very specifically, to refer to six species of small (generally between six and eight feet) Odontoceti with short snouts and spadelike teeth.

The Odontoceti group is divided into sperm whales, including pygmy and dwarf sperm whales; belugas and narwhals; beaked and bottlenosed whales (large, little-known denizens of the open ocean); porpoises; river dolphins; and Delphinidae,

the family that includes, essentially, everything else: all the familiar dolphins, such as bottlenose dolphins (the species used in dolphin shows), as well as pilot and killer whales.

But don't be distressed if, while traveling, you come upon "dolphin" on the menu of a seafood restaurant. Unless you've stumbled into a whale-meat restaurant in Japan, this refers to dorado, or *mahi-mahi*, also known as dolphin. This is one dolphin that really is a fish.

John Lilly was a man with a mission. He wanted to know more about the world of whales and dolphins than had been learned by all the other scientists in the world put together. In particular, he wanted to unlock the secrets of the minds of dolphins, to discover what they think and how they feel. It was a daunting task, to put it mildly, but Lilly believed he knew exactly how to reveal a dolphin's innermost thoughts. He planned to look one straight in the eye and ask it.   ◆   Lilly was convinced that cetaceans are extremely intelligent – that they are, in fact, at least the equal of humans. He was similarly adamant that they have a language, and that if only he could find out how to communicate with them, they would be able to share with us the benefits of the wisdom they had acquired over the millions of years they've been on this planet.   ◆   Lilly began his work in the 1960s. A physician by profession, he wanted to uncover the mind within the brain, to find out what it was about the human brain that made it such a power-house of intelligence. To do that, he needed to study a wild animal's brain of similar size. The bottlenose dolphin had such a brain.   ◆   So Lilly set about merrily implanting electrodes in the brains of captive bottlenose dolphins. One day, while playing back tapes of a dolphin making noises during a brain study, he thought the dolphin's sounds were remarkably similar to the verbal notes he had recorded on his dictation machine. The dolphin, he became convinced, was mimicking him.   ◆   From there, Lilly abruptly turned his attention to the question of whether dolphins could indeed communicate in English. He isolated one of the dolphins

What is the nature of cetacean intelligence, and how does it compare with human thought?

"**Dolphins**," wrote anthropologist Ashley Montagu, "have large brains. Possibly they will some day be able to teach us what brains are for."

from the others in the belief that, as a highly social mammal, the dolphin would be forced to direct its behavior toward Lilly and his assistants. In this way, Lilly hoped, the dolphin could be encouraged to repeat consistently the words and phrases of his human captors. It was asking a lot. To oblige, the dolphin would have to drop its voice to the lowest part of its vocal range and vocalize in the air with its blowhole closed. Remarkably, the dolphin did it, managing to repeat a number of words that Lilly and his associates spoke, and frequently in context.

There were, however, few signs that the dolphin could assemble these isolated words into phrases or sentences. Nonetheless, Lilly had seen enough for him to begin writing of dolphins having a language he called "delphinese." It was pure speculation, but that didn't prevent Lilly from presenting

it as fact; nor did it deter legions of supporters from accepting it as such.

Most scientists wasted little time in trashing Lilly's work. They said that all he had done was induce a dolphin to repeat a few random words – a feat performed by pet parrots and mynah birds the world over. And if Lilly's dolphins performed a little better than Polly and her peers, then that was only to be expected. Cetaceans, they noted, are naturally talented and varied vocalizers; they had adapted to their underwater world where sound travels farther than it does in the air and where vision can be drastically reduced. All Lilly's work showed was that dolphins are talented vocalizers and clever vocal mimics – which was never really in dispute.

Intelligent Signs

Nonetheless, there has emerged a popular conception that dolphins and whales are

somehow "intelligent," and much of that belief has sprung, consciously or not, from the work of John Lilly. If his work actually showed little of what he claimed he did, does that mean that speculation on cetacean intelligence is misplaced?

Not necessarily. Other researchers have been attempting to see if captive dolphins respond to sign language, and here at least there appears to have been more success than Lilly achieved. Dolphins have shown themselves able to understand simple sentence structure and seem also able to grasp abstract concepts. But, as one commentator has noted, while dolphins appear able to communicate *who*, *what*, *where*, and possibly *when*, there is no indication that they are particularly concerned with *how* or *why*.

Those who challenge the findings of captive studies argue that confining cetaceans to concrete pools and subjecting them to rote experiments are no more likely to produce an accurate understanding of dolphin intelligence than asking prisoners to perform tricks with the goal of obtaining a rounded picture of human society. Such critics suggest

Orcas (left) have the second largest brains of any animals, almost four times the size of a human brain, much of it apparently used for sonar processing.

Dolphins (opposite) spend as much as three-quarters of each day in creative play.

that only by watching dolphins and whales in their natural environment can we fully appreciate the nature of cetacean thought.

They may well have a point. Defining intelligence is notoriously difficult, even among humans. IQ tests are criticized frequently for being culturally biased. Thus far, attempts to assess intelligence in dolphins have been based very much on the kind of tests in which we as humans would expect to perform well. They are largely efforts to see how well dolphins do relative to human abilities, particularly in terms of language and communication. But if cetaceans are intelligent, then, because they have evolved in a completely different environment from ours, their intelligence will likely be of a totally different order than ours. As such, it may be extremely difficult to evaluate, or even recognize, in human terms.

For example, it has been suggested that dolphin echolocation may be so advanced that dolphins can actually "see" inside other living things and build up three-dimensional, holographic images of what they observe. If that is true, simply by examining a companion's heartbeat, a dolphin could tell whether that companion was relaxed or tense. Equally, it would be able to tell if the stomach of a nearby shark was empty (which might spell danger) or full (no cause for alarm). That being so, phrases such as

"How are you?" or "Are you hungry?" – which human researchers might take as a sign of high intelligence – would seem superfluous or even primitive to dolphins.

The problem with discussing the possibility of cetacean communication is that it's too easy to let our hearts rule our heads and accept vaguely defined theories as fact, simply

because the idea of whales and dolphins talking to each other is so attractive.

Wishful Thinking?

Too often the people who most strongly supported John Lilly's theories did so not because such theories were based on sound evidence – they clearly weren't – but because they were theories which, for various reasons, some people wanted desperately to be true.

Some saw the idea of cetacean language and intelligence as the perfect opportunity to put humans in their place and demonstrate that our species isn't quite so unusual as many of us like to think. Others, notably the ecological idealists of the 1960s and 1970s and their successors, argued, with some success, that if whales and dolphins really were intelligent, they were some-how "special" and their continued slaughter was therefore all the more morally repugnant.

The argument had a certain irony. Rather than showing, as its proponents intended, that humans' undoubted talents were no grounds for our species regarding itself as vastly superior to all other life-forms, it reinforced the prejudice that an animal species must share human characteristics before it can be regarded as truly special.

Today, most researchers say that whether or not whales and dolphins are intelligent communicators is irrelevant. What we already know about them is more than enough for them to be considered truly exceptional. We do not need to embroider the facts with half-truths and speculations about their brainpower.

If it turns out that cetaceans really are intelligent in a way we can understand, that will be all the more fascinating and exciting. Until and unless such a momentous discovery is made, perhaps we would do better not to paint cetaceans as aquatic images of our-selves, but to make a greater effort to appreciate them as the fundamentally different but extraordinary species that they are.

The Great Migration

The gray whale's 10,000-mile round-trip journey between Alaska and Baja California is probably the most famous whale migration in the world, but it is by no means the only one, nor the longest. Humpbacks journey each year from the Antarctic Peninsula to Colombia – a total of about 12,000 miles. Blue, fin, sei, right, sperm, and bottlenose whales, among others, also undertake migrations of various lengths at different times of the year.

Whale migration is governed by the two great constants in life: food and sex. During polar summers, when food is plentiful, whales concentrate their efforts on eating. As the food supply diminishes during polar winters, most whales head to warmer waters to breed and calve. Shortening days appear to inspire this move, but much remains uncertain. Some members of a whale population do not migrate: mature bull sperms, for example, travel to feed on squid in polar regions while females, immature males, and juveniles remain in the Caribbean.

How do cetaceans find their way during these long treks? One popular theory is that they follow a magnetic "map" across the oceans, like

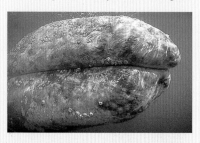

migrating birds. But cetaceans also may navigate using the sun or stars, the taste of different water masses, prevailing winds and swell patterns, even landmarks glimpsed by poking their heads above the surface, a behavior known as spyhopping.

Sperm whales (above, left) sound in the Sea of Cortez. Only mature males migrate long distances.

Pacific gray whales (left) migrate south in early winter, perhaps in response to shortening days.

Bottlenose dolphins like this one at the Institute for Marine Sciences in Honduras (right) seem to have a lot to teach us about having fun.

Cetacean Society

CHAPTER 7

What does it mean when a 40-ton humpback whale hurls itself out of the water and splashes down again? Scientists tell us this breaching behavior could be anything from a territorial display to long-distance communication to pure play. It certainly looks like fun.　◆　Therein lies the problem. Cetacean social behavior remains enigmatic, making it all too easy for humans to project familiar mammalian social patterns, including our own, onto animals we barely understand. What we do know about cetaceans – they have large brains, communicate, and live in organized social groups – is compelling. But we long to know more.　◆　One obstacle to more extensive study of cetaceans is that they inhabit a vastly different environment from our own. We have walked in outer space, but we are only beginning to explore the oceans here on Earth. It's easy to observe cetaceans on the ocean surface,

Like humans, many cetaceans appear to be social, to communicate, and to live in close-knit communities.

but they spend only a fraction of their lives there. Just imagine alien researchers thinking they understand human social behavior based on observations made at the bottom of a public swimming pool, and you start to grasp the problem. Until we can find ways to enter their realm, we will not be able to fully study the social structures and relationships of cetaceans, much less conclude anything.　◆　Despite these limitations, there is much we are beginning to understand about whale and dolphin society. Cetaceans, for example, are clearly social creatures and have been observed cooperatively rearing young, hunting, and engaging in courtship behavior. Toothed whales, such as orcas, pilot whales, sperm whales,

Atlantic spotted dolphins in the Bahamas may live in groups of 50 or more animals to protect themselves from predators and possibly to help with cooperative foraging.

and dolphins, generally have more structured societies than right, humpback, gray, and other baleen whales.

Wolf Packs of the Sea

Orcas may employ the most successful cooperative hunting techniques of all whales. Hunting in packs, like wolves, orca pods may move close to shore during seal-pupping season, when seals haul out on land to give birth, and seem to intentionally strand and capture seals in the coastal waters off Argentina. This learned skill apparently has been passed down from generation to generation in certain pods.

Orcas in Southeast Alaska have been observed herding sea lions against the hulls of large ships or into boat harbors, then darting through the corralled animals, killing as they go. Elsewhere, mariners tell of orcas coordinating attacks on great whales, driving them to the surface and preventing them from sounding, throwing themselves over the heads of their prey in an apparent attempt to asphyxiate whales by covering their blowholes, and generally harassing them into exhaustion. No one yet knows exactly how these skilled predators acquire effective new hunting skills within their social groups.

Hunting behaviors among baleen whales are far more methodical but no less fascinating. One of the most intensely studied is bubble-net feeding, a humpback behavior first noted in Alaska that allows 20 or more humpbacks to catch and feed on small fish, usually herring, trapped by a "net" of bubbles. Scientists are still unsure of the underwater process that produces the bubble net but speculate that a single humpback may initiate it by slowly emitting bubbles from its blowhole and spiraling gradually to the surface. Other whales join the herding effort until the schooling fish have been corralled in the bubble curtain. Lunging open-mouthed though the confused mass of fish and straining seawater through their baleen plates, the humpbacks appear to further herd the fish with their long pectoral flippers and to stun them with fluke slaps. They then banquet on several hundred pounds of fish each time.

This amazing spectacle may be coordinated, but it is not necessarily altruistic. It has been argued that some of the whales – maybe even most of them – are merely exploiting the net rather than working together to create it. A few hardworking whales may begin the process only to have a bunch of latecomers crash the party. Other researchers have noted that the bubble-netting group repeats the behavior over and over until full, and that every member of the group appears in the same place in the formation each time.

Bottlenose dolphins also use cooperative feeding

Spinner dolphins (top) travel in schools of 5 to 200 and sometimes coalesce into groups of 1,000.

Humpback bubble-net feeding (left) demonstrates the effectiveness of cooperative feeding, with up to 20 humpbacks working together to catch schooling fish.

Orca pods (right) take a divide-and-conquer approach to sea lions in Argentina, collectively stranding seal pups on the beach, then charging individuals.

techniques to herd large schools of fish – to their benefit and that of local fishermen. In South Carolina, onlookers have watched bottlenose dolphins drive fish onto the muddy beaches of the inner coast and then swim to the water's edge to catch them. As creative and successful as orcas are in their feeding techniques, bottlenose seem highly adaptive and intelligent, tailoring their foraging patterns and hunting techniques to their prey.

Competition and Cooperation

Cetacean courtship and mating also interest scientists. Like many land-based mammals, humpback males must often compete physically for mating privileges since there are generally fewer female humpbacks than males. This competition produces intriguing behaviors. The most fascinating may be the humpback song, a sequence of vocal sounds – grunts, howls, cackles, and melodic wailing – that may have much in common with birdsong. Interestingly, although the humpback song changes every breeding season, the males all sing the same song. Some scientists theorize that what may set apart the successfully reproducing males is the

strength and duration of their song; others suggest that the songs create a kind of acoustic territory warning off other males from a female or area.

Humpback mating techniques also involve competition, less artful to be sure but no less dramatic. Several males surround a female and try to win the opportunity to mate by getting closest to her. As the males jostle for position, they may lunge, fluke-strike, or slap their pectoral flippers to warn competitors away. Such behavior sounds relatively harmless, but it is common for males to be left considerably bloodied and scarred after such encounters. Researchers later use these distinguishing marks to identify individual whales. Not unlike another land-based mammal, the amount of time and effort a humpback male devotes to creating an opportunity to mate is disproportionate to the actual coupling. Humpbacks may sing their hearts out around the clock and brutally fight for a chance to mate, but pair-bonding is negligible at best and the male-female humpback relationship is fleeting. This is consistent with the typically temporary social arrangements and groupings of baleen whales during such times as feeding and birthing.

Their toothed cousins – the Odontoceti, or toothed whales – more than compensate for the lack of attachment among baleen

whales. One study in the Pacific Northwest found orcas residing in the same social group most of their lives, an estimated 29 to 50 years. Resident pods range in size from 7 to 50 members and remain within a more or less fixed territory. Transient pods, on the other hand, tend to live in smaller groups of around seven or fewer members. This may allow them to freely and quickly comb vast areas of coastline in search of prey.

Females Rule

Orcas are matriarchal, with mature females outnumbering mature males in most pods. This may contribute to the more leisurely mating style among orcas. During courtship, the mating pair swim slowly on their sides with ventral surfaces touching and heads gently butting. They then lie still during mating and remain this way until the male's penis is retracted. There are no competing suitors to fend off – most of the young males have left the pod to join others or form their own. This style of mating may help keep the peace and ensure the

diversity of the gene pool.

The closest relationship in cetacean society is between mother and calf. The bond apparently is central to the overall structure of any group of whales with young, but the length of the relationship varies widely. The gestation period for the world's largest whale, the blue, is about 11 months, but the calf may

suckle for only seven months after birth. In contrast, a pilot whale cow carries her fetus for 15 months and may nurse the calf for four to five years. This long nursing bond may account for the strength of the cow-calf bond in pilot whales, a relationship that appears to extend well into adulthood, and may offer clues about why the grand-

Humpbacks (opposite, top) breed and raise calves in protected Hawaiian waters.

A male Atlantic spotted dolphin (opposite, bottom) swims upside down beneath a female during courtship.

Southern right whales (right) breed in the shallow waters of a bay in Patagonia, Argentina.

The Reproductive Urge

If you watch nature documentaries, you're familiar with this story: A dominant male – be it lion, elk, or elephant seal – fights for the right to mate with a particular female or an entire harem and so passes on his genes to subsequent generations.

Certainly, some whales fit this model. Humpback bulls, for example, fight brutally among themselves to mate with a cow. But in species where all the bulls have easy access to fecund females, nature has come up with another scheme. The bull that produces the most copious amounts of sperm fertilizes the cow by displacing or diluting the sperm of rival males, and it is the most aggressive sperm, rather than the most aggressive whale, that passes on a genetic package.

So in this scenario, what gives the male a competitive edge? The testicles of a right whale weigh in at about two tons, the largest in the animal kingdom. The whale's penis is 14 percent of its overall body length, presumably to deliver the phenomenal numbers of sperm closer to the target. Gray and bowhead whales are not far behind in these statistical records.

Studies of a few other mammals indicate that those with large testicles display less aggressive sexual behavior than those with small testicles. Among primates, some monkey species with large testes seem to have relatively easygoing sex lives, while mountain gorillas, which have small testes, are far more sexually aggressive. Biologists are arriving at the same conclusions in regard to record-breaking right, gray, and bowhead bulls. They get along just fine without resorting to the "crimes of passion" observed among other mammals.

mother pilot whale seems to be the institutional figure of the group.

Bottlenose dolphins also seem to inhabit a matriarchal society. Slow breeders, bottlenoses calve only every four to five years. Males have had to develop strategies to make the most of limited mating opportunities, sometimes cooperating in separating available females from a social group but fighting for a chance to mate. Despite all their efforts, the romance is over relatively quickly, and the female-based social structure is restored.

In sperm whale society, groups of up to 50 adult females, calves, and juveniles live together, usually in warmer waters in what is dubbed a "nursery school." Wet nursing among females is popular; they also share the task of defending the school from marauding orcas and large sharks. The nursery school structure serves as a way of concentrating sexually mature females during the breeding season, and the largest males, colorfully known as harem masters, battle for the right to breed with the females of a particular nursery school, which then becomes the harem of the victor. Two harem masters may work together to fend off other males from their harems, but the master's hold on his harem seems to last only a few days. After that, he may take up with another nursery school in search of sexually receptive females. As they mature, young male sperm whales graduate from the nursery school into bachelor groups, which will decrease in size as the bachelors grow up. The largest among them will be the ones who roam the oceans by themselves or in pairs looking for harems.

Waiting for Answers

Feeding and breeding have been the areas of most fruitful

Inexplicable Strandings

Few observations of natural events are more wrenching than the sight of whales or dolphins stranded on a beach. While the stranding of a single whale usually can be explained by disease or injury, mass strandings of dozens or even hundreds of animals remain a mystery.

About the only thing that biologists know for certain is that mass strandings strike deep-water species far more often than coastal cetaceans. Such deep-diving species as sperm whales, false killer whales, and pilot whales may follow prey into unfamiliar coastlines and become disoriented. Strong social bonds among these animals may also be a factor: The members of a pod may be reluctant to abandon a sick or dying individual even at their own peril. Rescuers have often noted that "refloated" whales frequently try to rejoin their stranded mates.

Other theories suggest that infestations of parasitic worms in the inner ear may cause whales to become disoriented, or that certain topographical features such as shifting sandbars or beaches with a gradual slope may interfere with echolocation. One British researcher has even established a correlation between strandings and certain anomalies in the Earth's magnetic field that may hinder a whale's ability to navigate.

If you find a stranded whale, the best course of action is to contact a marine mammal center or the Marine Mammal Stranding Network (see the Resource Directory), which can dispatch trained rescuers to aid the animal.

Social whales, such as these long-finned pilot whales (above), may become beached while trying to assist sick or injured members of their pods.

Sperm whale cows, calves, and juveniles (right) live together in "nursery schools" in warm waters. Bulls, known as "harem masters," battle for the right to breed with females of a particular pod. Young adult males form bachelor groups, then head to cooler waters alone or in pairs.

study for scientists, while other cetacean social behaviors remain a mystery. Of course, like all intelligent species, cetaceans do more than breed and eat, so it's likely that many observed behaviors may turn out to be social. Why, for example, do humpbacks breach again and again – they have been observed breaching up to 100 times – whereas orcas and other species only occasionally breach? And what about spyhopping? Is the humpback or orca scanning its surroundings when it rises vertically out of the water some 10 or 12 feet, or is there some other explanation? Are lobtailing (in which a cetacean lifts its tail out of the water and slaps it back and forth) and fin slapping really forms of communication, as scientists conjecture? If a right whale points its flukes, is this a warning to

intruding whales, as some think? And, of course, the perennial questions: Why do dolphins enjoy riding in, or possibly playing in, the bow waves created by a moving vessel? And when two animals gently touch each other for no obvious reason, are they really being affectionate?

Cetacean sympathy, or "standing by," is another fascinating behavior associated with several of these mammals, including pilot and humpback whales, which often remain offshore if a pod member is stranded. In some species, pod members may even physically assist sick or injured members, although other whales seem to abandon compatriots in distress. As with so much cetacean behavior, the mechanism for this remains a mystery.

It's easy to fall into the trap of making behavioral

assumptions about cetaceans based on wishful thinking. The plight of intelligent captive killer whales like Keiko of *Free Willy* fame has been popularized by the media, but cinematic cetaceans seem to react in overly human ways to characters and events in the films. Their behavior seems to have more to do with storytelling on the part of the filmmakers than it does with real-life cetacean social behavior. Even researchers realize that they must overcome the tendency to anthropomorphize their subjects – as much an obstacle to good research as bad weather and rough seas. As for the rest of us, perhaps the best advice is to resist the temptation to project human behaviors onto wild animals and allow the mystery of wildness to have its moment.

hales produce the loudest sustained sounds in the animal kingdom. The moan of a blue whale can last up to 30 seconds at 188 decibels. By comparison, a 747 jet generates about 110 decibels of perceived sound at take-off. ◆ Scientists know little about the meaning of whale sounds. Contrary to a popular misconception, researchers have not isolated anything close to a language in whale songs. Rather, they have identified the repetitive sounds that comprise songs. To the untrained ear, whale songs sound random; to experienced researchers, however, they are long melodic patterns, repeated over and over. To the whales themselves, the songs may be a sexual come-on or a way to maintain space between individuals or establish a position in the social order. ◆ Maritime lore is filled with stories of sailors hearing siren songs and mysterious sounds at sea, but it wasn't until the 1950s that these underwater noises were first recorded

From clicks and groans to melodic themes, cetaceans produce a fascinating repertoire of sounds. Why do they do it, and what are they saying?

by the military. Now underwater recordings are relatively easy to make using a hydrophone – a specialized underwater microphone – and an ordinary tape recorder and receiver. Many whale-watching tours now carry hydrophones so that passengers can listen to nearby whales. This adds an entirely new and fascinating dimension to the experience. Often, the intervals between sighting the animals on the surface are filled with acoustic activity, some of it far more bizarre than the whale recordings many of us may have already heard.

A researcher records the sounds of gray whales from the beach at San Ignacio Lagoon in Baja California, Mexico.

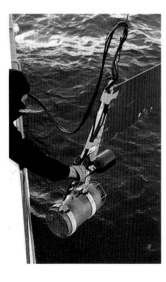

Name That Tune

Researchers place whale sounds into two categories: social sounds and song. Humpback whale song is composed of organized sequences of grunts, chirps, whistles, and wails known as themes. Themes can last from a few minutes to half an hour, and the songs may contain several themes.

Humpback songs are sung exclusively by bulls in tropical mating and calving grounds in winter. All males sing the same song, but over seasons, the pattern of notes changes gradually and the males all learn the revised song. Biologists have distinguished several geographically isolated populations of humpbacks with their own local song sequences. Humpbacks in the North Pacific, for example, sing a different song from those in the Caribbean.

Biologists have also recorded whale songs and fragments of song themes in the colder, northern waters where whales feed in summer. The separate stocks mingle in the feeding grounds, and it is possible that the new season's song is developed and passed among males while feeding. Prior to this discovery, scientists had few theories

about how whales managed to all learn the same song. According to one theory, whales broadcast the song over a deep-ocean thermocline, a layer of water of a temperature particularly suited to transmit the low frequencies of whale sounds. The likelihood of the song being learned in summer and fall while mingling opens up additional avenues for exploring whale behavior. Some scientists now speculate that males sing to trigger the estrous cycle in females.

We may never learn the actual purpose of whale song. There is abundant evidence suggesting that male humpbacks use song as a warning to other males, in effect to stake out an acoustic spatial territory. On the other hand, song may be a competitive display, and only the best and most powerful singers will attract sexually receptive females. Scientists

Whale researchers (top) have been studying whale sounds since 1949. Individual whales produce signature vocalizations, or ketophonations.

A dwarf minke whale (left) approaches a hydrophone off Australia.

Whale songs, like those of male humpbacks (opposite, top), peak during the mating season. Some whales seem to have "dialects," which may help researchers monitor populations.

Bob Bowman (opposite, bottom), a cetologist with the College of the Atlantic, records humpback songs in Samana Bay, Dominican Republic.

sometimes attempt to corroborate whale-song theory with information from elsewhere in the animal kingdom; the closest correlation may be the songs of birds. Songbirds also sing in identifiable, repetitive themes that vary according to the season and usually peak at breeding time. Geographically distinct bird populations also have different dialects. A lot of what we know about birdsong, however, is not really in dispute. Ornithologists can identify a singing bird and observe its behavior practically all the time. Whale biologists are almost never certain which animal is the one producing a specific sound and can catch only fleeting glimpses of their subjects. The study of birdsong is, literally and figuratively, on terra firma compared with that of whales.

Thanks to the trickledown of military acoustic technology, whale researchers have made great strides in their ability to monitor the audible activity of whales. Biologists have tracked individual blue whales for more than 1,500 miles. The great range of the acoustical equipment permits researchers to gather data on the geographical distribution of whales during their migrations. And new auditory information is coming to light all the time: The incredible moans of the blue whale are associated with reproductive behavior, and it seems likely that bowhead whales, like

humpbacks, may produce a complex repertoire of song.

Signature Sounds

Even less understood than song are the social sounds of humpback whales. Furthermore, social sounds are not limited to humpbacks. Drop a hydrophone in the water in the vicinity of any active group of cetaceans and you may hear an astonishing variety of sounds. Some researchers describe hearing a trumpeting or a train whistle when several humpbacks feed together. Other noises made by baleen whales can sound like monkeys, organs, groans, and knocks. Right whales produce sustained low moans among a number of other sounds, and bowheads

generate enough distinct sounds to allow researchers based on arctic shore ice to track their migrations far out at sea.

Dolphins and porpoises, including orcas, produce higher-frequency whistles and clicks than the baleen whales. Dolphins also clap their jaws in conflict situations (or to mug for the television camera, as Flipper did). Biologists are fairly certain that bottlenose and spinner dolphins have signature whistles that broadcast the identity of the whistler. Bottlenose dolphins not only possess signature whistles, they also mimic the whistles of others – likely memorizing each other's whistles in much the same way as we repeat a phone

number after snapping the directory shut.

Orcas go one step further and produce calls that may serve to identify an entire pod. The sounds produced by antarctic orcas are different from those recorded off the west coast of North America. These mostly pulsed, repetitive calls are regular enough for scientists to recognize basic patterns. The sounds are common during travel and feeding, perhaps serving as signals to help coordinate activity.

On the Radio

Orcas produce another set of calls when the pod is resting or "chatting." John Ford, director of conservation and research at the Vancouver Aquarium, has a unique

Seeing with Sound

Echolocation? It sounds like a science fantasy penned by Jules Verne. In fact, echolocation is an essential survival tool for toothed whales – a sophisticated form of radar that allows them to navigate and survive in the deep, murky waters of the world's oceans and rivers.

Echolocation is thought to work like this: Toothed whales send out short, high-frequency clicks from special fatty protrusions on their heads, called melons. These sounds bounce off objects and return as echoes, which are then received in another fatty area of the lower jaw, transmitted to the middle ear, then sent to the brain, where the information is interpreted.

Echolocation was first observed in captive dolphins in the 1950s, but it's believed that Odontoceti have been using this skill from their earliest beginnings, some 30 million years ago. Scientists think that dolphins can determine an object's distance, position, and size by echolocation alone. Some species can detect objects no bigger than one-sixteenth to one-eighth of an inch in diameter from up to 10 feet away.

This is a skill that apparently must be learned to some degree, and although it is used by all wild Odontoceti, it is not employed all of the time by all species. For example, orcas use echolocation to hunt fish but may resort to visual hunting of other cetaceans, such as gray whales. Toothless, or baleen, whales probably do not echolocate. Humpbacks are known to use low-frequency sounds for communication and courtship, but there is no evidence that they have any ability to "see" with sound. And so far, no scientist has blindfolded one to find out.

Resident orcas (opposite) off the coast of British Columbia create what one researcher calls "sound sculptures" that require a well-trained ear to decipher.

Eyes covered, a bottlenose dolphin (right) at the Institute of Marine Sciences in Roatan, Honduras, uses echolocation to retrieve a target.

approach to studying the sounds of killer whales. He has created a radio station devoted to picking up and broadcasting orca sounds: ORCA-FM. The station uses an underwater hydrophone in a popular whale-watching area and broadcasts the underwater sounds over a regular radio frequency. Boaters, kayakers, mechanics, schoolchildren – anyone on the water or on shore – can tune in and listen to orcas. They also hear the distinctive sounds of whale-watching boats. One of Ford's objectives is to increase public awareness of the intrusiveness of human noise in whale habitat.

On a purely scientific level, ORCA-FM is part of a larger project called Whale Link, which will maintain hydrophones in remote locations along the coast from Washington to Alaska. The hydrophones are linked to a computer that can discern underwater whale sounds. Ford is trying to distinguish different dialects among specific orca populations and hopes eventually to use dialects to unobtrusively track their movements.

When whale sounds are detected, Whale Link triggers a cell phone that allows researchers to listen in as whales move up and down the coast.

Even though they produce an astounding variety of sounds, cetaceans do not have vocal cords, and researchers still don't know how the creatures produce their sounds or from where baleen whales emit the sounds. Like other mammals, whales have lungs that drive air through the trachea and larynx, which in turn are connected by an air passageway to the mouth. A constriction between the back of the larynx and the trachea might serve as a kind of voice box, but baleen whales do not usually expel air from their mouths or blowholes during vocalization. Perhaps whale vocalization is physiologically separate from the respiratory system. Without a clear anatomical explanation, the apparatus used by whales to produce song remains a mystery.

Who's Watching Whom?

CHAPTER 9

Jan Sendall slowly eases his boat *Iolanthe* out of the harbor into St. David's Bay in Solva, Wales. Reaching a familiar patch of water, he slows down and begins scanning the waves excitedly, his normally taciturn features animated as he looks around in anticipation. Then, he hears a whoosh of air as a sleek, torpedo-shaped gray body streaks past. Jan's grizzled face erupts into a wide grin, and he pulls on his wetsuit as quickly as he can. In a flash, he's over the side, and Simo the dolphin is steaming toward him. Jan opens his arms wide to greet the creature swimming up to him, and the two tumble in the waves.   ◆   Jan was one of the first to discover Simo. After seemingly materializing from nowhere, the young male bottlenose hung around Solva and St. David's Bay for more than a year, playing with those who sailed out to watch and swim with him. Over time, he became a tourist attraction in his own right, and

Mutual curiosity and even a sense of protection and play characterize some encounters between humans and cetaceans.

then he disappeared as suddenly as he arrived.   ◆   To those who spent time with Simo, one thing seemed clear. As much as the many people who saw him were thrilled by the sight of the dolphin, Simo also seemed to enjoy playing with his human visitors. But he was discerning in his tastes. Although he appeared to revel in the company of virtually anybody, he had his favorites.   ◆   One of them was Tricia Kirkman. A young woman who could barely swim the width of a swimming pool, she could slip on a wetsuit and feel perfectly at ease in the sea with Simo. The dolphin, in turn, behaved completely differently around Tricia than he did with other people. With Jan Sendall, he was boisterous and uninhibited, happily

"**A whale's glimpse** of us is almost as rare as our glimpse of a whale," writes Diane Ackerman of her encounter with a right whale in Patagonia. "Her dark, plumlike eye fixed me and we stared at one another for some time."

roughhousing with the tough fisherman. But with Tricia, he appeared to sense her lack of confidence in the water. He would approach her gently, nudging her softly with his beak, supporting her from underneath, allowing her to ride on his back as he swam slowly at the surface. Simo was, it seemed, highly protective of her. He was also keen to spend time alone with her, away from the crowds of people who swarmed into the water as news of the dolphin's presence spread. When he felt crowded, he would gently steer Tricia away to a quiet area and play with her alone, splashing the water to warn the others to stay back.

Exchange of Worlds

Simo was by no means the first or only cetacean to show as much apparent interest in humans as people did in him. Anyone who has watched a pod of dolphins or porpoises make a beeline for the bow of a ship or boat and ride there for minutes at a time, then seen them twist and turn, gazing up at their human observers, must have wondered the same thing: Are they as curious about us as we are about them?

In numerous instances around the world, whales react with apparent fascination to the sound of instruments being played for their benefit by onboard musicians. A school of spotted dolphins happily plays and swims with divers and snorkelers in the Bahamas. At Monkey Mia in western Australia, a pod of bottlenose dolphins comes to shore every day to swim among the feet of fascinated visitors and to accept gifts of fish.

Two thousand years ago, the Roman historian Pliny the Elder wrote stories of the friendliness and playfulness of dolphins. One tale told of a boy and a dolphin who became devoted to each other, meeting at the shore and playing every day for years. One day, however, the

Diving with wild Atlantic spotted dolphins is permitted in the Bahamas (opposite, top) and gives humans an intimate look at the animals' highly social behavior.

Bottlenose dolphins (opposite, bottom) take advantage of a handout offered by a youngster in Monkey Mia, Australia. Dolphins seem to have a particular affinity for children.

An orca cow and calf (left) investigate a boat filled with whale watchers in the Pacific Northwest.

boy fell ill and died. After that the dolphin came to shore every day looking for its companion. When the dolphin's dead body was found in the surf, the local people mourned and said that the dolphin had died of grief over the loss of its friend.

One of the earliest documented stories of close contact between humans and wild cetaceans involved Pelorus Jack. From 1888 to 1911, Jack, a male Risso's dolphin, took it upon himself to act as unpaid pilot for mail steamers entering Pelorus Sound between the North and South Islands of New Zealand. So popular did Jack become that a special law was passed to protect him. This, however, may not have been enough; it is believed that Jack met his maker at the hands of a Norwegian whaling boat anchored in Pelorus Sound

in 1912. In more modern times, the "friendly wild dolphin" has found popular resonance in such fictionalized accounts as the TV series *Flipper* and the 1950s movie *Boy on a Dolphin* — although the latter earned its place in cultural history primarily for introducing the world to the sight of Sophia Loren in a wet T-shirt.

Interest in cetaceans has mushroomed since the mid-1970s, with stories and sightings of friendly cetaceans flooding in from places as diverse as England, Ireland, France, Italy, Australia, New Zealand, Brazil, and Alaska.

Besides such "friendlies," there are numerous brief encounters between cetaceans and swimmers, divers, and boaters. One humpback whale in Antarctica circled a ship while apparently gazing at the crew and rubbing its

back against the keel. A pair of fin whales off New England surfaced on either side of an inflatable boat and swam alongside as if escorting the boat operator into the shallows. And a young right whale in the Bay of Fundy swam up to a small boat, lifted it gently into the air with its nose, then set it back down softly on the surface of the water. There are also stories of dolphins saving the lives of exhausted swimmers by supporting them gently from underneath and even carrying them toward shore.

Transformative Encounters

Perhaps the most frequent site of close interactions between humans and wild cetaceans is in Baja California, where nursing migratory gray whales in San Ignacio Lagoon attract

thousands of sightseers every winter. The friendliness of these gray whales was not immediately evident to the first tourists and researchers to visit the area. Indeed, the grays' reputation, earned from the accounts of whalers, was of a species that would fiercely resist and attack any boat that came too close. Then, in the 1960s, stories began emerging of grays approaching skiffs and tour boats, and in 1975 some whales were reported hanging around boats for hours.

In 1977, Bill and Mia Rossiter were members of an expedition to San Ignacio

Lagoon. Several whales had approached to within several feet of their boat. Then, one afternoon, an adult whale appeared and surfaced alongside. To attract its interest, the Rossiters began singing to the whale; suddenly, the object of their attention gently lifted the boat up on its head. As they continued to sing, the Rossiters leaned over the side of the boat and rubbed the whale. It presented a flipper, which they pulled gently, then it opened its mouth and allowed the humans to rub its gums and baleen. They named her Amazing Grace.

The popularity and familiarity of these whales provided much of the impetus behind the international campaigns to free three grays trapped in the ice off Alaska in 1988 and against the proposed resumption of subsistence whaling by the Makah Indians of Washington State 10 years later. Close encounters with cetaceans, particularly when the interest seems to be mutual, can be extremely moving and profound experiences for many people.

In his book *Encounters with Whales and Dolphins*, Wade Doak recounts how photographer Dotte Larsen, who had visited the whales of San Ignacio in 1976, found them to be completely different when she returned in 1981. A mother and calf surfaced alongside her boat, gently rubbing and rocking it. Larsen was in awe. "They wanted to be petted, vying for attention, splashing us with their tails. [We] stroked them on the head, mouth, chin and back, but it was the eye – that four-inch, unblinking, benign eye – that penetrated my very being. It seemed to speak to me of all the pain inflicted by my ancestors ... I felt shame and guilt on behalf of all mankind."

Why do some wild cetaceans spend their time apparently not only enjoying human company but even, at times, seemingly seeking it out? There are no firm answers. Maybe there is no real explanation. Perhaps, like us, they are simply curious or playful.

One thing, however, is certain. Whatever their reason for doing so, those wild cetaceans that interact with humans are powerful ambassadors for their species. As Dotte Larsen's account vividly highlights, people who enjoy the cetaceans' company and attention almost invariably come away awed by the experience, filled with a fondness and respect for the marine mammals, and, in most cases, urgently wanting to add their voices to those calling for their protection.

A trainer (opposite, top) uses a series of whistle commands to motivate a bottlenose dolphin in Honduras.

Close encounter (left). Few people are unmoved after making contact with a gray whale in Baja's San Ignacio Lagoon, a designated safe haven for breeding and calving whales.

Questions surround dolphin therapy programs such as this one in Israel's Red Sea (right), but many people have a faith in the healing power of dolphins.

Dolphin Therapy

Do dolphins have special healing powers? Around the world, an increasing number of people think they do.

Dr. Horace Dobbs, director of International Dolphin Watch, was one of the first to popularize the theory. While studying wild dolphins in the mid-1980s, he noted that perennially shy, introverted humans became more relaxed and cheerful while swimming with dolphins and remained that way, for the most part, days later. Dolphins reputedly have a similar effect on clinically depressed individuals and autistic children.

One explanation may be that such playful, excitable, and affectionate creatures benefit the human psyche by offering unconditional affection like pets. Some scientists have drawn fire for suggesting that there also may be a physiological effect; they claim, for example, that dolphin sonar aids in the production of disease-fighting T-cells or the release of relaxing endorphins. More controversial still are various New Age authors who claim that "dolphin therapy" is some-how connected to the animals' spiritual nature and that swimming with them affects both body and soul.

Could such claims lead to a burgeoning trade in the captive-dolphin industry? Some conservationists think so. They also fear that tourists will become more aggressive in their efforts to swim with wild dolphins. As always, the goal of any sort of wildlife encounter is to be as unintrusive as possible. These curious creatures may approach you in the wild, but you should never intentionally try to bring them near, grab them, or chase after them in boats.

◆

Whale-Watching Destinations

◆

*Visit the top places in North America to view
migrating grays, thrill to breaching humpbacks,
kayak among orcas, mingle with wild dolphins,
and experience whales, dolphins, and porpoises
on their own terms.*

St. Lawrence River
Québec

Dress for cold, says the boat captain. "And I mean winter cold." It's late August, and some three dozen whale-watch passengers are toasty as they bask in abundant sunshine on the shores of Québec's **St. Lawrence River**. A sort of collective chuckle resonates from the group. The chuckle doesn't last long. ◆ The captain finishes her spiel, and the passengers watch as she dons two layers of fleece, heavy gloves, a fleece hat, a bright yellow two-piece Mustang survival suit, and clunky rubber boots. The passengers quietly scurry about to extricate spare clothes from their cars, then squirm and wriggle into survival suits and high-topped boots dispensed from the whale-watching company's shed. En masse, like a parade of one-color crayons, everyone waddles down the road to the beach and clambers aboard a small fleet of rigid-hulled, inflatable Zodiacs. ◆ The Zodiacs putter away from the beach toward the mouth of the harbor, picking up speed as they pull out of **Baie de Tadoussac** into the St. Lawrence. The temperature steadily drops out of summer and heads deep into autumn. Damp spray atomizes over the bow as each raft starts pounding the chop with jackhammer strength. The brassiness of the cockier passengers, who at first leaned out of the rafts and into the wind, soon falters and they too finally hunker down and grab hold of the safety ropes. ◆ The fleet streaks toward the offshore Prince Shoals lighthouse, which juts up improbably from the middle of the river, and the boats then fan out like a squadron of fighter jets, carving a wide, buzzing arc downstream. The indomitable St. Lawrence River is Canada's

Venture onto Canada's largest river to seek North America's only year-round population of beluga whales.

A population of about 650 belugas is now isolated in the St. Lawrence River and no longer migrates.

Preceding pages: Humpbacks sport unique tail flukes, which allow them to be identified by researchers.

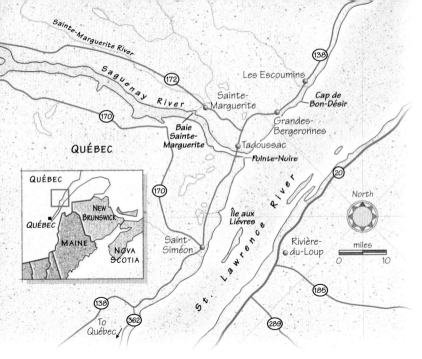

some former screwballs (now considered visionaries) decided that people would happily part with good money to view a small part of a large animal.

When you glance out over the wind-rippled surface of the wide river, it doesn't seem to hold any special qualities. The distant south shore is low and flat, scattered with homes and commercial businesses. The north shore, outside Tadoussac, is wilder and more remote, with high, sandy bluffs and eroded ridges topped with a prickly boreal forest.

So why are whales drawn here? The answer lies in large part on the bottom of the river. From the Gulf of St. Lawrence inland to Tadoussac, the river bottom is carved into a deep trough more than 1,000 feet deep in spots. At Tadoussac, however, the river bottom suddenly and steeply rises to about 100 feet. A complicated interaction of tides, currents, and temperature gradients ushers krill upstream along the river bottom to Tadoussac, where vigorous upwelling

Amazon, draining the Great Lakes and much of southern Québec eastward into the Atlantic Ocean. It seems a peculiar place for whales, so far from the deep ocean. Yet here, some 170 miles inland from the **Bay of St. Lawrence**, belugas, humpbacks, finbacks, minkes, and blues, among other whales, congregate in teeming numbers throughout the summer and fall. So consistent is their presence that the first commercial whale-watching tours took root in the 1970s in the Edwardian village of **Tadoussac**, when

Belugas (left) are wrapped in thick blubber, lack a dorsal fin, and have small front flippers and tail flukes that keep exposure to icy water minimal.

Sightings of endangered belugas (opposite) are frequent at the confluence of the Saguenay and St. Lawrence Rivers, but rarely do belugas come this close to a tour boat.

forces the food to the surface. Coupled with
the nutrient-rich waters from the Saguenay
River (look for the river's "plume" as it
trails out into the St. Lawrence), the region
is just too much for the whales to resist. It's
an all-you-can-eat smorgasbord.

Ice Age Relicts

The fleet of Zodiacs scuds along the river's
surface, then one, two, three engines suddenly
cut off. The boat captains point. The
chilled passengers unfurl stiffly from their
hunched positions and stand to scan the
waters, some fumbling with binoculars,
others with cameras. Maybe 200 yards
off to the south the group spots what looks
like a wayward arctic ice flow – gleaming
white slabs of ice tightly packed together.
But the ice seems to move. It undulates.
And it disappears. Belugas.

Belugas are commonly associated with
the shores of Greenland, the Canadian
Arctic, Alaska, and Russia; at the time of the
Ice Age, belugas could be found continuously
from the Arctic into the St. Lawrence. When
the ice sheet receded 10,000 years ago, the
St. Lawrence belugas were isolated from
their arctic cousins and formed a colony
that remained year-round. (Belugas are the

only whale to winter over in the St.
Lawrence.) While estimates have varied
widely over the years, current thinking
suggests that about 650 belugas now reside
in the St. Lawrence, down from an estimated
5,000 at the time of the first European settlers.
After years of being hunted, they are now
struggling with another foe: toxic pollution
in the St. Lawrence. Right now, their future
seems far from certain.

The Zodiacs don't approach the belugas.
These whales are protected, and commercial
outfitters aren't allowed to target them for
observation – they can't even drift toward
them. This sighting is a matter of happen-
stance, a fortuitous sighting on the way to
scouting for other whales. The passengers
murmur appreciatively, then the Zodiacs
throttle up and speed eastward.

Commercial boat tours aren't the only
way to view belugas. Following the lead of
the locals, you also can spot these whales
from the open deck of the 65-minute car ferry
that shuttles across the St. Lawrence between
Rivière-du-Loup and **Saint-Siméon**, a short
drive upstream from Tadoussac. Travel close
to high tide and keep binoculars handy as
you cruise along the shores of **Île aux
Lièvres**, the large island near Saint-Siméon.

Belugas also are spotted frequently from the shore, if you know where to go. Following the food supply, they swim far up the **Saguenay River** (it's technically a fjord) and congregate at remote **Baie Sainte-Marguerite**, about 24 miles upstream of Tadoussac. There's a new visitor center accessible by car (off Route 172) and a 2.1-mile nature trail that winds along the bay. Adventurous sorts can spend several days hiking and kayaking along the fjord from Tadoussac, camping at waterside sites, and admiring the glacially sculpted valley while watching for pods of belugas. Kayakers often report that the whales are naturally inquisitive and often surface next to the boats seemingly just to say hello.

Another good location is the juncture of the St. Lawrence and the Saguenay Rivers, across from Tadoussac, at **Pointe-Noire**, a Canadian heritage park. An observation center sits atop a high bluff here and is

staffed in summer with helpful naturalists who can guide visitors through the compact interpretive exhibits and help aim the spotting scopes in the right direction. Eastward along the St. Lawrence is **Cap de Bon-Désir**, another brawny and handsome park where you can rent binoculars to search the river for belugas and other whales.

Up Close or Too Close?

Out on the Zodiacs, the motors fall silent again as the fleet spots a pod of minke whales knifing gracefully through the water. Then, to the north, more whales surface – one, two, then three finbacks. Their prominent dorsal fins slice gracefully through the river, and they clear their blowholes forcefully and loudly. After a few passes, they arch sharply and dive deep and out of view.

And then, a real treat: The boats spot a great behemoth of the deep. A blue whale, the largest mammal on Earth, surfaces several times as it feeds enthusiastically along the river's surface. At one point, swimming on its side, it waggles a flipper, as if offering a greeting. Camera shutters click in unison.

The blue whale hasn't escaped the attention of about a dozen boats now on the river, including the open Zodiacs, an enclosed Zodiac, and a pair of larger double-decker whale-watch ships. All cluster around the spot the blue was last sighted, their bows pointed in a semicircle. It's like the whale paparazzi, and it brings to mind a cartoon taped to an office door at Le Centre d'Interprétation des Mammifères Marins (CIMM), the whale research center located on a small in-town isthmus between the Saguenay River and Tadoussac's harbor: Two whales besieged by tour boats are commiserating; one says, "Now I know how Princess Di felt."

Among the topics the center's researchers are delving into is the impact of tourism on whales. Radio beacons attached temporarily to the whales with suction cups measure the time they spend feeding and diving, both when tour boats are present and when they are alone. The early results are encouraging. All the attention seems to alter the feeding patterns slightly but not enough to make a difference. "If I interrupt your dessert, you may take a little longer to eat," says CIMM director Patrice Corbeil. "But is that really a problem?"

The blue whale soon sinks out of sight, and the feeding slows down all around. The river ripples into tight ridges as a cold wind rises, and the late summer twilight starts to spread. After nearly three hours on the water, the Zodiacs turn back toward Tadoussac, and the throttles open up. After 15 long minutes of cold and damp, the lipstick-red roof of the historic Tadoussac Hotel appears on the shore. Marking the harbor, the hotel is a welcome sight for the passengers. Thoughts of sipping a cocktail in the warm and gracious lobby help distract everyone from the one thing now on their mind: It's damn cold. Winter cold.

Canaries of the Sea

At birth they are dark gray, but they grow progressively lighter until they bleach pigment-free at about age six. They are belugas, often called white whales, a small, toothed whale with a stout body and round head.

Belugas are frequently referred to as the "canaries of the sea," a tribute to the way their wide repertoire of clicks, chirps, and whistles floods the world beneath the waves with sound. One purpose of the beluga's animated chatter is to communicate with its own kind. The whales also use sound, or echolocation, to hunt and to navigate through dense ice cover and shallow water.

But in the St. Lawrence River, the beluga might more accurately be likened to the "canary in the coal mine." Its demise is symbolic of the impact humans continue to have on the marine environment. Toxic chemicals, notably PCBs and pesticides, have been found in high levels in the whales' organs and blubber. Some have concentrations of pollutants as high as 600 parts per million (ppm); most countries consider fish unsuitable for human consumption if they contain 2 ppm of pollutants.

Autopsies conducted on belugas washed ashore have revealed an array of disorders. One young beluga had a perforated gastric ulcer with peritonitis, broncho-pneumonia, dermatitis associated with a herpes-like virus, immune suppression, and chronic hepatitis. Others suffered from the likes of cancer, ruptures of the pulmonary artery, and skin fibrosis. One beluga even had both male and female genital organs.

Through all this, the population continues to fall and is now about 650 – far less than the many thousands of belugas that swam in the river a century ago. For the St. Lawrence beluga, the future is seemingly bleak. – *Kieran Mulvaney and Beth Livermore*

Belugas in the St. Lawrence River (above) have been found to contain harmful compounds released from surrounding industrial areas.

Blue whales (opposite, top) occasionally venture into the river.

French explorer Jacques Cartier was the first European to view belugas (opposite, bottom) in the St. Lawrence River, in 1535.

TRAVEL TIPS

DETAILS

When to Go

Belugas can be seen in any season, but summer and early fall are the best times to see a variety of whales. Dress for subzero temperatures in winter. Summers are warm and buggy.

How to Get There

Major airlines serve Québec Airport in Québec City, about 135 miles southwest of Tadoussac via Route 138. Montréal International Airport is about 290 miles southwest of Tadoussac. Car rentals are available at the airports.

Getting Around

Tadoussac, at the confluence of the Saguenay and St. Lawrence Rivers, is reached via Route 138, on the north side of the St. Lawrence. From the southeast (including northern Maine), travelers can take a daily 65-minute ferry ride (April to December) from Rivière-du-Loup to Saint-Siméon. A free, year-round, 24-hour ferry crosses the mouth of the Saguenay, linking Pointe-Noir and Tadoussac.

INFORMATION

Association Touristique du Saguenay Lac-Saint-Jean

198 rue Racine est, bureau 210; Chicoutimi, Québec G7H 1R9, Canada; tel: 418-543-9778.

Parc du Saguenay

Ministère de l'Environment et de la Faune, 3415 boulevard de la Grande-Baie Sud, La Baie, Québec G7B 1G3, Canada; tel: 418-544-7388.

Parks Canada

Parc Marin Saguenay-St. Laurent, 182 rue de l'Église, Tadoussac, Québec G0T 2A0, Canada; tel: 418-235-4703.

CAMPING

Parc du Saguenay, 418-544-7388, operates a campground at Baie Éternité for campers with automobiles, and 10 primitive campgrounds along 37 miles of the fjord, reached by canoe or kayak, or on foot.

LODGING

PRICE GUIDE – double occupancy

$ = up to $49 $$ = $50–$99

$$$ = $100–$149 $$$$ = $150+

Hôtel Le Pionnier

263 rue des Pionniers, Tadoussac, Québec G0T 2A0, Canada; tel: 418-235-4666 or 418-236-9271.

This intimate hotel, set in the heart of Tadoussac, offers 25 guest rooms, most with views of the St. Lawrence River. A large terrace also overlooks the river. Breakfast, included in the price, is served in a breezy dining room. $$–$$$

Hôtel-Motel Baie Sainte-Catherine

294 Route 138, Baie-Sainte-Catherine, Québec G0T 1A0, Canada; tel: 877-444-7247 or 418-237-4271.

This quaint hotel at the mouth of Saguenay Fjord, facing the St. Lawrence River, has 16 renovated guest rooms with private baths and balconies; 11 have river views. Chalet-style motel units with kitchenettes are available. A restaurant serves breakfast, lunch, and dinner. $–$$

Hôtel-Motel Le Béluga

191 rue des Pionniers, Tadoussac, Québec G0T 2A0, Canada; tel: 418-235-4784.

This hotel in the heart of Tadoussac has 39 tastefully appointed guest rooms with one or two double beds, private baths, and river views. Le Beluga's adjacent restaurant, Auberge du Lac, is open daily, serving breakfast, lunch, and dinner. $$

Hôtel Tadoussac

165 rue Bord de l'Eau, Tadoussac, Québec G0T 2A0, Canada; tel: 800-463-5250 (winter), 800-561-0718 (summer), or 418-235-4421.

Perched high on a bluff above the harbor, the old beachfront hotel is the premier destination for whale watchers. Whales are visible from the lawn. Four boats, including a 500-passenger cruiser, make daily whale-watching trips. The hotel's 149 rooms have private baths, hand-woven bedspreads, and maple furniture; some have river views. Frescoes grace the dining room. A nine-hole golf course and swimming pool are on the premises. $$–$$$$

TOURS & OUTFITTERS

A number of whale-watching tours are available, typically lasting three hours. Vessels range from large catamarans with indoor seating to high-powered inflatable Zodiacs. Larger ships, warmer and more comfortable, permit better views of subsurface whales from upper decks. But for sheer exhilaration, however, nothing beats a Zodiac. Passengers are provided with waterproof coveralls and boots, and should dress warmly.

Compagnie de la Baie de Tadoussac

145 rue du Bord-de-l'Eau, Tadoussac, Québec, Canada, G0T 2A0; tel: 800-757 4548 or 418-235-4548.

The company's fleet of Zodiacs departs from Tadoussac four times daily in season. Dawn excursions (at 5 A.M.) are available upon request.

Les Croisières Express

161 rue des Pionniers, Tadoussac, Québec, G0T 2A0, Canada; tel: 888-235-6842 or 418-235-4770.

Whale-watching tours are conducted aboard three 12-passenger motor boats, including a covered Zodiac. Trips depart from Tadoussac and Baie Ste.-Catherine four times a day in season.

Mingan Island Cetacean Study

124 boulevard de la Mer, Longue-Pointe-de-Mingan, Québec C0G 1V0, Canada; tel: 418-949-2845 (June to October) or 514-465-9176 (November to May).

Naturalists lead multiday whale-watching trips aboard a research boat equipped with hydrophones.

MUSEUMS

Le Centre d'Interprétation des Mammifères Marins

108 rue de la Cale-Sèche; Tadoussac, Québec G0T 2A0, Canada; tel: 418-235-4701.

An essential stop for whale enthusiasts, the Marine Mammal Interpretive Center offers an 18-minute film on marine research, whale exhibits (including a half-scale model of a finback), and a map pinpointing daily whale sightings.

Pointe-Noir

Route 138, Baie-Sainte-Catherine, Québec G0T 1A0, Canada; tel: 418-237-4383 or 418-237-4703.

Across the mouth of the Saguenay River, this free interpretation and observation center is part of the Saguenay-St. Lawrence Marine Park. Guides assist visitors with spotter scopes, used to pick out and identify whales offshore. Some exhibits are available for inspection. Open mid-June to mid-October.

Excursions

Lower St. Lawrence Islands

Société Duvetnor Limitée, 200 rue Hayward, C.P. 305, Rivière-du-Loup, Québec G5R 3Y9, Canada; tel: 418-867-1660.

Near the confluence of the Saguenay and St. Lawrence Rivers, these small, rugged islands are owned by the Société Duvetnor Limitée, a conservation organization. Colonies of seabirds, including an estimated 25,000 pairs of eiders, inhabit the islands and estuaries; beluga whales are regularly seen from shore. In addition to research and conservation efforts, the organization offers ferry service and ecotourism programs. Participants stay in cottages, campgrounds, a lodge, or a restored lighthouse.

Mingan Archipelago National Park Reserve

1303 rue de la Digue, P.O. Box 1180, Havre-St.-Pierre, Québec G0G 1P0, Canada; tel: 800-463-6769 or 418-538-3331.

The reserve encompasses 40 islands and 800 islets near the north coast of the Gulf of St. Lawrence. Carved by the sea, the uniquely shaped limestone islands sustain 200 species of birds, including common eiders and large colonies of Atlantic puffins. Nine species of cetaceans inhabit the surrounding waters, where Atlantic white-sided dolphins and minke whales are commonly seen. Blue, humpback, and fin whales are seen farther offshore. The Mingan Island Cetacean Study offers day tours and extended research trips.

Percé

Information Touristique de Percé, C.P. 99, Percé, Québec G0C 2L0, Canada; tel: 418-782-5448.

Situated on the Gulf of St. Lawrence, Percé is the most remote of the Gaspé Peninsula towns, a tourist capital teeming with hotels, bed-and-breakfasts, and campgrounds. Whale-watching tours are conducted aboard a glass-bottomed catamaran. Cruises visit L'île-Bonaventure-et-du-Rocher-Percé Provincial Park, an offshore bird sanctuary. The massive Percé Rock, which rises a sheer 290 feet from the sea, is a popular hiking destination. An interpretive center focuses on the gulf's ecosystem.

Atlantic Provinces
Canada

CHAPTER **11**

ar out in the **Bay of Fundy**, with distant spruce-covered islands low and soft in the salty haze, a tour boat edges along the "footprint" of a whale. This somewhat fanciful term describes the glossy slick that lingers amid rough chop for a few moments after a whale disappears beneath the surface. A whale's mass and power are displayed most dramatically during a full breach, when it leaps into the air and roils the water all around. But the quiet afterimage left in its footprint also testifies to its size and might. A whale can both raise up the seas and calm them. ◆ The footprint seen today was left by a northern right whale, which migrated here to feast in this wedge-shaped bay on the northeast edge of the **Gulf of Maine**. The right whale is rather easy to identify. It lacks a dorsal fin, has a low spout that forms a distinctive V when seen from front or back, and its rounded head is encrusted with rough white patches, called callosities, which are often covered with barnacles and tiny crablike

The endangered right whale and other cetaceans find refuge in the nutrient-rich coastal waters of Newfoundland, Nova Scotia, and New Brunswick.

creatures known as sea lice. When you come upon the broad, blubbery back of a slow-moving right whale, you might guess how it got its name: Whalers regarded it as the "right" whale to hunt, because it provided abundant blubber, preferred calm inshore waters, and tended to float after it was killed. ◆ Seeing the ghostly footprint of a right whale imbues the tour with a melancholy air, since those aboard have been told about the species' precarious existence. The right whale was abundant in these coastal waters before the arrival of European whalers in the late 16th century. About 1,000 were killed each year during the height of the

Newfoundland sea cliffs. The local lingo, always colorful, describes harbor porpoises as "puffing pigs" and dolphins as "squid hounds."

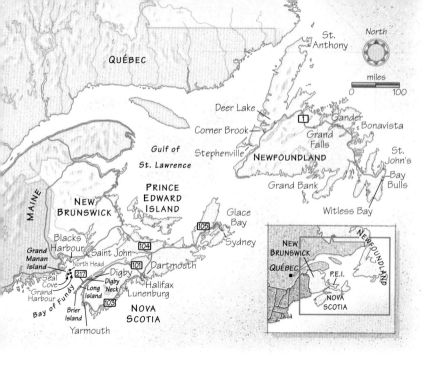

QUÉBEC

St. Anthony

miles
0   100

Deer Lake

Corner Brook

Gander

Bonavista

Grand Falls

NEWFOUNDLAND

St. John's

Bay Bulls

Grand Bank

Witless Bay

Gulf of St. Lawrence

Stephenville

PRINCE EDWARD ISLAND

MAINE

NEW BRUNSWICK

Glace Bay

Sydney

Blacks Harbour

Grand Manan Island

Saint John

North Head

Dartmouth

Digby

Halifax

Seal Cove

Long Neck Island

Grand Harbour

Lunenburg

Bay of Fundy

Brier Island

NOVA SCOTIA

Yarmouth

NEW BRUNSWICK

QUÉBEC

P.E.I.

NOVA SCOTIA

NEWFOUNDLAND

shipping traffic protocols have been altered, for example – but the sad fact remains that the species may be headed for extinction.

Summer Sanctuary

Northern right whales winter off Florida, Georgia, and the Carolinas, then migrate in summer to Cape Cod, Stellwagen Bank, and the cold, productive waters of the Bay of Fundy. The greatest concentrations – and the best place and time to spot them – are during the prime feeding months of July and August near **Passamaquoddy Bay** (on the Maine-New Brunswick border) and off the long, lonesome island of **Grand Manan**, the largest of the **Fundy Isles**.

Grand Manan is a 90-minute ferry ride from **Blacks Harbour** on the **New Brunswick** mainland. The island has some 2,800 year-round residents spread along its 15-mile length, mostly along the gentle eastern shore. A handful of inns and cottages caters to summer travelers, and bird-watchers gather here in great number during migrations, when they've cataloged as many as 275 avian species. Among those smitten by the island's seductive languor was the novelist Willa Cather, who wrote many of her best-known stories in a quiet summer cottage.

Right whales come not for the easy summer pace, of course, but for the copious krill and copepods. The powerful tides and topographically varied ocean floor combine with the cold Labrador Current near Grand Manan to provide vigorous upwellings of nutrient-rich water. Right whales typically skim food from the surface, but here they often dive deep, finding krill stretching out in long, deepwater trails that outdoor writer Harry Thurston has likened to rich seams of coal.

Several outfitters offer whale-watching

slaughter; their bleached bones still litter the shores of Red Bay, Labrador, along a once-popular migratory route. Twice the right whale was thought to be extinct – in the early 18th and mid-19th centuries – and twice it reappeared. As few as 20 animals were left in the 1930s when a global ban on hunting was imposed on the whaling industry.

Today, only about 300 northern right whales survive, and the future looks grim. Studies suggest that the population may be declining. Mortality from fishing nets and ship collisions is on the rise, and the whale's birth rate is dropping. Several steps have been taken in recent years to protect the right whale – commercial fishing and

trips ranging from two hours to an entire day. Boats also sail from **Campobello** and **Deer Islands**, and the towns of **Eastport, Maine**, and **St. Andrews, New Brunswick**. On the *D'Sonoqua*, a traditional 50-foot schooner, seven-hour whale excursions run throughout the summer, weather permitting. The boat sails past Atlantic salmon farms and islands populated with puffins, then angles offshore encountering pelagic birds such as storm petrels, shearwaters, and phalaropes. The pace slackens as the boat reaches an area dubbed the **Bulkhead**, where lively upwellings attract ravenous whales. Travelers themselves enjoy a meal of fresh seafood chowder while awaiting cetacean company. Captain James Bates says that whales are sometimes abundant here, sometimes not. He notes with concern that right whales haven't been seen with calves for the past two years, and that the whales have been returning to the open ocean much earlier in the season.

If right whales decline to make an appearance, others invariably fill in. Compact and sleek minke whales feed and cavort. Sei or humpback whales occasionally pass through the bay, but it's the fin whales – the second largest of all cetaceans – that

often steal the show. Some 35,000 populate the northern Atlantic, and by some estimates their numbers on the East Coast equal that of all other whales combined. "They've got a really powerful blow," says Bates. He also reports seeing four to eight fin whales feeding in groups just off the shore of Grand Manan.

End of the Road

The Bay of Fundy is shaped a bit like a battered trumpet – Grand Manan marks one side of the flared horn, and **Digby Neck**, Nova Scotia, the other. It's about 25 miles as the whale swims but nearly 400 by car. (You can trim that by hopping the ferry from Saint John, New Brunswick, to Digby, Nova Scotia, which itself provides a good platform for spotting whales.)

Cetologists (above) identify whales using photos of head callosities, patches of roughened skin called "bonnets" by early whalers.

Humpbacks (left) are identified by the distinct light and dark patterns on the underside of their tail flukes.

Peggy's Cove, a fishing village near Halifax, Nova Scotia (opposite). Nearby is the Bay of Fundy, whose famous "Fundy fogs" may have discouraged whalers and protected wildlife.

Digby Neck – a lanky peninsula and a pair of islands that extend about 40 miles southwest of the town of **Digby** – is more readily reached than Grand Manan but has a similarly remote character. To reach the end of the road requires two crossings on quick, inexpensive ferries – the first puts you on **Long Island**, another takes you to salty **Brier Island**, where roads weren't paved until the 1960s.

Situated at the vague boundary between open ocean and the Bay of Fundy, the neck was populated with thriving fishing communities until recently. The collapse of the region's fishing stocks left fishermen almost as endangered as the right whale. Saddled with boats and hefty payments, quite a few have turned to whale watching, outfitting their boats to accommodate passengers rather than cod. These are more homespun operations than the slick outfits in New England, but the boats are safe (Canadian Coast Guard regulations are enforced) and the crews have lived with the sea much of their lives. Many of the same whales seen off Grand Manan can be seen along these shores, as can the great leviathan of the sea, the blue whale.

Just beyond the **Tiverton** ferry on Long Island is Ocean Explorations, operated by marine biologist Tom Goodwin. He offers a damper perspective on whale tours aboard rigid-hulled Zodiacs, which power through the choppy waves and strong currents. Don't expect much in the way of luxe touches; do expect to wear a survival suit and be thrilled by the experience.

On the Rock

When right whales venture beyond the Bay of Fundy, they often edge north past the ragged Atlantic coast of Nova Scotia and the rounded headlands of **Cape Breton Island** to the icy waters off **Newfoundland**, known as "The Rock" to natives. Right whales aren't the chief reason to venture here – the Bay of Fundy is the safer bet for them. But if you're a lover of wild, lonely places, you'll appreciate the stern boreal landscape of bogs, berries, sea cliffs, and icebergs.

Newfoundland is the tenth largest island in the world, about a third larger than Ireland. The northern and eastern coastlines are wrinkled with peninsulas and bays and dotted with tiny fishing villages called outports. One of the best destinations for whale watching is the **Avalon Peninsula**, a vaguely H-shaped landmass off the island's southeast corner. Not only is it well populated with whales and whale-watching outfitters, it is reasonably compact and accessible. It's also home to **St. John's**, the island's largest and most vibrant city, and connected to the outside world with frequent commercial air service.

St. John's makes a superb base for whale scouts. From the downtown hotels, visitors can walk to dramatic **North Head Trail**, which follows the rocky northern edge of the harbor. From the bluffs at the harbor's mouth, the view of the rugged coastline is sweeping and remarkably unchanged since the region was first visited by Europeans 500 years ago. Bring a picnic lunch and binoculars and watch for whales and icebergs. Some 17 species of whales have been sighted off Newfoundland, with humpback and minkes among the most common. Keep an eye out for fin, pilot, blue, sperm, and sei whales, too. Less common are belugas and narwhals.

Whale-watching tours are available in several harbor towns along the Avalon Peninsula. From St. John's itself you have a number of choices, ranging from a 90-foot schooner to sea kayaks. Pilots also offer whale watching from helicopters. Heading south along the coast, you'll find whale-watching tours in **Bay Bulls** and **Witless Bay**, two villages that offer the added advantage of being near the offshore **Witless Bay Ecological Preserve**, famous for its teeming, screeching masses of seabirds. In Newfoundland you can do something remarkable: watch whales, puffins, and icebergs all at once, without even shifting in your seat.

Wherever your adventure in the Atlantic Provinces takes you, a trip is likely to be tinged with both awe and melancholy – awe at the vast and austere landscape, and sadness that such abundant waters have been so depleted. There's still time to change that, and with every glimpse of a right whale, one hopes that others, too, will take up the challenge.

Flights of Fancy

The puffin is Newfoundland's provincial bird, and it's emblazoned everywhere – on brochures, T-shirts, and all manner of souvenirs. As official symbols go, it's certainly among the best – comical yet regal, colorful and lively. Puffins fail to shake the impression that they're cute little penguins who've run amok at the cosmetics counter.

In their own way, the seabirds of Newfoundland are as exotic and curious as anything found in the tropical jungles. Puffins lead the weirdness parade, with their stumpy profile, fancy colors, and cliffside burrows. They nest in areas safe from predators, which usually means islands or sea stacks, and can be viewed on boat tours from the **Avalon Peninsula**.

Among other birds that can be observed in the region are murres with their garish red legs, razorbills, guillemots, and black-legged kittiwakes. Some 3.3 million Leach's storm petrels inhabit **Baccalieu Island** to the north-west of **St. John's**. At Cape St. Mary, more than 5,000 gannets – beautiful, swan-sized birds with latte-colored heads – nest cacophonously on an impressive sea stack that's easily viewed from a mainland wildlife preserve.

Northern gannets (above) live in large colonies on the coastal cliffs of Newfoundland.

Atlantic puffins (left), also called sea parrots, catch fish in their large, colorful bills as they "fly" underwater.

Round bumps known as tubercles are visible on the head of a surfacing humpback whale (opposite, top).

DETAILS

When to Go

Most whale-watching companies offer tours in summer only. Summer temperatures in Nova Scotia occasionally reach into the low 90s, but are considerably cooler offshore. Newfoundland tends to be cooler, with coastal temperatures peaking around 70°F. Prepare for intermittent cold and fog. Summer nights average in the 50s and 60s.

How to Get There

Major airlines serve Saint John Airport in New Brunswick, Halifax International Airport in Nova Scotia, and St. John's Airport in Newfoundland. Ferries to Grand Manan operate year-round. For information, call 506-662-3724. Marine Atlantic ferries operate between North Sydney, Nova Scotia, and Port aux Basques and Argentia, Newfoundland. For information, call 902-794-5700. St. John's, Newfoundland, is about a 20-hour drive (plus a 5-hour ferry ride) from Halifax, Nova Scotia.

Getting Around

A car is essential for getting around Nova Scotia and Newfoundland. Grand Manan is best traveled by car or bike.

INFORMATION

Grand Manan Tourism Association

P.O. Box 193, North Head, Grand Manan, NB E0G 2M0, Canada; tel: 506-662-3442.

Newfoundland and Labrador Department of Tourism

P.O. Box 8730, St. John's, NF A1B 4K2, Canada; tel: 800-563-6353 or 709-729-2830.

Nova Scotia Department of Tourism

Box 130, Halifax, NS B3J 2M7, Canada; tel: 800-341-6096 or 902-424-5000.

CAMPING

Anchorage Provincial Park

Seal Cove, Grand Manan, NB E0G 1L0, Canada; tel: 506-662-7022.

This Grand Manan park has 100 campsites available by reservation or on a first-come, first-served basis. Open from May to October.

Pippy Park Campground

P.O. Box 8861, St. John's, NF A1B 3T2, Canada; tel: 709-737-3669.

Situated in the city of St. John's, the campground offers 184 tent and RV sites with bath and shower facilities.

LODGING

PRICE GUIDE – double occupancy

$ = up to $49	$$ = $50–$99
$$$ = $100–$149	$$$$ = $150+

Inn at Whale Cove Cottages

P.O. Box 233, North Head, Grand Manan, NB E0G 2M0, Canada; tel: 506-662-3181.

The inn's main house was built between 1816 and 1860 and is decorated with Shaker furniture. Guest rooms have private entrances and baths. Housekeeping cottages are available for weekly rental. A restaurant and gourmet take-out shop are available. $$

McCoubrey Manor Bed-and-Breakfast

8 Ordnance Street, St. John's, NF A1C 3K7, Canada; tel: 888-753-7577 or 709-722-7577.

Situated in the historic district of St. John's, this striking 1904 townhouse was the home of James McCoubrey, a prominent merchant. The bed-and-breakfast offers four guest rooms with private baths; three of the rooms have fireplaces, two have Jacuzzis. All are furnished with antiques. Breakfast, evening snacks, and the use of laundry facilities are included. $$–$$$

Monkstown Manor Bed-and-Breakfast

51 Monkstown Road, St. John's, NF A1C 3T4, Canada; tel: 888-754-7377 or 709-754-7324.

Built in 1890, this downtown St. John's bed-and-breakfast has four guest rooms with shared bathrooms. Rooms are replete with Newfoundland art and memorabilia. Hosts arrange wildlife tour packages. A patio, garden, and large Jacuzzi are on the premises. $$

Oakwood Manor

250 Northside Road, Cape North, NS B0C 1G0, Canada; tel: 902-383-2317.

Built in 1930, this manor occupies a 150-acre farm in Cape Breton's Sunrise Valley, about two miles off the Cabot Trail. The interior is enriched by oak walls, floors, doors, and ceilings, with bird's-eye maple inserts. Guest rooms have private baths; some have queen-size beds and Jacuzzis. A suite has two single beds, a sofa bed, private bath, Jacuzzi, and private patio. A full breakfast is included. $$

Westport Bed-and-Breakfast Inn

Box 1226, Westport, NS B0V 1H0, Canada; tel: 902-839-2675.

Homey and affordable, this inn occupies a turn-of-the-century house on the Bay of Fundy. Six comfortably appointed rooms are available, five with shared baths, three with bay views. A glass sun porch and veranda offer a full view of the bay. The price includes breakfast at the inn's restaurant, next door. $–$$

TOURS & OUTFITTERS

Island Coast Boat Tours

P.O. Box 59, Castalia, Grand Manan, NB E0G 1L0, Canada; tel: 506-662-8181.

A 25-passenger boat departs from Grand Manan daily from July 1 to September 15. Narrated tours focus on whales, island life, the commercial fishing industry, and birds. Whale sightings are guaranteed.

O'Brien's Whales and Birds Tour

150 Old Topsail Road, St. John's, NF A1E 2B1, Canada; tel: 877-639-4253 or 709-753-4850.

Two 90-passenger boats depart from Witless Bay and explore the waters around Gull and Green Islands.

Pirate's Cove Whale and Seabird Cruises

Box 624, Tiverton, NS B0V 1G0, Canada; tel: 888-480-0004 or 902-839-2242.

The operator's 40- and 20-passenger boats depart three or more times daily from June to October. A naturalist narrates the trips, which frequently result in sightings of humpback, northern right and minke whales, Atlantic white-sided dolphins, harbor porpoises, seals, and many types of seabirds.

Brier Island Whale and Seabird Cruises

Water Street, Westport, NS, Canada; tel: 902-839-2995.

Four-hour whale-watching tours are offered in the Bay of Fundy aboard vessels each carrying about 45 passengers.

MUSEUMS

Grand Manan Whale and Seabird Research Station

Box 9, North Head, Grand Manan, NB E0G 2M0, Canada..

This small museum focuses on the marine ecology of the Bay of Fundy.

Excursions

Cape Breton Highlands National Park

Ingonish Beach, NS B0C 1L0, Canada; tel: 902-285-2270 or 902-285-2691.

Near the northern tip of Cape Breton Island about 290 miles from Halifax, the park preserves Nova Scotia's largest wilderness area. The highland plateau abounds with lakes, bogs, forests, canyons, and river gorges. Twenty-seven hiking trails wind through the park, which is bordered by the Cabot Trail, one of the most beautiful sightseeing tracks in North America. Moose, minks, red foxes, and bald eagles are often spotted along the trails; whales are seen offshore from Meat Cove, just north of the park.

Gros Morne National Park

P.O. Box 130, Rocky Harbour, NF A0K 4N0, Canada; tel: 709-458-2417.

This park, situated along the Gulf of St. Lawrence in western Newfoundland, was designated a UNESCO World Heritage Site in 1987. In addition to the sublime Long Range Mountains, Gros Morne features four freshwater fjords, towering waterfalls, marine inlets, sea stacks, and sandy beaches. Tour boats transport passengers into the fjords. Pilot whales are seen from the park in July and August.

Lunenburg

Town of Lunenburg, 119 Cumberland Street, P.O. Box 129, Lunenburg, NS B0J 2C0, Canada; tel: 902-634-4410.

This historic coastal town, about 100 miles south of Halifax, was established in 1753 and designated a UNESCO World Heritage Site in 1995. Strewn with charming 18th-century buildings, the former British colonial settlement is home to the excellent Fisheries Museum of the Atlantic, which examines the town's maritime history and German heritage. *Bluenose II*, a replica of Canada's most famous tall ship, may be visited in its home port. Boat tours and whale-watching trips are available at the harbor.

Gulf of Maine

CHAPTER 12

A sleek, three-decker catamaran of gleaming brushed aluminum cruises in large, lazy circles about 20 miles off **Mount Desert Island**. On a clear day, the fabled Maine coast rises distantly to the north, with the rounded peaks of **Acadia National Park** the most prominent landmarks. But today the seascape is swaddled in a dense and muffling fog, with visibility of just 50 yards or so. It's like being inside a Ping-Pong ball.   ◆   What's most impressive isn't the seascape but the absolute silence. The whale watchers clustered tightly along the rails are soundless, listening intently, cocking their heads this way and that, hoping to hear the blow of a whale. The only interruption in the silence is the deep thrum of the idling engines, the gentle chop as the boat rises and falls on glassy swells, and the man in the maroon windbreaker indelicately transferring his lunch back into a paper bag.   ◆   Exhaling

A boat from Bar Harbor is the ticket to the Ballpark, the watery haven of finback, minke, humpback, and rare right whales.

whales can be heard up to a half-mile away, but so far today they've refused to come near. After 15 minutes, the silence begins to erode. Kids no longer find it entertaining to peer through the wrong end of their binoculars. Elderly passengers start whispering about heading down to the galley for a nice cup of chowder. Zack, the onboard naturalist, notices the shift in attention and, like a comedian whose routines are falling flat, resumes his banter and starts to talk faster. Over the boat's booming sound system he recalls wonderful sightings from last year and speaks poetically of humpbacks in full breach and of whales returning from deep dives, their heads smeared with mud. The ship continues in large, lazy circles,

A curious humpback pokes its head out of the water, a behavior known as spyhopping, and reveals the pleated throat common to all rorqual whales.

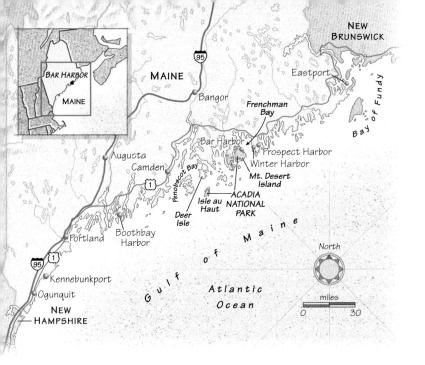

diner for the Atlantic's cetaceans, which migrate here through the summer and early fall to indulge in a banquet of plankton, krill, and copepods.

Oceanographers describe the Gulf of Maine as somewhat like a shallow bathtub perched at the edge of the much deeper Atlantic Ocean. Whereas the Atlantic can plunge to depths of 11,000 feet, the Gulf of Maine is only some 900 feet at its deepest point, and it is frequently much shallower due to isolated banks that rise from the ocean floor.

the passengers hoping and listening.

The **Gulf of Maine** is that vast swath of sea that falls between the pincers of Cape Cod to the south and Nova Scotia to the north. It's edged by thousands of miles of coastline (were one to straighten the kinks out of Maine's coast, it would run more than 3,000 miles) and dotted with thousands of remote islands. The Gulf of Maine isn't especially well known among tourists – most know it by component parts like Penobscot Bay or the Bay of Fundy – but it stands out as prominently as a neon-lighted, 24-hour

From the perspective of the marine mammal, the Gulf has much to recommend itself. It's blessed with delightfully frigid waters, for starters. The warm Gulf Stream trends north from the Caribbean to Cape Cod, but it then arcs eastward toward Europe, bypassing the Gulf of Maine entirely. The Gulf is flushed with currents from the Arctic, which arc southward around Nova Scotia. A rich soup of microscopic nutrients thrives in the cold, oxygen-loaded water, which attracts marine creatures all the way up the food chain to whales. The

Boothbay Harbor, Maine (right), has been serving travelers ever since steamer service was established in the 1870s. Whale-watching tours abound.

Lunge-feeding (opposite, top). A humpback surfaces with jaws agape, its distended throat filled with water and food.

Lobster buoys (opposite, bottom) at Bass Harbor, Mount Desert Island, near Acadia National Park.

whole process is helped along by underwater turbulence that propels a steady flow of food toward the surface – a result of local currents pairing up with unusually high tides (about 8 to 12 feet at Bar Harbor and exceeding 50 feet far up Canada's Bay of Fundy).

Back from the Brink

The tremendous whales off Newfoundland caught the attention of Basque whalers as early as the 16th century, but hunters set up bases all along the Maine coast, in ports like **Winter Harbor** and **Prospect Harbor**. The prized right whale was depleted by 1750, but whalers were still stalking humpback and finback whales as late as the mid-19th century. By 1900, with whales dwindling from overhunting, whaling had more or less ceased in the Gulf of Maine.

Three-quarters of a century later, with the help of

protective laws, whales had re-established themselves in the Gulf and were again enjoying the banquet in increasing numbers. This time they caught the attention of entrepreneurs, who, like the whalers before them, established bases in ports along the Maine coast. Travelers today can set out into the Gulf of Maine on whale-watch boats from several picturesque harbor towns, including **Ogunquit**, **Kennebunkport**, **Portland**, **Boothbay Harbor**, and **Eastport**.

Maine's premier location for whale watchers is **Bar Harbor**, the de facto capital of Acadia National Park, one of the most heavily visited national parks in the United States. Bar Harbor is scenically located on the northeast corner of Mount Desert Island (connected to the mainland via a short, two-lane causeway) between the rugged islands of Frenchman Bay and the hulking, glacially sculpted

hills of the island's interior, which rise to heights of 1,500 feet.

Bar Harbor is a love-it-or-leave-it kind of place. Many visitors savor the human scale of the downtown and its elegant, turn-of-the-century commercial architecture. They love the stout shingled summer homes (many converted to inns) that line the bay and recall the region's golden days, when Bar Harbor was the summer colony to some of the nation's most affluent families, including the Rockefellers, Carnegies, and Fords. Others find the town rather cheesy, given over wholesale to tourists who elbow their way into shops for overpriced T-shirts and ice-cream cones. The traffic can be aggravating during the peak summer season.

In Bar Harbor, whale watching happens to be an adjunct activity, not the main event. Mountain biking on the extraordinary network of park carriage roads is the chief attraction. Yet whale watching plays a significant role in the local economy, as just a

few minutes of wandering downtown will attest. You'll be handed brochures picturing humpback whales breaching. You'll stop to view television monitors in storefronts running video loops of finbacks feeding and contented tourists snapping photos. You may wander into a purported whale museum only to discover that it's a well-done ploy for what amounts to an ambitious trinket shop. Competition for tourist dollars is keen, which results in a sort of superlatives inflation: the four tour-boat operators variously claim to be the fastest, smoothest riding, best located, and most comfortable.

One trait the tour companies do share is a knack for efficiently herding large numbers of people; the intimate whale-watch adventure you might find elsewhere along the Maine coast or in Atlantic Canada isn't the allure here. But there's something to be said for being on a fast and modern boat – with heated cabins and a galley offering hot chocolate – when most of the action is miles offshore. The less time in transit, the more time spent scanning the seas for whales.

At the Ballpark

As the whale watchers aboard the aluminum catamaran have discovered this day, the trips also share an element of chance, no matter which boat company you select. Before the ship pulled away from the dock this morning, the captain announced that a persistent fog was present offshore (in contrast to the brilliant sunshine onshore), and this would limit chances of a sighting. Anyone who wanted to disembark could get a full refund. No one did.

The boat motored slowly past downtown Bar Harbor, past the stately summer mansions, past Bar Island studded with spruce and fir and connected to the mainland via a low-tide sandbar (hence the town's name). After steering wide of a group of sea kayakers, the ship aimed for the open sea, the

engines throttled up, and soon the catamaran hit its cruising speed of 40 knots. A gauzy curtain of fog rose seamlessly from the steely sea ahead, and the ship plowed full speed into it. A sort of early, unearthly twilight descended over the ship.

The boat slowed and began its lazy circling at The Ballpark, so named by local fishermen because they often hit "home runs" here. The depth of outer Frenchman Bay is typically about 200 to 300 feet, but at the Ballpark there's a ridge where the floor abruptly drops off to 500 feet. As a result, there's lots of upwelling, and lots of whales. In theory, at

The Craft of Scrimshaw

It would be nice to think that the majesty of the whale or the mystique of the hunt gave birth to what some people claim is the only nonaboriginal American folk art: scrimshaw. But the real reason is much more prosaic. It was sheer boredom that drove sailors to whittling, sculpting, and etching the only material they had at hand – the bones and teeth of whales and dolphins.

The most popular scrimshaw themes are almost always related to the sea or the opposite sex. Lassies in tartan, hula dancers, Greek goddesses, Madonnas, mermaids, and trollops were carved by sailors longing for homegrown pleasures. Religious and patriotic themes also recurred, with crucifixions and eagles among the most common. Sometimes scrimshaw served practical purposes; men carved nautical gear, combs, brushes, and belt buckles for their own use, and corset stays, hairpins, clothespins, and pie crimpers for their ladies back home.

The art of scrimshaw is still very much alive in the United States, primarily in New England, Alaska, the West Coast, and on the Hawaiian island of Maui, which is said to be the largest market today.– *Rita Ariyoshi*

This dolphin jaw (above) was carved by a 19th-century scrimshander. Today "sim-shaw," an artificial alternative, is also available.

Whale watchers (top) get a close look at a pod of humpback whales feeding in the Gulf of Maine.

Fin whales (opposite), often confused with blue and sei whales, have asymmetrical coloring: white on the lower right side of the head and black on the lower left.

least. Today, in the heavy fog, the light wind casts a mackerel pattern on the water, and the diffused sunlight reflects back into the fog off the brushed aluminum, creating evanescent rainbows visible out of the corner of one's eye. The more intrepid passengers maintain their vigil at the rail. Others head inside to view Zack's photos of whales and to pass around the weirdly bony baleen plate recovered from a deceased whale.

Star Performers

Other days, whales surface. Lots of them. The most commonly spotted whales hereabouts are the finback and minke. The graceful finback, the second largest whale after the blue whale, is impressive in many ways. A finback can measure up to 80 feet long, can live to 90 years old, and has a powerful spout that can rise as high as 20 feet. For all that, however, experienced whale watchers often affect a shruggy, "been-there-done-that" attitude around finbacks, in part because they're so common and in part because they feed less exuberantly than other whales. They're also rather shy about exposing their flukes, reducing chances of that great photo opportunity.

Minkes are the most abundant of the Atlantic whales and among the smallest, topping out at just 28 feet in length. They tend

A rare and thrilling sight, this endangered northern right whale (top) is one of just a few hundred. Populations have never recovered from overhunting.

A sailboat captain (right) guides his vessel through Penobscot Bay; cetaceans are often sighted on multiday sailing tours.

Maine's scenic lighthouses (opposite) are excellent places to spot whales from shore.

to be bashful and keep their distance from tour boats, but it's not uncommon to catch sight of one or more prominently hooked dorsal fins arcing out of the water as they breathe two or three times before diving deeper. Though small, minkes tend to elicit a soothing chorus of "ooohs" from the rails.

"Home runs" for whale watchers at the Ballpark usually involve the spotting of a humpback or right whale. The burly humpbacks have been deepwater celebrities among whale lovers ever since their haunting underwater songs were first recorded, although the males rarely sing during the summer, reserving that for their wintering grounds in the Caribbean. But whale watchers here may see a good show when the humpbacks feed. They are known to lunge at schools of fish near the surface, stun them with a smart thwack of a flipper on the water's surface, or work in small groups to cut off the escape routes of prey schools. More than a century ago, a boat sank near Portland after being caught in a humpback bubble net. And one of the most dramatic of sights on the open ocean is that of a humpback all but exploding out of the water in full breach.

While somewhat less showy, the right whale is prized for its extreme rarity. Only some 300 to 400 right whales are thought to survive in this part of the Atlantic (other diminished populations are found near South Africa, Argentina, and Australia) after having been hunted almost to extinction by whalers after their oil. You'll know if it's a right by the bumpy callosities on the head and by its distinctive spout, which, when seen from front or back, forms a prominent V, like old rabbit-ear TV antennas.

Occasional Strikeouts

It's a nice touch of irony that the fog that obscures the whales from view today is in part the reason

they are here: Fog forms offshore where the cold currents full of nutrients mix at the surface with the warm summer air, resulting in condensation and zero visibility. After more than an hour of circling and listening, nothing is seen, nothing is heard. Today, alas, the Ballpark produces only strikeouts.

The boat revs up, starts back to shore, and streaks out of the fog and into sunshine as it speeds past Egg Rock Light. The passengers, now lolling about on the open decks, seem curiously content and relaxed. While no one can guarantee that they'll see a whale every time, this boat does hand your money back if no whales are spotted. For whale watchers, the afternoon was a bust. But for the passengers now enjoying the sun, the islands, and the sweeping views, this excursion was made somewhat sweeter by Zack's words, heard all too rarely where tourists congregate: Enjoy it. It's free.

TRAVEL TIPS

DETAILS

When to Go

Midsummer is the best season for whale-watching in the Gulf of Maine. Coastal temperatures reach the 80s; fog, wind, and rain are intermittent. Temperatures at sea are much cooler; bring warm clothing.

How to Get There

Major airlines serve Bangor International Airport, about an hour's drive from Bar Harbor. Colgan Air, 800-272-5488, offers commuter flights from Boston to Trenton, across the bay from Bar Harbor.

Getting Around

Most whale-watching companies are based in or around Bar Harbor, at the gateway to Acadia National Park. Mass transit is limited. Cars, available for rent at the airports, are essential for travel afield.

INFORMATION

Bar Harbor Chamber of Commerce

93 Cottage Street, Bar Harbor, ME 04644; tel: 207-288-5103.

Maine Tourism

P.O. Box 2300; Hallowell, ME 04347; tel: 800-533-9595 or 207-623-0363.

CAMPING

Acadia National Park

P.O. Box 177; Bar Harbor, ME 04609; tel: 800-365-2267.

The park has more than 500 campsites. Reservations are required for some sites from June 15 to September 15.

LODGING

PRICE GUIDE – double occupancy

$ = up to $49 $$ = $50–$99

$$$ = $100–$149 $$$$ = $150+

Bar Harbor Inn

Newport Drive, Bar Harbor, ME 04609; tel: 800-248-3351 or 207-288-3351.

The inn's three buildings, situated at the head of Frenchman Bay, offer 153 rooms, many with bay views. Live music, seafood dinners, and views of lobster boats, yachts, and schooners are available in the inn's two restaurants. Amenities include a spa and heated swimming pool. $$-$$$$

Bar Harbor Tides

119 West Street, Bar Harbor, ME 04609; tel: 207-288-4968.

The inn occupies an 1887 Greek Revival mansion overlooking Frenchman Bay, five minutes from Acadia National Park. Three suites have ocean views, king-size beds, and private parlors; two have fireplaces. An economy suite has a four-poster queen-size bed and a private bath. Gourmet breakfasts are served on the veranda or near the fireplace. The inn is situated on one and a half acres, with gardens and shade trees. $$-$$$$.

Breakwater 1904

45 Hancock Street, Bar Harbor, ME 04609; tel: 207-288-2377.

This turn-of-the-century Tudor cottage is set on four waterfront acres. The inn has six guest rooms. An adjoining carriage house has two-bedroom efficiency apartments, available for weekly rental year-round. $$$$

Inn at Canoe Point

Eden Street, P.O. Box 216, Bar Harbor, ME 04609; tel: 207-288-9511.

The inn, nestled among pines on Frenchman's Bay, is two miles from downtown Bar Harbor, within walking distance of the entrance to Acadia National Park. Built in 1889, the large Tudor house offers ocean views from two suites and three guest rooms. A common room has a granite fireplace and views of the sea and mountains. Breakfast is served on a large deck overlooking the water. $$-$$$$

Kingsleigh Inn

373 Main Street, P.O. Box 1426, Southwest Harbor, ME 04679; tel: 207-244-5302.

This turreted Colonial Revival, built in 1904, was once the custom house for Southwest Harbor's schooner fleet. Fifteen minutes from Bar Harbor, the inn has eight guest rooms with private baths, lace curtains, and period antiques; most rooms have views of the harbor. A spacious third-floor suite offers a panoramic view, living room, fireplace, and four-poster king-size bed. A library, sitting room, and wraparound veranda are available. Breakfast is served on a sun porch. $$-$$$$

Pilgrim's Inn

P.O. Box 69, Deer Isle, ME 04627; 207-348-6615.

This four-story inn, built in 1793, is distinguished by a warm and cultivated atmosphere. Thirteen guest rooms are furnished with antiques; 10 have private baths; a cottage has a kitchen and fireplace. Amenities include a parlor, library, and two sitting rooms with fireplaces. A swimming pool and beach are available on the inn's two waterfront acres. Egrets, blue herons, and ospreys inhabit the tidal pond off the rear lawn. Gourmet dinners are served in a rustic dining room. $$-$$$$

TOURS & OUTFITTERS

Acadian Whale Watcher

Golden Anchor Pier, 56 West Street, Bar Harbor, ME 04609; tel: 800-421-3307 or 207-288-9794.

The operator offers four-hour

trips and a shorter sunset cruise daily from mid-May to late October. Excursions are led by a naturalist from Acadia National Park. The boat accommodates 150 passengers.

Bar Harbor Whale Watch Company

39 Cottage Street, Bar Harbor, ME 04609; tel: 800-942 5374 or 207-288-2386.

Based at the Regency Holiday Inn, this company operates *Friendship V*, a three-deck, 200-seat catamaran. Two- to three-hour trips sail from the inn's pier daily between mid-June and late September.

Maine Whalewatch

P.O. Box 78, Northeast Harbor, ME 04662; tel: 207-228-5803.

Nine-hour trips are offered daily from June to September in association with Allied Whale, a cetacean research group at the College of the Atlantic. Naturalists lead research-oriented trips aboard a 38-passenger boat.

Seafarers Expeditions

P.O. Box 691; Bangor, ME 04401; tel: 207-942-7942.

Founded in 1981, this company offers two five-day packages to Grand Manan Island in July and August. Passengers ride aboard the 42-foot *Sea Princess*, a converted fishing boat. Price includes ground transportation, lodging, meals, and professional guides, including naturalists from New England Whale Watch and the New England Aquarium.

MUSEUMS

Bar Harbor Whale Museum

52 West Street; Bar Harbor, ME 04609; tel: 207-288-2339.

This small museum explores whaling history and the natural history of cetaceans in the Gulf of Maine. Open in summer only.

Excursions

Deer Isle

Deer Isle/Stonington Chamber of Commerce, Deer Isle, ME 04627; tel: 207-348-6124.

Dubbed Avalon by John Steinbeck, this unspoiled isle on Penobscot Bay is about 60 miles south of Bangor. Home to fishermen and quarrymen for centuries, the nine-mile-long body has four villages – Deer Isle, Sunset, Sunshine, and Stonington Harbor – and an abundance of hiking, boating, kayaking, and fishing. The Nature Conservancy maintains two preserves on the island. Craftsmen teach summer classes in weaving, smithery, pottery, and glasswork at Haystack Mountain School of Crafts.

Isle au Haut

Acadia National Park, P.O. Box 177, Bar Harbor, ME 04609; tel: 207-288-3338.

Fabulous hiking and camping are available on this rugged, six-by-three-mile island, the southern half of which is part of Acadia National Park. Trails wind along cobblestone coves and up rocky peaks scoured by sea breezes and ringed with blueberry bushes. The trails offer fine vantages for whale watching. Mail boats provide twice-daily transportation between Stonington and the island.

Roosevelt Campobello International Park

Roosevelt Campobello International Park, P.O. Box 97, Lubec, ME 04652; tel: 506-752-2922 or P.O. Box 9, Welshpool, Campobello, NB E0G 3H0, Canada.

This unique international park, about two hours from Bar Harbor, is managed jointly by the United States and Canada. The 2,700-acre park includes much of Campobello Island's southern shore.

Wonderful seaside hikes sometimes result in sightings of endangered right whales. The focus of the park is Franklin D. Roosevelt's family cottage (more like a mansion), where young Franklin summered for four decades before developing polio in 1921. Beware of the massive tides, which exceed 20 feet.

Stellwagen Bank
National Marine Sanctuary
Massachusetts

CHAPTER **13**

On a clear day in winter, you can stand on the pristine beaches of **Provincetown**, at the tip of **Cape Cod**, and watch for whales much as the colonists did. Perhaps you will glimpse dorsal fins cleaving the horizon or whale spouts blowing like geysers. At such times, it's not difficult to imagine men pushing dories after right whales, Indians boiling blubber on the beach, and three-masted clipper ships on the watery horizon.   ◆   But for a close encounter with North Atlantic whales, return to Cape Cod between June and September and take to the seas. Every summer, just seven miles offshore at the 842-square-mile **Stellwagen Bank National Marine Sanctuary**, one of the world's greatest gatherings of whales takes place.   ◆   As many as 17 species of whales, dolphins, and porpoises visit these waters. Common part-time residents include the endangered finback and the diminutive minke whale, plentiful here all summer. In spring, Atlantic white-sided dolphins play in bow wakes, and harbor porpoises frolic on the horizon.

The historic center of American whaling is now one of the most popular spots for summer whale watching.

Blue whales and sei whales are occasionally spotted. And though rare, sperm, killer, and northern right whales have been seen in the sanctuary. Of the many whales swimming these waters, the humpback is the most common. Approximately 100 humpbacks spend about six months here, feeding on sand lance and other small fish.   ◆   Boat trips to the sanctuary commonly encounter more than 10 species of marine birds, including gannets, storm petrels, loons, shearwaters, phalaropes, and fulmars. Bluefin tuna, sunfish, and the enormous basking shark fatten up here. So do harbor seals and leatherback turtles. But

Provincetown, described by Henry David Thoreau as the "sandy fist" at the tip of arm-shaped Cape Cod, is the scenic home of several whale-watching companies.

Stellwagen Bank's most conspicuous marine creatures are cetaceans.

Quintessential New England

Cape Cod is one of the easiest and most inexpensive places to watch whales in the United States. Several times daily, a small fleet of 100-foot-long, double-decked boats departs MacMillan Wharf in Provincetown for half-day whale-watching trips, while nearby **Nantucket** and other ports along this stretch of the New England coast also offer half-day and full-day tours. Rough waters are common, and whale watchers are always advised to come prepared with sea-sickness medications.

The view from the stern, beyond the sunbathers, sailboats, and gaudy storefronts that crowd Provincetown's inner harbor, is of clapboard houses, tall white church steeples, and buckling docks – a quintessential New England scene. To the left is Long Point, a wide swath of white sand beach that curls back around the harbor; to the right is Cape Cod's North Shore, which stretches 35 miles west to Massachusetts proper. Beyond this, facing the North Atlantic, there's nothing but deep green swells.

Ahead lies Stellwagen Bank, a 19-mile-long underwater plateau of sand and gravel left behind, like Cape Cod, by the Laurentide ice sheet. The bank runs north to south, from Cape Ann on Boston's North Shore to Cape Cod. It rises steeply from the seafloor and is buffeted by deep waters transporting a rich broth of mineral debris and organic matter. Here the fast-growing microscopic plants known as phytoplankton multiply quickly in the warm, sun-drenched environment and lure equally microscopic marine animals called zooplankton, the main food of whales and fish. Think of it as a great big restaurant, says the onboard naturalist from the Center for Coastal Studies.

As the whale-watch boat motors across **Cape Cod Bay**, the naturalist discusses the area's rich whaling history and passes around what looks like a thin, slightly curved rectangle of polished wood. It is, in fact, whale baleen. The passengers take turns stroking the fibrous ends and scratch the hard surface. Once used for making everything from venetian blinds to umbrella

ribs to buggy whips, baleen was as useful to people in the past as plastic is to us today.

Wampanoag Indians were some of North America's first whalers. They cut away the blubber of pilot whales stranded on Cape Cod beaches in the fall and winter and boiled it down into oil. The Wampanoag were the first to build canoes and hunt whales with stone-tipped arrows and spears attached to short lines – a technique they taught to the first American colonists on Cape Cod.

But it was oil, not baleen, that lured Cape Codders into the whaling business. First they hunted right whales, then they built larger boats and moved out to Middle Bank, now known as Stellwagen Bank. Eventually they sailed three-masted factory ships to distant oceans like the Pacific to hunt sperm whales for their oil and spermaceti. The bustling summer resort town of Provincetown was a famous whaling port, host to as many

as 175 whalers in the mid-1800s, its shoreline packed with shipbuilding yards, blacksmith shops, and sail lofts.

Big Wings and Watery Footprints

After about 30 minutes at sea, there is still no sign of whales. The closest thing to a humpback is the boat wake, which resembles a humpback's fluke as it fans behind. Within minutes, the water starts to get shallow, just 100 feet deep, and a yellow buoy bobs on the horizon. The boat is now entering

A humpback (above) slips beneath the surface with a flourish of its tail flukes.

Whale watchers (opposite) spot a humpback off Cape Ann.

Unspoiled beaches (left) attract summer visitors to Cape Cod. Much of the upper Cape is protected by a national seashore.

New Bedford Whaling Museum

The wealth of New Bedford, said Herman Melville, was "harpooned and dragged up hither from the bottom of the sea." **New Bedford Whaling National Historical Park** preserves the city's whaling past, and its centerpiece is the **New Bedford Whaling Museum**.

Dominating the museum's entrance hall is the *Lagoda*, an 89-foot-long, fully rigged ship model. Assembled in 1916 by a local boat builder, this half-scale bark – like the museum itself – is known as one of the world's largest of its kind. The whaler's dangerous life is well documented through a collection of logbooks, charts, harpoons, and navigational instruments and is vividly portrayed in more than 800 paintings, prints, and drawings. Two sections of the 1,275-foot Russell-Purrington *Panorama of a Whaling Voyage Round the World* dominate a small back room. A black-and-white documentary film, *Down to The Sea in Ships*, provides an onboard view of an actual whale hunt.

To while away long hours at sea, many whale men turned to making scrimshaw, beautiful yet functional objects carved from ivory and whalebone. Among the 2,000 pieces of scrimshaw on display are intricately decorated corset stays and pie crimpers.

The whales themselves are celebrated in all their glory. A 35-foot humpback skeleton hangs overhead on the way downstairs, and a 98-foot sperm-whale mural by the noted marine artist Richard Ellis sprawls across an entire wall. The museum has recently acquired the skeleton of a blue whale, the world's largest creature.

Across the cobblestone street is the **Seamen's Bethel**, where Melville attended worship services before boarding the *Acushnet* in 1841. And be sure to take a stroll to the waterfront, where the historic schooner *Ernestina* sits next to present-day fishing boats. You can sense the romance that lured Melville and a whole generation of young men to adventures on the high seas.

The New Bedford Whaling Museum (above) houses one of the world's largest collections of whaling art, artifacts, and manuscripts from the late 18th to early 20th centuries.

Seawater streams from the body of a breaching humpback (opposite, top). Biologists often know whales by name in these well-studied, whale-rich waters.

Nantucket Harbor (opposite, bottom), quiet now, was an early leader in New England's whaling industry.

Stellwagen Bank National Marine Sanctuary. And this almost always means whales.

"Whale at 11 o'clock," shouts the naturalist from the bridge. "About a mile away." The droopy, somewhat seasick passengers rise to their feet and rush for the rails.

"Two feet on the deck, everyone. Two feet."

The boat plows ahead, its bow throwing off a rainbow of spray while anxious whale watchers lean forward over the rails and stare hard at the horizon. At first, there is nothing but black water and a circle of white birds. But as the boat draws closer to its intended destination, we can see misty plumes of warm air blow up from heaving bodies. Humpbacks! As the boat slows, the giddy crowd grows silent. Flapping windbreakers are the only sound.

Suddenly a huge black back, shining like patent leather, eases out of the waves, and pauses. Before it bends toward the seafloor, it kicks up a huge rubbery fluke and waves it in the air, then sinks, leaving behind only its footprint, a smooth round patch of surface water. Moments later, off the starboard side, another humpback moves swiftly through the swells toward the boat, its body making an eerie green glow in the water. As it draws closer, it slows down, and just five yards from the boat, shifts course and seems to swim away.

The humpback has a pronounced hump in front of its stubby dorsal fin and 15-foot pectoral fins, or flippers, the longest of any whale. Taking up one-third the length of its body, the flippers gave rise to the humpback's

Latin name, *Megaptera novaeangliae*, "big wing of New England." The white flippers appear fluorescent green as the whales near the surface.

"Humpbacks are the most gamesome and lighthearted of all the whales, making more gay foam and white water generally than any other of them," wrote Herman Melville. The whale watchers now get to see this for themselves. A small juvenile male eases up to the boat, then periscopes straight out of the water, exposing his wide snout, chunky body, and long flippers. He hangs there, seemingly for inspection, close enough for everyone to study the golf-ball-sized knobs that spread all over the top of his head and jaw. A hair grows out of each bump, which are in fact tubercles, or extra-large hair follicles.

Stellwagen Stalwarts

As if to show up the youngster, an adult female breaches just 20 yards away. Forty tons of humpback shoots straight out of the surf like a missile. Only a shower of spray seems to keep her waterbound. Then she twists exuberantly in the air with the finesse of Esther Williams. For a grand finale she crashes backward onto a white-capped sea, using the full weight of her massive body. Her audience vigorously applauds.

These humpbacks are known to the whale-boat crew by name, each one identified by the patterns on the underside of their scalloped tails. About the size of a billboard, their tails are as unique as a human

fingerprint. The acrobatic humpback cow is Apostrophe. Glacier's fluke is mostly white underneath. Othello has a large black O on his left fluke. Researchers catalogue everyday sightings and keep track of the local whale population and its activities. Stellwagen whales, some of the most studied in the world, have given scientists lots of information to analyze.

Humpbacks arrive at Stellwagen Bank and the surrounding waters in spring, feed here for about six months, then travel to Silver Bank Marine Sanctuary, some 65 miles off the coast of the Dominican Republic, where they breed and give birth. After breeding, the whales begin their northward journey. Even young whales return to their mothers' feeding grounds. Some swim as far north as Nova Scotia. Marine biologists have been studying various humpback behaviors, such as cooperative bubble-net feeding, chin breaching, lobtailing, or tail and flipper slapping, which are not yet fully understood.

Rights at Risk

Although humpbacks steal the show, they are by no means Stellwagen Bank's only attraction. The rarest, and most poignant, of all sights is a glimpse of the greatly endangered North Atlantic right whale. Averaging 50 feet in length and weighing 70 tons, the northern right resides in Cape Cod Bay from January through April, foraging for copepods, small planktonic crustaceans. In April and May, visiting right whales may also be accompanied by newborn calves. Once abundant from the Azores to Spitsbergen, the species is now the world's most endangered cetacean. Studies show that nearly three-quarters of the known northern right whale population has swum these waters since the 1980s. About 300 are in the North Atlantic, and just a few are in the North Pacific. Breeding grounds have been reported near Georgia and Florida.

Look for the northern right's distinctive V-shaped blow, which shoots up to 16 feet in the air. The right lacks a dorsal fin on its smooth black back, but it has large spatulate flippers and sleek flukes with pointed tips and a deep median notch. Most distinctive, though, are the right's "callosities," or raised patches of rough, thickened skin, which may appear whitish yellow, pink, or orange from the "whale lice," or cymid crustaceans, that collect on them. Callosities are found on the chin, lower lips, and sides of the right's head, as well as above its eyes and near its blowhole. Each pattern is unique, so scientists use them to identify and catalogue individuals.

Cape Cod whalers dubbed them the "right" whales to catch because of their thick blubber, six-foot baleen plates, and habit of floating when dead. They quickly reduced the huge numbers of rights swimming near shore. Northern right whales were all but gone by the mid-1700s, and even though they have been protected since 1935, their numbers have still not recovered.

In an ironic twist of fate, several descendants of yesterday's whalers now help run Cape Cod whale-watching excursions and champion the right whale's cause. There is reason to believe they will meet with success. In 1992, after substantial lobbying, members of this same group succeeded in getting Stellwagen Bank designated as New England's first national marine sanctuary. But whether it is too little, too late for right whales remains to be seen.

Long-finned pilot whales (above) are sometimes seen resting motionless at the surface, a behavior known as logging.

Minke whales (top) are the smallest and most abundant of the rorqual whales and are often sighted at Stellwagen Bank.

Martha's Vineyard (opposite) owes much of its architectural charm to wealthy whalemen who built fine homes on the island.

Long-Finned Pilot Whale

Blackfish. Potheads. These aren't rock groups but nicknames for long-finned pilot whales – the ocean's natural-born leaders.

Long-finned pilot whales, seen in the North Atlantic and also found in the Southern Hemisphere, are so called because of their huge pectoral fins and a tendency to swim in herds behind one leader. The name blackfish refers to their dark color; pothead is a nod to their bulbous forehead.

These toothed whales, 13 to 20 feet long, have flippers that extend 18 to 27 percent of their body length. Ranging from slate gray to jet black, long-finned pilots have light W-shaped patches on their throats and anchor-shaped marks on their bellies, and some have a gray streak behind their eyes and dorsal fins. These gregarious whales live in herds and mingle with dolphins and other small Odontoceti. When a boat is near, they nonchalantly allow it to come close before diving straight down to great depths.

Long-finned pilots may be subject to more mass strandings than any other cetacean. Researchers don't know exactly why, although some speculate that pod members may be reluctant to abandon an ill or injured mate. The worst case may have been the 1985 stranding of 400 whales on a New Zealand beach.

TRAVEL TIPS

DETAILS

When to Go

Whale watching is available from late spring to early fall. Humpbacks, minkes, fins, and small cetaceans arrive in April and May, and peak from June to October. It can be drizzly in April and early May, warm to hot in summer. Pepare for cool and breezy conditions at sea.

How to Get There

Major airlines serve Logan International Airport in Boston. Cape Air, 800-352-0714, offers daily, 18-minute flights from Logan to Provincetown Airport. Bonanza Bus Lines, 800-556-3815, run between Boston and Hyannis. Amtrak, 800-872-7245, runs between Providence, Rhode Island, and Hyannis on summer weekends. Passenger ferries serve Cape Cod and the islands year-round.

Getting Around

Traveling on foot or by bicycle suffices in most towns. Cars, available for rent at Logan International Airport, are convenient for those traveling afield; parking may be limited.

INFORMATION

Cape Cod Chamber of Commerce

307 Main Street, Hyannis, MA 02601; tel: 888-332-2732 or 508-362-3225.

Massachusetts Office of Travel and Tourism

100 Cambridge Street, 13th Floor, Boston, MA 02202; tel: 800-447-6277 or 617-727-3201.

Province Lands Visitor Center

Race Point Road, Provincetown, MA 02657; tel: 508-487-1256.

Stellwagen Bank National Marine Sanctuary

175 Edward Foster Road, Scituate, MA 02066-4342; tel: 781-545-8026.

CAMPING

Outermost Hostel

Winslow Street, Provincetown, MA 02657; tel: 508-487-4378.

The hostel affords plain accommodations – $15 per person – in four vintage cabins, each with six or seven beds and a bathroom.

Roland C. Nickerson State Park

3488 Main Street, Brewster, MA 02631; tel: 508-896-3491.

Camping is available on a first-come, first-served basis from mid-April to mid-October.

LODGING

PRICE GUIDE – double occupancy

$ = up to $49 $$ = $50–$99

$$$ = $100–$149 $$$$ = $150+

Captain's House Inn of Chatham

371 Old Harbor Road, Chatham, MA 02633; tel: 800-315-0728 or 508-945-0127.

Built in 1839 by Captain Hiram Hardin, this Greek Revival has original plank floors and antiques, and four-poster beds. Two suites and 14 guest rooms, some with fireplaces, are divided between the carriage house and cottage. Large formal gardens, a fountain, and a croquet lawn are on the premises. $$$–$$$$

Charlotte Inn

27 South Summer Street, Edgartown, MA 02539; tel: 508-627-4751.

An elegant Martha's Vineyard inn, the Charlotte is comprised of the 1860 Captain's House, a 200-year-old garden house, and carriage, summer, and coach houses. Twenty-three guest rooms and two suites are available; a restaurant serves French cuisine. $$$–$$$$

Colonial House

Route 6A and Strawberry Lane, Yarmouth Port, MA 02675; tel: 508-362-4348.

This rambling Cape Cod hotel has sections dating back to the 1730s. The inn's 21 rooms, which range considerably in size, have private baths and canopy beds. Common areas have fireplaces and overstuffed armchairs A Jacuzzi and pool are on the premises. $$

Jared Coffin House

29 Broad Street, Nantucket, MA 02554; tel: 800-248-2405 or 508-228-2400.

Once the grande dame of Nantucket inns, this 1845 brick Georgian is where Herman Melville spotted the real Ahab of *Moby Dick* renown. The house has five attached wings, some dating back to the 1700s. $$–$$$$

Whalewalk Inn

220 Bridge Road, Eastham, MA 02642; tel: 508-255-0617.

This Federal-style house, set in a salt meadow near Rock Harbor, was built by a whaling captain in the 1830s. Cozy accommodations, decorated in a light country style, are available in a cottage, four suites, and seven guest rooms. Most rooms have kitchens and gas or wood-burning stoves; three have balconies. $$$–$$$$

TOURS & OUTFITTERS

Cape Ann Whale Watch

Rose's Wharf, Gloucester, MA 01930; tel: 508-283-5110.

The company offers research-oriented excursions off Cape Ann. The trips, led by naturalists from the Cetacean Research Unit, depart twice daily in summer, once daily in early spring and late fall.

Cape Cod Whale Watcher
P.O. Box 254, Barnstable, MA 02630; tel: 508-747-2400.

Three trips led by naturalists depart daily from Provincetown and Barnstable aboard 150-passenger vessels.

Dolphin Fleet of Provincetown
MacMillan Wharf, Provincetown, MA 02657; tel: 508-349-1900.

The East Coast's "oldest whale-watching business" conducts trips aboard a fleet of three 145-passenger boats. Four-hour trips, hosted by naturalists from the Center for Coastal Studies, depart daily.

Provincetown Whale Watch
MacMillan Wharf, Provincetown, MA 02657; tel: 508-487-3322.

Three daily whale-watching trips, led by a naturalist, accommodate up to 415 passengers aboard the *Ranger IV*.

MUSEUMS

Kendall Whaling Museum
27 Everett Street, Sharon, MA 02067; tel: 781-784-5642.
Twelve galleries house an international collection of whaling art, literature, and history spanning more than a thousand years.

New Bedford Whaling Museum
18 Johnny Cake Hill, New Bedford, MA 02740; tel: 508-997-0046.

The museum features an extensive collection of whaling art and artifacts from the age of sail.

Whaling Museum
15 Broad Street, Nantucket, MA 02554; tel: 508-228-1736.

Originally a candle factory, this superb museum displays whaling equipment, scrimshaw, early whaling records, and the skeleton of a 43-foot finback whale.

Excursions

Cape Ann
Cape Ann Chamber of Commerce, 33 Commercial Street, Gloucester, MA 01930; tel: 800-321-0133 or 978-283-1601.

Situated north of Boston, Cape Ann has earned its living from the sea since 1623. One of the nation's oldest artist colonies, Cape Ann was once home to Winslow Homer, Milton Avery, and John Sloan, all of whose works are on display at the historical museum. Whale-watching tours depart from Gloucester harbor to view whales feeding at Stellwagen Bank and Jeffrey's Ledge, east of Cape Ann.

Martha's Vineyard
Martha's Vineyard Chamber of Commerce, P.O. Box 1698, Vineyard Haven, MA 02568; tel: 508-693-0085.

On this tony island, the wealth of 19th-century whalers, who erected huge homes in the Federal and Greek Revival styles, has become the good fortune of visitors. Many of the mansions, now inns and restaurants, line North Water Street and Main Street in Edgartown and William Street in Vineyard Haven. In Edgartown, look for the 1840 home of Dr. Daniel Fisher (99 Main Street), a noted physician and whaling mogul, and the 1843 Old Whaling Church (89 Main Street), whose 50-foot hand-hewn beams were assembled with wooden pegs in the style of a whaling ship.

Nantucket
Nantucket Chamber of Commerce, 48 Main Street, Nantucket, MA 02554; tel: 508-228-1700.

New England's oldest whaling port is chock-full of whaling history. Bone up on the island's seafaring heritage at the excellent whaling museum, then stroll past the lavish 18th- and 19th-century buildings constructed by whaling merchants on Upper Main Street. Of particular interest are "Three-Bricks," identical redbrick mansions with columned, Greek Revival porches built in the mid-1830s by Joseph Starbuck for his three sons. The 1818 Pacific National Bank commemorates epic whaling voyages, many of which it financed, with murals of port scenes and whaling expeditions. Whale-watching cruises sail from the island in summer.

Bimini Islands
Bahamas

CHAPTER **14**

Snug against the dark-blue waters of the **Gulf Stream**, the long, thin spindle of **Bimini** rises from an unusually flat sea. The wisp of a pine-blown island looks hardly big enough to support the 1,600 people who live here. Seven miles long but not more than 700 feet wide, it is the first sign of land during the 25-minute seaplane flight from **Miami** to the **Bahamas**, an archipelago of about 700 islands, some no bigger than a spit of sand that comes and goes with the tides. ◆ The economy of Bimini depends upon tourism, as it has for decades, although Bahamian divers still plumb ocean depths to spear fish. Strong women pound open coconut shells and peel away thick fibrous husks to grate dry coconut into their tasty Bimini bread. ◆ On the north end of Bimini, a sickle of wild beach curves into the Atlantic. Beyond that, in the far blue, are the dolphins. Bimini looks as if it should belong to dolphins. Near a sand reef

Spotted and bottlenose dolphins thread the Gulf Stream waters that lap the shores of these Bahamian islands.

north of the main island – past the red mangroves that spawn game fish like the famous bluefish and tarpon, past nesting kingfishers and peregrine falcons hunting mice, far from human cares – a community of spotted dolphins regularly appears. Spotted dolphins dwell only in the tropical to warm temperate Atlantic, and perhaps 100 live in this pod, cavorting, fending off sharks, mating energetically, and raising their young. The elders of Bimini say that historically dolphins by the hundreds frequented the reefs and shallows around the island. Sometimes Atlantic bottlenose dolphins, common in Florida's coastal waters, are among the spotted dolphins. ◆ Since 1995 Nowdla Keefe has been taking tourists to

Long, prominent beaks lined with up to 260 teeth are characteristic of oceanic dolphins like this inquisitive bottlenose.

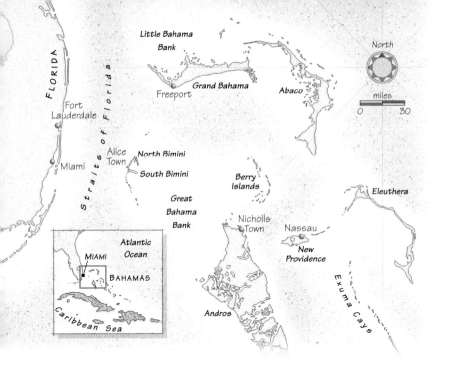

recognize the staff and the sound of the boat.

Spotted dolphins are extremely social and curious animals. They do not flee the tour boat but approach it, rejoicing in their play and snatching every opportunity to bow ride, breach, and roll in the boat's wake. No one aboard is permitted to feed the dolphins or attract them to the boat in any way, but passengers may slip into the water and swim among them, if the dolphins approach of their own volition.

see wild dolphins, one of the most playful and cooperative animals on the planet, and to swim with them if the dolphins allow it. Eleven years before, she and her husband Bill took over Bimini Undersea, a dive excursion business, and began noticing how regularly they encountered dolphins in a certain area. Noting the times of day and tides when she spotted them, Nowdla read all the literature she could find, and from that data organized her trips.

Two or three times a week Nowdla hauls a small group of tourists out to the dolphins at sunset, the dolphin "happy hour," as Nowdla dubs it, because the animals feed all day and rest at night. After years of interactions, the tour operator can now identify about 10 dolphins, which seem to

The boat leaves from a crumbling concrete dock. Across the lagoon rises a small cay, thick with green vegetation. Nowdla loads the boat with gear – flippers and masks and a cooler for drinks – then slips the moorings and heads the boat out of the lagoon. It takes an hour to get to the dolphins. Traveling south, the boat cuts through the channel separating **North** and **South Bimini**. The point is guarded by a beautiful graveyard, where morning glories sprawl among the headstones and racerunner lizards dart among saltwort.

Near the 2,000-foot drop-off from the **Grand Bahama Sand Bank** to the Gulf Stream, the turquoise water darkens to purple. The Gulf Stream continually brings fresh nutrients into the area, enriching the sea for all manner of sea life, including pilot whales that grow up to 28 feet in the deep Gulf Stream waters. The constant renewal of plankton feeds invertebrates that sustain small fish which, in turn, are eaten by progressively larger fish up the marine food chain. Dolphins thrive on this abundance.

The boat passes the wild north beach, where shorebirds probe wet sand. Five brown pelicans wing by in formation. Somewhere

out there are dolphins. At a small beacon Nowdla cuts the motor and begins cruising. She tells us not to worry – it may take a while to find them. For 20 or 30 minutes she allows the boat to putter, then turns south. Thirty more minutes and still nothing.

Suddenly a teenage girl notices a charcoal gray fin cutting the water. Then another. One of the dolphins surfaces alongside the prow, actually pushed along by the boat's wake. The creature cuts through the roll of water, falls back, then slices through again, with movements that are both fluid and powerful. His body is a dark, fat quarter-moon breaching against the foil of ocean. It is freckled with white spots that fuse along the back, indicating that this is no youngster. He moves to the bow and is joined by a cohort as everyone coos and exclaims.

Acrobats of the Sea

Perhaps these two acrobats are scouts leading the way to the community, for soon the boat is surrounded by spotted dolphins and, one by one, the passengers dive into the wide clear ocean. At least 15 dolphins surround the group, but more than 100 dolphins have been known to arrive on a particularly good day. Spotted dolphins are typically 6½ to 7½ feet long and weigh about 200 pounds, but they don't seem fierce.

Someone dives from the boat toward the dappled sea floor, and immediately two or three dolphins follow, ready to play. They twirl and circle in twos and threes, then, like the snorkelers, rise to the surface to blow and breathe. Fine mists of seawater

Secluded beaches (above) on hundreds of islands make the Bahamas an ideal destination for divers, boaters, and dolphin watchers.

Bottlenose dolphins (left and opposite) seem to take pleasure in accompanying boats and are sometimes seen riding their wakes or bows or leaping nearby.

spray into the air. All around, the water is filled with splashes and lappings and dolphin clicks and whistles.

We humans, for some reason, have a great desire to be close to dolphins, to touch them. Maybe, when we are with them, we remember how to have fun, how to play, how to live in joyful abandon in the human body. Maybe we want to witness their great intelligence and know what they are thinking. Poet Pattiann Rogers suggests, in "Animals and People," that "we want to know what they see when they look at us." Humans want to be privy to the mysteries of dolphins. Perhaps a secret part of the soul wants to be dolphin.

The dolphins, of course, are beyond reach. Although they appear so like humans – with the ability to give birth, nurse their young, and breathe air – we are not of their ilk. They are of water. They have been around for 65 million years, humans for a little over two million. Even

their famed intelligence can't be measured in the same terms as our own.

Dolphin Smarts

"We have no objective criteria for intelligence that allows us to cross species lines," states Dr. Randy Wells, cetacean researcher with the Chicago Zoological Society. "Their brain size in relation to body weight is larger than humans. But much of the space is used for processing sound information, which we can't even begin to understand. One of the greatest fascinations of these animals is how well they have adapted to a life so foreign to our own. We can't even begin to dream about mimicking them."

One thing is clear today: The more the snorkelers look like dolphins, keeping their arms to the side, the more comfortable the dolphins seem. They dash in closer, but they dart away when snorkelers use their arms. They remain with the boat for 15 minutes, circling and cavorting, clicking, flipping into the waves, and brushing against a young girl.

Nowdla explains that the dolphins always show total acceptance, allowing their human companions to be who they are, weak or macho, anorexic or over-weight. Time and again, she has seen how the dolphins manage to touch – and emotionally move – every person in the group.

Almost imperceptibly, the spotted dolphins are joined by a couple of spotless dolphins. These Atlantic bottlenose dolphins are mistakenly called porpoises. The adults are typically eight to nine feet long, larger than the spotted dolphins, with robust, powerful bodies colored gray on top and whitish underneath. They live both inshore and offshore at temperate and tropical coasts worldwide, eating mullet, pinfish, and marine invertebrates. Today's tour is in luck. Bottlenoses, though very trainable, are wary of humans in the wild.

One female with a young calf, no more than three feet long, hangs back.

Human Hazards

Bottlenose dolphins are commonly found throughout Florida's coastal waters from north to south. They may be seen by boat or from the beach, on guided tours or on personal forays. More than 550 dolphins live in the Tampa Bay area alone. They exist in communities of some 100 animals, but they travel about their home ranges in groups of four to seven in shallow waters and in groups of more than 20 in deeper areas, where they interact and form subgroups at will, like a kaleidoscope.

In the busy Florida waters, manmade dangers threaten dolphins at every turn.

Endangered manatees (above) congregate around Florida's warm springs in winter.

Atlantic spotted dolphins (top and opposite) often seem more curious than fearful of humans. "The dolphin does not dread man," wrote the Roman scholar Pliny the Elder nearly 2,000 years ago, "but comes to meet ships, leaps and bounds to and fro, vies with them in swiftness, and passes them in full sail."

Sea Cow Serenade

One of the star attractions in Florida is the gentle, slow-moving manatee, or sea cow, colossal silver-gray marine mammal of the order *Sirenia*. They are unrelated to cetaceans but have a special charisma that draws thousands to view them every winter.

Sea cows browse on sea grasses and vegetation growing along the Florida coast. Occasionally they range as far north as the Carolinas and as far west as Louisiana, but when water temperature falls below 68°F they return to the year-round, 72°F warmth of Florida's springs. In cold weather as many as 30 manatees have been spotted in the brackish waters of **Moore's Creek** in Fort Pierce, where the warm-water outflow of a generating plant meets the waters of the **Indian River Lagoon**.

The **Manatee Observation and Education Center** in Fort Pierce (561-466-1600) has covered walkways and an observation platform to facilitate viewing, which is usually best during the first few days following a cold front. Despite being shy and reclusive, sea cows are curious creatures, agile for their size, and playful. Feeding or swimming with the manatees is not allowed, because a natural fear of humans is their main source of protection.

The manatees' need for Florida's warm water puts them directly in harm's way. Manatees feeding in shallow areas are easily trapped when motorboats suddenly appear. Thirty percent of deaths are the result of boat collisions, either on impact or later from internal injuries. Propellers also inflict wounds that easily become infected. About 2,500 manatees remain in Florida, but dozens, sometimes hundreds, die each year. The species is gravely endangered and under federal protection.

The greatest of these is also the most common: marine debris. Dolphins, especially youngsters, may end up choking on ingested plastic or becoming entangled in fishing lines, which can amputate appendages. Collisions with boats pose another threat. Between three and five percent of Florida's dolphins have been struck by boats, especially in shallow waters where they can't dive down and escape. Heavy-metal pollution, with its powerful effect on the immune system, is yet another hazard.

Off Bimini, where most of the garbage disposal is done at sea, debris is the gravest threat to dolphins. The beaches are littered with trash, but none of that is visible now, as the dolphins fade into the recesses of the sea. The excited snorkelers begin climbing back into Nowdla's boat. Many say they have never experienced anything so powerful. Above, a pair of oystercatchers fly like twin W's into the gold sun.

Then, from out of the blue, a dolphin breaches high into the cloudless sky, twists, and lands in a huge splash. It sails out again and, seemingly for no reason, leaps and falls. For a moment the dolphin is a magnificent bridge between the world of air and water, linking creatures dependent on land with those who have mastered the sea, and in that moment we understand how much we have to learn.

Dolphin Alliances

Bottlenose dolphins are the gold-medal acrobats of the ocean and are among the most highly social and communicative of all marine mammals. One of 25 species of oceanic dolphins – the largest group of cetaceans – bottlenose dolphins live in pods throughout the world's warm and temperate seas and display extraordinary unity and mutual support, perhaps best demonstrated in cooperative birthing and feeding.

Midwifery is a fine dolphin art. During calving season, in spring and summer, several dolphins may surround a laboring mother and whistle as two female "midwives" yank on the baby's tail fluke to help it emerge. Once the calf is born, the midwives close in and float the baby to the surface for its first breath. Later, they may baby-sit the youngster while its mother forages for food.

Bottlenose dolphins draw on an array of cooperative hunting strategies, including a method of corralling schools of fish. Two or three dolphins keep the fish in position, while the others gorge themselves. Most dramatic of all, however, is a hunting technique observed in South Carolina and Baja California. There, the dolphins chase their prey onto the shore, then deliberately beach themselves and feast on the flailing fish before working their bodies back into the water. It gives new meaning to a beach picnic. – *Beth Livermore*

Common dolphins (above) herd a "bait ball' of horse mackerel in the eastern Atlantic.

The wind stirs palm trees on a Bimini beach (top).

A diver shares a moment of communion with a wild dolphin (right). Swimming with dolphins is unregulated in the Bahamas; the onus is on tour operators and passengers to decide what is ethical.

TRAVEL TIPS

DETAILS

When to Go

The best dolphin watching in the Bahamas is from May to September. Unfortunately, this overlaps hurricane season, although, for the most part, the weather is calm and warm.

How to Get There

Major airlines serve Miami and Fort Lauderdale-Hollywood International Airports in Florida. Pan Am Air Bridge, 305-371-8628, operates 25-minute seaplane trips from Miami to Bimini. Charter and private planes to Bimini also are available.

Getting Around

Walk, bicycle, or rent a golf cart to get around Bimini. See Tours & Outfitters for a list of companies that offer dolphin-watching excursions.

INFORMATION

Bahamas Tourist Office

19495 Biscayne Boulevard, Aventura, FL 33180; tel: 800-224-3681 or 305-932-0051.

LODGING

PRICE GUIDE – double occupancy

$ = up to $49 $$ = $50–$99
$$$ = $100–$149 $$$$ = $150+

Abaco Beach Resort and Boat Harbour

AB 20511
Marsh Harbour, Abaco, Bahamas; tel: 242-367-2158.

The resort offers 80 guest rooms and six two-bedroom villas on a 52-acre beachfront property overlooking the Sea of Abaco. A marina, restaurant, pool, and dive center are on the premises. Bicycle, windsurfer, and sailboat rentals are available. $$$–$$$$

Bimini Big Game Fishing Club and Hotel

King's Highway, P.O. Box 699, Alice Town, Bimini, Bahamas; or P.O. Box 523238, Miami, FL 33152; tel: 800-737-1007 or 242-347-3391.

This classic Bahamian hotel, the largest on the island, has been used by film stars, writers, and other celebrities since it opened in 1946. Now owned by Bacardi International, the hotel has 35 rooms, 12 cottages, and four penthouse apartments. Many of the rooms have patios or porches overlooking the marina and pool. Cottages have kitchenettes and outdoor grills. A restaurant is on the premises. $$$$

Bimini Blue Water Resort

King's Highway, P.O. Box 601, Alice Town, Bimini, Bahamas; tel: 242-347-3166.

Geared toward sportfishers, this resort has complete dockside services, including 32 slips. The resort's 12 units have private baths, double beds, and private patios. The white-frame Bahamian-style main building once was home to Michael Lerner, a noted fisherman. Ernest Hemingway used the Marlin Cottage, the most expensive unit, as a retreat; it was the setting of *Islands in the Stream*. A restaurant and bar are on the premises. Bicycles, mopeds, scooters, and golf carts are available to rent. $$–$$$$

Compleat Angler Hotel

King's Highway, P.O. Box 601, Alice Town, Bimini, Bahamas; tel: 242-347-3122.

This weathered hotel, built in

the 1930s, is sided with wood taken from rum barrels used during Prohibition. Hemingway lived here from 1935 to 1937 while writing *To Have and Have Not*. The hotel, in the middle of Alice Town, has 12 guest rooms and a small Hemingway museum. Fishing boat charters are available. $$

Running Mon Marina & Resort

208 Kelly Court, Box F-42663, Freeport, Bahamas; tel: 242-352-6834.

All 32 guest rooms at this peaceful and reasonably priced two-story hotel face the 66-slip marina, its main attraction. Rooms have floral decor, wicker furniture, and a refrigerator. The grounds include a sandy beach, man-made saltwater lagoon, diving facility, and full-service restaurant. $$

TOURS & OUTFITTERS

Bimini Undersea Adventure

P.O. Box 693515, Miami, FL 33269; tel: 800-348-4644 or 305-653-5572.

The company offers scuba diving and swimming with wild dolphins two to three times a week. A variety of dive/hotel packages is available.

Dolphin Experience

Underwater Explorers Society, 5601 Powerline Road, Suite 206, Fort Lauderdale, FL 33309; tel: 800-992-3483 or 242-373-1250.

This diving operator, located on Grand Bahama Island, instructs visitors about wild bottlenose dolphins before swimming with the creatures. Snorkeling trips and shark dives are available.

Dolphin Research Center

P.O. Box 522875, Marathon Shores, FL 33052; tel: 305-289-1121.

This nonprofit education and research center, based in Grassy Key, offers a walking tour and a chance to swim with dolphins. A workshop on bottlenose dolphins is conducted.

Earthwatch

680 Mount Auburn Street, P.O. Box 9104, Watertown, MA 02471; tel: 800-776-0188 or 617-926-8200.

Ten-day research trips are dedicated to identifying and conducting a census of whale and dolphin species in Bahamian waters. The data will be used to inform government policy on marine mammal conservation.

Oceanic Society Expeditions

Fort Mason Center, Building E, San Francisco, CA 94123; tel: 800-326-7491 or 415-441-1106.

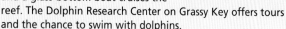

Swimming with free-ranging Atlantic spotted dolphins is the highlight of this interactive, six-day research project. Participants collect data on dolphin family and social structure, behavior and habitat. Accommodations are provided aboard a 68-foot motor yacht.

Underwater Explorers Society

Royal Palm Way, Box F-42433, Freeport, Bahamas; tel: 242-373-1244.

This educational and research organization is dedicated to the conservation of the marine environment, with a special emphasis on dolphins. Scuba-diving and dolphin-encounter tours are offered daily. Those with a keen interest in dolphins can assist at the facility for a full week.

Wild Dolphin Project

P.O. Box 8436, Jupiter, FL 33468; tel: 561-575-5660.

This organization offers weeklong boat tours in the waters around Bimini and other Bahamian islands. Research focuses on social behavior and communication of Atlantic spotted dolphins.

Excursions

Florida Keys

Florida Keys and Key West Visitors Bureau, P.O. Box 1147, Key West, FL 33041; tel: 800-352-5397 or 305-296-1552.

Florida Keys National Marine Sanctuary protects the waters off the 120-mile-long Florida Keys. John Pennekamp Coral Reef State Park on Key Largo is a popular spot for scuba diving and snorkeling, and a glass-bottom boat cruises the reef. The Dolphin Research Center on Grassy Key offers tours and the chance to swim with dolphins.

Grand Bahama Island

Bahamas Tourist Office, 19495 Biscayne Boulevard, Aventura, FL 33180; tel: 800-224-3681 or 305-932-0051.

Grand Bahama Island has attracted dolphin watchers since the 1970s, when schools of Atlantic spotted dolphins began approaching boaters. Three- to 11-day tours depart from Freeport, West End, and Port Lucaya and typically anchor about 30 miles from land on Little Bahama Bank, giving passengers plenty of opportunities to view and sometimes swim with wild dolphins. Research trips sponsored by Earthwatch are also based in the Bahamas. The trips last from a week to 10 days; participants assist in an ongoing survey of whale and dolphin species.

Sarasota

Sarasota Visitors Information Center, 655 Tamiami Trail, Sarasota, FL 34236; tel: 941-957-1877.

Sarasota and Tampa Bay offer year-round dolphin watching, marvelous sandy beaches, and a low-key seaside environment along the Gulf Coast. Tampa Bay has an assortment of tour operators. One option is to sign up for the daily ecotour of Sarasota Bay run by Mote Marine Lab (800-691-6683 or 941-388-4441), a marine science research and rescue center with a strong educational mission. Tours are by motorboat or kayak. Migrating right whales can be seen off northern Florida between late November and March.

Dominica
Lesser Antilles

A sperm whale calf, left alone at the surface while its elders are far below, approaches a party of whale watchers leaning over the side of their boat. The calm Caribbean waters part as the young whale lifts its head above the water to get a better look at the strangers.   ◆   The baby is about 15 feet long and its black, wrinkled skin is studded with remoras, the parasitic, eel-like hitchhikers that attach themselves to their hosts. No remora could withstand the pressure of a deep-diving adult, so the baby must be less than three months old, too young to plummet to such depths. It stares with a baseball-sized eye at the human faces, moving its head back and forth, perhaps introducing itself. It's hard to tell who is more fascinated: the watcher or the watched.   ◆   Whale calves like this one can be found investigating the underwater arches, pinnacles, and craters of **Soufriere Bay** off the volcanic island of **Dominica**, about 1,500 miles

Sperm whales, the deep-sea divers of the ocean abyss, and pods of acrobatic dolphins thrive in clear Caribbean waters.

southeast of Florida in the center of the **Lesser Antilles**. Less than a mile from shore, the sea floor plunges to more than 3,300 feet, and upwellings of cold, nutrient-rich water attract whale species that are rarely seen close to land. Many kinds of whales – sperm, pilot, false killer, pygmy sperm, dwarf sperm, orca, melon-headed, and rare beaked – along with spinner, spotted, bottlenose, Risso's, and Fraser dolphins, frequent the 29-mile-long leeward coast of Dominica. Baleen species such as Bryde's, sei, and humpback whales occasionally languish in the shallows, at less than 100 fathoms, or 600 feet. Humpbacks are plentiful in the Dominican Republic's Silver Bank Marine Sanctuary and Samana Bay, where bulls compete for

The village of Soufriere, on the southwest coast of the volcanic island of Dominica in the Lesser Antilles, was named for nearby sulfur springs.

with an upper viewing station and a covered deck to escape the salt spray and sun. Half-day and full-day whale-watch tours depart daily from the port of **Castle Bruce** for the deep waters off the west coast. Passengers are usually asked to bring a lunch, fruit, and plenty to drink to stay hydrated under the hot sun.

These lazy blue latitudes are so calming it's easy to forget that you are here to spot whales. The languid heat stretches seconds into hours. On any given day, though, the captain of the whale-watching boat keeps passengers on their toes, urging them to look for spouts or splashes or a sperm whale's low, slanted blows. Diving seabirds are a good indicator that bait fish are plentiful – a sign that dolphins may be nearby, too. Some passengers gaze through an underwater viewing window, hoping to catch a fleeting glance at a school of squid or fish.

Motoring through the forest-green waters of Soufriere Bay in the channel between Dominica and Martinique, fishing boats disappear in the troughs between waves and then reemerge just as suddenly. Strong currents in the area create a constant show of whitecaps. The captain slows the engines, and the crew lowers a hydrophone into the water and uses headphones to listen for the distinctive clicking of a sperm whale or the swooping whistles of dolphins. When they hit the jackpot and locate whales, they flick on the loudspeakers and the balmy air fills with a strange static cacophony of clicks. It is a large group of sperm whales, making a sound similar to the tapping of Morse code.

Home Schooling

Herman Melville's *Moby Dick* cast sperm whales as creatures of "great ferocity, cunning, and malice," but their social life in the waters of Dominica tells a different story. Sperm-whale society is intimate and extremely cooperative. Adult sperm whales feed at depths where calves never venture. While calves wait near the surface, females take turns baby-sitting; an adult is always

females and mothers rear newborn calves, but here on Dominica, sperm whales are the big draw.

Whale-Watch Central

Whale watching in the eastern Caribbean began on the island of Dominica in 1988 with these resident sperm whales. The best time for watching is in the dry months between January and June, with the peak occurring around March. June through September is uncomfortably rainy, although whales appear with or without an audience. Most boats are large motorized sportfishing vessels or flat-hulled craft

nearby to defend a calf from attacks by sharks or killer whales. Like other mammals, sperm whales nurse their calves until they can forage for food by themselves.

Thirty minutes pass. The steady clicks subside as the cows rise to the surface and rejoin their calves. Their black skin gleaming, they mass together like a raft of logs and remain still except for an occasional breath. You can count the seconds between their blows – 53, 54, 55 – and the sunlight makes a rainbow out of their misty exhalations as they rest and restore vital oxygen to their blood.

Then comes a loud trumpeting blow followed by a few splashes, a great head thrust forward, an arch of the back, a tail raised high. The whales are getting ready for a deep dive. Sperm whales are champion divers and can hold their breath for more than 90 minutes. Whales around Dominica hold the world record for the deepest dive – some 8,000 feet to the sea floor below. You might wonder what they do for a breathless hour. In fact, these giants spend three-quarters of their day searching for food. The biggest sperm whales eat giant squid up to 40 feet long and consume an average of 800 pounds of fish and squid a day.

After they dive, no trace remains except for a smooth, round slick on the surface. Soon a lone male announces itself on the hydrophone with a metallic clang like a jail door slamming shut, perhaps a call to attract females or intimidate other males. Sperm whales live in extended family units. For females this is a lifelong association; they rarely stray from their natal group. Males leave the family at age six to roam the cooler waters of the north, where they occasionally travel in small bachelor groups. While females and their offspring travel in larger groups, fully grown males lead a solitary, nomadic life, roaming frigid, high-latitude waters to satisfy their enormous appetites.

This bull sperm whale resembles a tarred log from a distance but is graceful and maneuverable underwater. As the boat inches closer, he lifts his massive head out

Sperm whales (above) are the largest toothed whale; males can measure more than 60 feet long, females up to 56 feet.

of the water and spyhops 360 degrees. Wounds and scars clearly visible on his head indicate his status among the bulls. These distinguishing marks and the irregularities on his 12-foot-wide flukes serve as identification markers for researchers. One enormous male is nicknamed Moby for a prominent white scar on his lower jaw.

Dolphin Consorts

The trade winds drop as the sultry afternoon wears on. White thunderheads are building to the south. The whale-watch boat now motors along the coast looking for dolphins. Spotting these acrobats of the sea takes practice. Often all you can see are blips on the horizon or splashes from an agile member of the pod.

"Man, look at them there!" shouts one of the crew. "They're chasing tuna."

From the upper deck, the passengers have a good view as the tuna launch themselves into the air, breast fins opening like wings, allowing the fish to fly along until momentum is lost. A school of spotted dolphins breaks the surface in hot pursuit. Eight dolphins race rapidly into the boat's bow wave, positioning themselves three layers deep. Their flukes rapidly propel them in a zigzag formation, weaving from side to side, never touching, but remaining within inches of the other. The position in which a dolphin swims may indicate its relationship to other dolphins in the group. A larger individual, freckled with prominent spots on both the upper and lower half, keeps pace with an effortless grace. Those jumping through the wake look like small torpedoes catapulted six feet into the air and gracefully slipping through the chop.

A mother and her calf parallel the boat for 30 seconds, then fall behind. The calf learns how to position itself high against the mother's side and rides along on the waves generated by her movements, pumping its flukes to maintain its place. Then it gradually switches to the "infant" position below and slight-

Deep Divers

Like actor John Barrymore, the sperm whale has an unmistakable profile. Who could fail to recognize that boxlike snout and blunt, enormous head? At 12 to 16 feet long, a sperm whale's head typically measures a third of its body length. But it is the spermaceti organ, which sits in the snout, that gives rise to its name and may contribute much to the behemoth's legendary diving abilities.

This organ is a massive cavity containing numerous weblike ducts, the conduits for a waxy yellow liquid used by whalers to make dripless candles. Biologists are not sure what function the spermaceti serves in whales. They speculate that it may focus sonar clicks like a "lens" during echolocation and also help control buoyancy during dives.

Throwing flukes high into the air, sperm whales routinely plunge more than 3,300 feet below the surface and can stay submerged for 90 minutes or more. They are known to dive 8,000 feet; some evidence suggests that they occasionally plummet more than 10,000 feet. Once at these great depths, they wait to snare one of the swift, luminous giant squids that haunt the world's oceanic canyons.

How does a sperm whale accomplish this feat? Researchers believe that the whale may inhale water through its blowhole and circulate the cool rush through its nasal passages. This causes the surrounding spermaceti to become denser and may help the whale control its depth. A sperm whale may also deflate its lungs to decrease buoyancy, then conserve oxygen by slowing the heart rate and rerouting blood only to the brain, heart, and other vital organs. – Beth Livermore

Scars on the bodies of sperm whales testify to their battles with giant squids (left).

Schools of Atlantic spotted dolphins (opposite, top) often number up to a dozen or more animals. They are still hunted by fishers in the eastern Caribbean.

Colorful fishing boats (right) line the beach at Scott's Head Village, Dominica.

ly to the side of the mammary area.

Color conveys the age and social status of spotted dolphins. Calves are born without spots. As the dolphin ages, its color pattern changes. Just as a male lion grows a mane as testament to his authority, a mature male spotted dolphin at the peak of his prowess possesses white jaw tips, an unmistakable status symbol that no dolphin is apt to miss.

Surprise Companions

The boat turns in wide circles. Spinner dolphins join the group, twirling and displaying their repertoire of acrobatic behaviors: breaching, porpoising upside down, and turning flips and cartwheels when leaping from the water. A half-mile offshore, in sight of the port of **Roseau**, six melon-head-ed whales come into view. They are lined up in a neat row with backs and fins as straight as the creases on a freshly-pressed pair of pants.

On the way back to Castle Bruce, Dominica's backbone appears solidly mountainous, with ribs of sharp ridges punctuating the coast and jungle-green valleys sifting back down to the sea. Rain falls on the volcanic peaks of Mounts Diablo and Soufriere almost daily and feeds more than 200 rivers that empty into the Caribbean Sea. To the north, the outline of Guadeloupe is barely visible.

As the boat comes into port, a swarm of boys swims out to greet it. At the dock, a man sits on his heels ready to catch the boat lines. A big tamarind tree at the end of the dock casts a welcome shadow in the glare of the white sun. The captain says goodbye to the passengers. Whale watching, he says, is an unpredictable adventure, and there is no guarantee of a sighting. Today they were lucky. It was an exceptional day to see whales.

TRAVEL TIPS

DETAILS

When to Go

Weather is finest from December through May, when temperatures average in the 70s and 80s. Whale watching is best from May to October, when several species, including humpback, sperm, and pilot whales, gather offshore. July through October is hurricane season, with frequent clouds and rain. The coolest months, December and January, remain relatively mild, with daytime temperatures in the 70s.

How to Get There

Dominca has two airports: Melville Hall, a 90-minute car ride from Roseau, and Canefield, a 15-minute ride. There are no direct flights to Dominica from the United States. Travel from the United States is best negotiated via Puerto Rico aboard the daily American Eagle, 800-433-7300, and from Puerto Rico to Dominica via a puddle jumper. Small aircraft also fly to the island from Antigua, Guadeloupe, and Martinique. Dominica is reached by ferries from neighboring islands.

Getting Around

Travel by taxi, island minibus, or rental car, available at the airports. A Dominica driver's-license fee is charged in addition to the rental rate. Arrange rentals well ahead of your arrival.

INFORMATION

Caribbean Tourism Organization
80 Broad Street, 32nd Floor, New York, NY l0004; tel: 212-682-0435.

Dominica Tourist Office
10 East 21st Street, Suite 600, New York, NY 10010; tel: 212-475-7542.

LODGING

PRICE GUIDE – double occupancy

$ = up to $49 $$ = $50–$99
$$$ = $100–$149 $$$$ = $150+

Anchorage Lodge
P.O. Box 34, Roseau, Dominica, W.I.; tel: 800-742-4276 or 767-448-2638.

Part of the island's most complete diving resort, the Dive Center, this lodge has a private dock, swimming pool, viewing deck, squash courts, dive boats, and restaurant with terraces. The lodge's 32 guest rooms have private baths and patios overlooking the ocean. An afternoon whale-watching tour is one of the main draws, along with diving lessons and trips. $$–$$$

Castle Comfort Hotel
Castle Comfort, P.O. Box 63, Roseau, Dominica, W.I.; tel: 800-544-7631.

The lodge offers 15 basic guest rooms with air conditioning and ceiling fans. Eight-day diving packages include lodging, breakfast, and dinner, as well as dives, equipment, and transportation to and from the airport. A bar and hot tub are on the premises. Dive Dominica, a dive shop, is located behind the hotel. $$$$

Fort Young Hotel
Victoria Street, P.O. Box 519, Roseau, Dominica, W.I.; tel: 800-223-1588 or 767-448-5000.

This 33-room hotel, on the edge of a cliff above the Caribbean Sea, occupies a 1770 fort (you can still see the cannon). A new facility below the hotel offers 21 oceanfront rooms. The hotel is a favorite with travelers, who come for its ambience and location above the mosquito zone. A restaurant serves West Indian cuisine. A fitness room and swimming pool are available. $$–$$$

Petit Coulibri
P.O. Box 331, Roseau, Dominica, W.I.; tel: 767-446-3150.

You'll need a four-wheel-drive vehicle to get here, but this solar-powered retreat amid Dominica's lush vegetation is worth the trouble. An expatriate U.S. couple has built three two-bedroom cottages and two stone-and-glass studios with stained-glass details. Cottages have verandas and kitchens; studios have small verandas. The complex overlooks Martinique Channel, a thousand feet below. A swimming pool and both breakfast and dinner are available. $$–$$$$

Portsmouth Beach Hotel
P.O. Box 34, Roseau, Dominica, W.I.; tel: 767-445-5131.

This beachfront hotel is less than a mile from the northwest town of Portsmouth. The 170 guest rooms have private baths and terraces. A restaurant, bar, lounge, and swimming pool are on the premises. The hotel offers birding and safari tours of the surrounding mountains and rain forest. $–$$

Sutton Place Hotel
25 Old Street, Roseau, Dominica, W.I.; tel: 767-449-8700.

A mile from the beach, the original Sutton Place Hotel was built in the 1930s as a guest house. Destroyed by Hurricane David in 1979, this small, historic hotel was rebuilt and upgraded. The eight guest rooms have antiques, four-poster beds, and teak bathroom furnishings. The hotel's Cellar Bar is original. A restaurant, one of the better dining establishments in Roseau, serves Creole and international cuisine. The nearest beach is about a mile away. $$–$$$

TOURS & OUTFITTERS

Anchorage Dive Center

P.O. Box 34, Roseau, Dominica, W.I.; tel: 767-448-2638.

Four-hour whale-watching tours are offered twice a week aboard a 30-foot, 20-passenger vessel. The operator is affiliated with the Anchorage Hotel at the dock in Soufriere Bay.

Dive Dominica

P.O. Box 2253, Roseau, Dominica, W.I.; tel: 800-544-7631 or 767-448-2188.

One of the longest-running whale-watching operations in Dominica offers four-hour tours on Sunday and Wednesday. Accommodations are available in the adjacent Castle Comfort Diving Lodge.

Natural Habitat

2945 Center Green Court, Suite H, Boulder, CO 80301; 800-543-8917 or 303-449-3711.

Natural Habitat offers trips to Silver Bank National Marine Sanctuary, north of the Dominican Republic, to view breeding humpbacks. Breeding in the only humpback sanctuary in the Caribbean occurs during a one- to two-week period each year.

Oceanic Society Expeditions

Fort Mason Center, Building E, San Francisco, CA 94123; tel: 800-326-7491 or 415-441-1106.

The society offers weeklong research trips to Silver Bank National Marine Sanctuary to study humpback whales during the winter calving and mating season. Participants live and travel aboard an 86-foot motorized catamaran. Using snorkels to observe the whales underwater is one of the highlights of the trip.

Excursions

Puerto Rico

Puerto Rico Tourism, P.O. Box 902, Old San Juan Station, San Juan, PR 00902-3960; tel: 787-721-2400.

Lush and verdant, Puerto Rico packs an awful lot into an island about half the size of New Jersey, including sandy beaches, rain forests, plantations, and remnants of its 2,000-year-old Carib culture and 500-year-old Spanish colonial history. Opportunities abound for golf, tennis, sportfishing, snorkeling, and scuba diving. Humpback whales winter at Navidad Bank on the west side of the island.

Silver Bank National Marine Sanctuary

Dominican Republic Tourism, Mexico Avenue, Government Building B, 2nd Floor, Ministry of Tourism, Santo Domingo, Dominican Republic; tel: 809-221-4660.

The only humpback sanctuary in the eastern Caribbean makes for an ideal whale-watching adventure, although it may be difficult to find space aboard a vessel during the winter calving and breeding season. Book a tour from the United States or try operators in the Dominican Republic. Some 3,000 humpbacks gather and breed on Silver Bank. Expect to see lively courtship, rowdy males, and newborn calves, and to hear humpback songs.

St. Vincent and the Grenadines

St. Vincent and the Grenadines Tourist Office, Edgemont Street, P.O. Box 834, Kingston, St. Vincent and the Grenadines; tel: 809-457-1502.

The mountainous island state of St. Vincent, which includes the Grenadine islands, lies in the southern West Indies. St. Vincent's 4,000-foot-high volcano makes for a challenging hike with stunning views; it last erupted in 1979. Guides lead visitors to the island's Falls of Baleine, where swimmers can cool off in a plunge pool at the base of a 500-foot cascade. Tour boats cruise among spinner, spotted, and Fraser's dolphins, and pilot, sperm, and pygmy sperm whales.

San Ignacio
Lagoon
Baja California, Mexico

CHAPTER **16**

The water is tranquil and glistening on a mid-March morning as a 26-foot-long motorized skiff rounds Rocky Point. Approaching the mouth of **San Ignacio Lagoon**, it skirts the nearby shore lined with leathery-leafed mangroves. Flocks of cormorants pass overhead. Caspian terns with bright orange bills and black crowns flap their wings, preparing to dive at the silvery flash of mullet near the surface. ◆ This is the most pristine and remote of three lagoons along the Pacific coast of **Baja California**, midway between the Mexican border city of Tijuana and the peninsula's southern tip at Cabo San Lucas. Long before any trace of humankind appeared, gray whales began coming to breed and bear their young in these warm, calm Baja waters. Their migration, all the way from arctic feeding grounds, is the second longest of any mammal – a round-trip of more than 10,000 miles. And their interaction with people, especially here at San Ignacio

At a remote lagoon, gray whales and their calves introduce themselves to skiffs full of awestruck visitors.

Lagoon, offers a wilderness experience that many visitors describe as life-changing. ◆ What scientists have come to call "the friendly gray whale phenomenon" began in the 1970s. For reasons that remain a mystery, mother whales started bringing their offspring over and "introducing" them, first to local fishermen, then to marine biologists, and now to boats filled with tourists. Often a mother and calf linger alongside for what seems like an eternity, allowing themselves to be rubbed and petted. No other whale species is known to exhibit this type of behavior in the wild. ◆ Twice during the past century and a half, this majestic creature was hunted to near extinction by humans. So fierce were the mothers in protecting their

A gray whale thrusts its immense barnacle-covered head above the waters of San Ignacio Lagoon.

calves from harpoons, they often capsized the wooden whaleboats, earning the designation "devilfish" from lagoon hunters. Today, the gentle visitations of the gray whale are one of our planet's natural wonders.

Close Approach

While whale-watching excursions also take place during the winter months at the calving lagoons of Guerrero Negro and Magdalena Bay, it's San Ignacio where one is likely to enjoy the closest encounters. Here, three safari-style campgrounds are interspersed along the shell-laden shoreline, each with its own fleet of skiffs (known as *pangas* in Mexico). No more than a dozen *pangas* are allowed in the whale observation area near the lagoon's mouth at any one time. Nor are the skippers permitted to approach the whales directly. It is the animal's choice whether to initiate contact.

The Mexican guide points to a geyser of seawater that erupts, then subsides about 50 yards ahead. He cuts back on the throttle, moving in slowly toward the site of the whale's spouting. A mother, followed closely by her baby, swims just ahead. The *panga* stays parallel and a little behind at first, letting the whales take the lead. Gradually the skipper overtakes them, passes about 30 feet beyond the pair, then puts the motor into idle. Nine passengers, maximum capacity for the *panga*, lean over the sides and commence splashing with both hands. The sound attracts the whales, as does the boat's engine. During the 1980s, one scientist discovered that the outboards emit noise along the same frequency range as the vocalizations of the gray whales.

Yes, suddenly, magically, there they are, inches below the surface and only a few feet away from the starboard side. The temptation for everyone aboard to leap to that side is discouraged, so the *panga* doesn't overturn. Each passenger will get a turn.

Already the calf, perhaps a month old, is almost one-third her mother's size. Even at birth in the shallowest reaches of the lagoon, a baby gray whale weighs upward of 1,500 pounds and is 15 feet long. It gains about 200 pounds a day while nursing on milk rich in fat. By the time it departs with its mother for the long arctic migration, the calf will have doubled in size.

The mother uses her massive body as a natural breakwater for her newborn, seeming to coax it toward the boat. Slowly, the baby makes the rounds of each person's out-stretched hands. Its mottled, charcoal-gray skin is rubbery, shiny, and surprisingly soft to the touch. The thick, widely spaced bristles that sprout from the top of its head and along the lower jaw are more notice-able than on its mother. Each of their triangular, bow-shaped heads is massive, about one-sixth of the total body length.

The whales circle the bow, advancing again down the port side. Trailing close to her calf, considerably longer than the *panga*, the mother raises herself to be petted. Her flippers, back, and tail flukes are covered with dense clusters of white barnacles and pink sea-lice. Grays can be recognized by two characteristics: They lack dorsal fins – a series of knucklelike ridges covers their broad backs instead – and only this species has an upper jaw that overhangs the lower one, giving it a kind of "parrot-beaked" facial appearance.

Scientific facts are far from everyone's minds as the two whales reach out to commune with the human realm. For the timeless minutes that the whales are alongside, you feel as if you are almost holding your breath. The heart pounds; tears may well up. There is no trace of fear. An ineffable fusion of worlds is occurring. There can be no better definition for the word *awestruck*.

Taking simultaneous breaths through their oval blowholes that leave behind a foam of bubbles, the cow and calf disappear beneath the surface and with extraordinary grace glide away smoothly, as if they are taking extreme care not to rock the boat. The senses feel magnified a

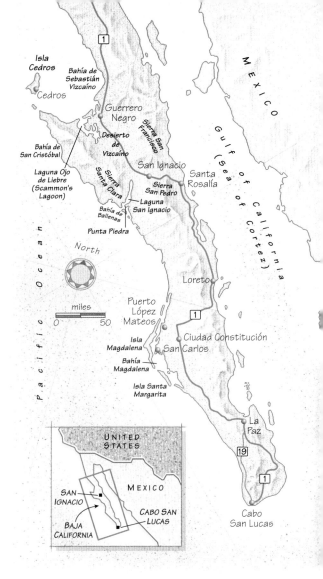

thousandfold. The visitors are enveloped by silence in this whale domain.

Breeding and Spring Training

All around the main channel of the lagoon, in waters between 60 and 100 feet deep, many more whales are visible as noon approaches. At the height of the breeding season, at least 600 have been counted along San Ignacio's 60 square miles.

Giant barrel cactus on Santa Catalina Island (opposite). Baja's desert landscape contrasts dramat-ically with its blue waters.

Distinctive markings on tail flukes (left) are used to identify individual whales.

A baby gray whale (left) enjoys having its jaw rubbed. Grays that approach boats are dubbed *las amistosas,* the friendlies.

Elephant seals and whale watchers share a beach at San Ignacio Lagoon (below).

Ancient pictographs of whales (opposite, top) adorn the ceiling of a cave in San Gregorio Canyon.

A gray whale spyhops (opposite, bottom) amid a clutch of small tour boats known as *pangas.*

Although boats are banned from the inner sanctums where gray whales give birth, courtship between the sexes may be observed in February where the lagoon meets the Pacific. By mid-March, the males wait just outside the lagoon to be joined by their herd.

Meanwhile, the calves go through a kind of "spring training" in preparation for their coming journey. They gather strength by swimming, as on a treadmill, against strong tidal currents. And they greet, for the first time, the human race that will follow their path from points on shore and from whale-watching boats as the grays pass within a few miles of the California, Oregon, Washington, British Columbia, and Alaska coasts.

About a thousand people annually make this pilgrimage to Laguna San Ignacio, usually in February and March. They arrive either by chartered plane or along the spectacular trans-peninsular

Highway One that winds through coastline, mountains, and desert about a day-and-a-half's drive from the U.S. border. The final stretch is a rough one – 30 miles of rutted dirt road leading out of the oasis town of San Ignacio and along the salt flats of the **Vizcaino Desert**. But this, all would agree, is a token price for admission.

Whale Communion

Framed by the volcanic peaks of the Santa Clara Mountains northwest of the lagoon, the *panga* comes to within 30 feet or so of another small vessel. There, excited voices blend with the upsurge of a new duo, and the scene offers passengers on the nearby boat the best opportunity for photographs. A woman leans far over the bow rail. From the depths, the mother rises and sends a fountain of spray that resembles a hibiscus flower opening its petals. The woman, shouting with joy, her clothes more wet than dry, flashes a look of surprise and wonder. Baptized.

Another passenger begins humming a tune. Both whales swim right up to him, their huge faces craning out of the water. Along the edge of the boat now, once more the mother arcs upward in a single motion. She turns on her side and gazes up at a woman sitting beside her own young boy. This whale's eye is moonstone blue, the size of a baseball. The look penetrates to the very depths of a human being. It feels as though one is being "read" by the whale, that an entire life is, for one endless moment, an open book.

Mother and baby dive directly under the *panga* and resurface on the other side. With one of her powerful pectoral flippers, mom pushes the "little one" up until its head is level with the stern. An outstretched hand touches something fine and bristly. It takes a minute to realize that this is the baleen of the baby's mouth, the natural sieve that lets water pass through while the food remains. In one's hand, it feels like a thick moustache. Gray whales like to have their gums rubbed. The baby wriggles, slaps the water with its fluke, and emits a gentle plume of sweet-smelling vapor.

Take a Bow

If there is even a slight chop on the water, the gray whales will not approach a boat. Instead, they are content with "performing" for camera-laden viewers. Bursting from the water, they launch as much as three-quarters of their body skyward and turn onto their back or side before hurtling back into the sea. Sometimes first the mother and then the calf breach, several times in a row with about a 15-second interval in between. Yet the whales maintain enough distance from the *panga* to scarcely make waves. They spyhop for up to 30 seconds after a dive, lingering above water and scanning the horizon. Then their 12-foot-long tail flukes arch into the air before descending with a mighty splash.

After three hours on the lagoon, the skipper revs the engine and prepares to head back to camp. Off to starboard, the last two whale visitors hover in the turquoise sea, side by side, motionless, bidding farewell. As a single unit, all nine people aboard the *panga* stand and face them. Nobody speaks.

TRAVEL TIPS

DETAILS

When to Go

Gray whales breed in Baja lagoons between January and April before migrating north. Blue, Bryde's, fin, humpback, and minke whales visit the Gulf of California year-round, as do Pacific white-sided, common, bottlenose, and various tropical dolphins. The Pacific Coast is sunny and generally dry, with temperatures close to the mid-80s, somewhat cooler in winter. In sharp contrast, the interior desert can be brutally hot and dry, with summer temperatures routinely above 110°F. Polarized sunglasses, a broad-brimmed hat, and sunscreen with a high SPF factor are essential.

How to Get There

International airports are located in Tijuana, Mexicali, Loreto, La Paz, Los Cabos, and San Jose del Cabos. Seven- to 10-day, self-contained cruises are available from San Diego, or you can fly in and drive to Guerrero Negro, near Scammon's Lagoon, or Adolfo Lopez Mateos, at Magdalena Bay, and hire small boats called *pangas*.

Getting Around

Car rentals are available at all Baja airports. Consider using a four-wheel-drive vehicle on remote, unpaved roads. Carry plenty of water, food, and break-down equipment and buy good car and health insurance when traveling in Mexico (U.S. insurance policies usually do not extend south of the border). Information about long-distance bus service in Baja California is available from Tijuana's Central de Autobuses, 52-66-86-9060.

INFORMATION

Baja Information

7860 Mission Center Court No. 2, San Diego, CA 92108; tel: 800-225-2786 or 800-522-1516 (from California).

Gobierno del Estado de Baja California Sur

Coordinacion Estata de Turismo, Apartado Postal 419, Edif. Fedepaz, La Paz, Baja California Sur, Mexico; tel: 52-112-31702.

CAMPING

Baja Discovery

P.O. Box 152527, San Diego, CA 92195; tel: 800-829-2252 or 619-262-0700.

Rocky Point Camp is situated on a low bluff overlooking San Ignacio Lagoon, providing round-the-clock whale-watching opportunities. Visitors stay in roomy tents with comfortable cots. The camp has modern bathroom facilities and solar showers. Meals, served inside a large dining and activity tent, are a cut above ordinary camp food.

Ecoturismo Kuyima

Apartado Postal 53, San Ignacio, Baja California Sur, Mexico; tel: 52-115-40070.

The operator runs the only two Mexican-owned campgrounds on San Ignacio Lagoon – one with tent sites, the other with cabins. A reasonable daily fee includes a three-hour whale-watching tour. Inexpensive meals are available.

LODGING

PRICE GUIDE – double occupancy

$ = up to $49 $$ = $50–$99

$$$ = $100–$149 $$$$ = $150+

Hotel Blanco y Negro

Avenida Sarabia 1, Santa Rosalia, Baja California Sur, Mexico; tel: 52-115-20080.

The hotel offers basic but comfortable lodging with reliable hot water. Some rooms have private baths. $

Hotel del Real

Avenida Montoya, Santa Rosalia, Baja California Sur, Mexico; tel: 52-115-20068.

This attractive hotel has a terrace, restaurant, and long-distance phone. Guest rooms are small but air-conditioned. $

Hotel El Morro

Apartado Postal 76, Santa Rosalia, Baja California Sur, Mexico; tel: 52-115-20414.

Situated one mile south of the Santa Rosalia ferry terminal, this Spanish-style hotel overlooks the Gulf of California. Rooms have two beds and shower/baths; some have private patios. Amenities include a swimming pool, dining room, and bar.

Hotel La Pinta

P.O. Box 37, San Ignacio, Baja California Sur 23930, Mexico; tel: 800-336-5454.

Located on the main road into San Ignacio, this pseudocolonial hotel offers comparatively fine accommodations, including a tiled courtyard, swimming pool, and groves of date palms and citrus. $$

TOURS & OUTFITTERS

American Cetacean Society Expeditions

P.O. Box 2639, San Pedro, CA 90731; tel: 213-548-6279.

The society conducts eight- and nine-day whale-watching tours from San Diego to San Ignacio Lagoon in February, with stops at Scammon's Lagoon, San Martin Island, San Benito Islands, Cedros Island, and Todos Santos Island. As many as 31 passengers live aboard a 95-foot sportfishing vessel and use small skiffs for whale-watching. The society also offers eight- and 10-day tours to the Sea of Cortez in March and April to see minkes, blues, finbacks, pilots, and dolphins. Naturalists accompany all trips.

Baja Discovery

P.O. Box 152527, San Diego, CA 92115; tel: 800-829-2252 or 619-262-0700.

Baja Discovery leads custom adventure tours of Baja. Whale-watching tours include trips to San Ignacio Lagoon to see grays, combining hotel stays with beach camping. Whale- and dolphin-watching tours of the Sea of Cortez are also available.

Baja Expeditions

2625 Garnet Avenue, San Diego, CA 92109; tel: 800-843-6967 or 619-581-3311.

"Mexico's largest and oldest outfitter of adventure travel" offers flexible itineraries for whale watching, sea kayaking, sailing, and scuba diving. Whale-watching tours include flights to San Ignacio Lagoon and boat tours of Magdalena Bay. Sea of Cortez trips include viewing blue whales and other cetaceans as well as beachcombing, snorkeling, and hiking.

Oceanic Society Expeditions

Fort Mason Center, Building E; San Francisco, CA 94123; tel: 415-441-1106.

The organization offers four eight-day whale-watching trips to San Ignacio Lagoon from mid-February to late March. Tours leave from San Diego and stop at San Benito Island, Cedros Island, and Todos Santos Island. Participants live aboard a 36-passenger cabin cruiser; whale watching is conducted aboard small skiffs. Trips include slide shows, informal evening lectures, and varied daytime activities. Tours also leave from La Paz for the Sea of Cortez to see blue, humpback, and sperm whales, and other cetaceans. Naturalists accompany all trips.

Excursions

Bahia Magdalena

Baja Information, 7860 Mission Center Court No. 2, San Diego, CA 92108; tel: 800-225-2786 or 800-522-1516 (from California).

"Mag Bay" to many English speakers, Bahia Magdalena is the gateway to the Pacific. Gray whales arrive from January to March, transforming the area into one of the coast's most important whale-breeding sites. Magdalena and Margarita Islands protect the 50-mile-long bay from the Pacific's strong waves. Beaches, inlets, marshes, and mangrove swamps offer sanctuary to a variety of resident and migratory seabirds.

Laguna Ojo de Liebre

Baja Information, 7860 Mission Center Court No. 2, San Diego, CA 92108; tel: 800-225-2786 or 800-522-1516 (from California).

Ojo de Liebre, also known as Scammon's Lagoon, is the largest gathering place of California gray whales in Baja. Ironically, it is named for 19th-century whaling captain Charles M. Scammon, who discovered the lagoon and then killed the whales gathered there. The lagoon, designated the world's first whale sanctuary in 1972, has witnessed the renewal of the gray-whale population. Unfortunately, another threat looms: The lagoon is the site of the world's largest evaporative salt works, which may radically alter the habitat.

Upper Gulf of California and Colorado River Delta Biosphere Reserve

Sonora Information, tel: 800-476-6672.

Set aside in 1993, this is Mexico's newest reserve, established to protect the vaquita, a small endangered porpoise endemic to the area. Vaquitas may be hard to spot, but humpback whales are sometimes seen, and finback whales and common dolphins are plentiful. Other attractions include hiking, birding, desert wildlife watching, and volcano viewing. Tours depart from the popular tourist town of Puerto Peñasco, Sonora, just south of the Arizona border.

Santa Barbara
and the Channel Islands
California

CHAPTER **17**

S anta Barbara is an uncommonly wealthy community, in terms of both per-capita income and natural beauty. The azure Pacific lies to the west, and rugged mountains rise directly behind the town. Pine, oak, and chaparral cloak most of this cordillera, except at the lower elevations, where mansions predominate. Lavish fetes are thrown here, and invitations are much coveted. ◆ But you don't need an invitation to attend another kind of soirée. Whale tea parties are held regularly in the kelp beds just offshore, and newcomers are always welcome. Not that tea is actually served, of course. "Tea party" is a term coined by local skippers to describe the phenomenon of several female gray whales resting together in the kelp, nursing their young. ◆ Whale-watching boats approach to about 100 yards of the groups, which can number five or more mother-offspring pairs. The calves – curious, like most children – leave their mothers to

Attend a gray whale "tea party," with guest appearances by blue and humpback whales and dolphins of many species.

investigate the boats, much to the delight of the passengers. The mothers loll in the seaweed, using the respite from their demanding young to socialize among themselves. After a while, the youngsters return for another feeding, spyhopping occasionally to see what the boats are doing. ◆ Tea parties mark the end of the gray whale's northward migration for the **Santa Barbara** area, a wondrous climax to a season replete with wonders. The whales swim past Santa Barbara from mid-February to May as they head north from Mexico to their summer feeding grounds in the North Pacific. And they come in force: More than 22,000 of these gentle, gregarious giants negotiate the 25-mile strait between Santa Barbara and the

Seaside daisies bloom at Harris Point on San Miguel Island, Channel Islands National Park. Gray whales are sometimes spotted in offshore kelp beds.

Gray whales (left) have made a successful recovery in the Pacific. Up to 22,000 whales now migrate between Mexico and Alaska.

Bat stars (below) are often found along the shore. Some Pacific tide pools contain as many as 4,000 organisms per square foot.

California sea lions (opposite) frolic in the shallow waters of a Channel Islands kelp forest.

Channel Islands each year. And big as this once-endangered population is, it's still growing, by about two percent annually.

Migratory Routes

The **Santa Barbara Channel** constricts the whales along the mainland shore and affords close-up views of one of the most spectacular wildlife migrations on the planet. This is particularly true of northward-bound whales. Grays tend to stay farther out to sea during their autumnal southward migration, sometimes venturing windward of the Channel Islands. During the spring, the whales take three distinct routes through the Santa Barbara Channel. The outside track traverses Coal Oil Point near the Isla Vista campus of the University of California at Santa Barbara. This route is about five miles offshore. The middle track is just west of several oil platforms located in the channel, about three miles from the beach. Whales seem to favor these tracks early in the

season, and both are easily accessed by boats leaving daily from the Santa Barbara waterfront from late winter through early summer. Trips are short, averaging two and a half to three hours in length, because the whales are usually close to shore.

The inside track lies right along the kelp line, sometimes no more than a hundred yards from shore. This is the route favored by late-season cows escorting their calves to Alaska. Biologists think the mothers may be attempting to avoid attacks by orcas and great white sharks by keeping close to the kelp, which affords some protective cover from predators. These luxuriant forests of marine vegetation also provide a safe place for the cows to feed, rest, and suckle their young. The **Hope Ranch** area just north of downtown Santa Barbara is a particularly good place to observe whales lounging in the kelp. Grays sometimes can be seen from the beach here, as well as from **Devereux Point** near the University of California at Santa Barbara, about five miles north of Hope Ranch.

Southward migrating gray whales

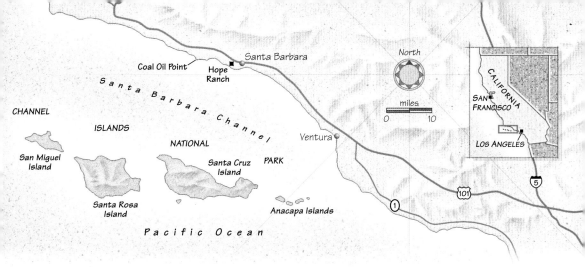

Santa Barbara · *Coal Oil Point* · *Hope Ranch* · *North* · *miles* · *CALIFORNIA* · *SAN FRANCISCO* · *CHANNEL* · *ISLANDS* · *NATIONAL* · *Ventura* · *LOS ANGELES* · *San Miguel Island* · *PARK* · *Santa Cruz Island* · *Santa Rosa Island* · *Anacapa Islands* · *Pacific Ocean* · *Santa Barbara Channel*

demand more time and effort to observe since they often travel farther seaward, but they are well worth the trouble to find. Mating pods of grays may be observed through October, providing what the skippers jocularly term "X-rated" trips. A typical mating pod consists of two males and one female. Breeding is something that gray whales have trouble accomplishing one-on-one. Usually one male positions and subdues the female while the other accomplishes penetration. Consummation is achieved only with a great deal of exuberant fluke splashing and pectoral fin flipping.

Curious Humpbacks and Big Blues

Gray whales are by no means the only whales to frequent the channel. Humpbacks and blues usually show up in force during the spring and summer months to graze on the vast shoals of krill and bait fish that congregate in the deeper water.

Humpbacks are the first to arrive, with initial sightings typically logged in March or April. They are probably the most inquisitive and active of the baleen whales and usually put on a good show for visitors to their pelagic realm, spyhopping and breaching over and over – the latter a truly marvelous spectacle when you consider that the whales are more than 50 feet long and weigh in excess of 30 tons. The sight and sound of a mature humpback lifting completely out of the water, then falling back to the surface with a resounding report, will stay etched into an observer's brain for a

lifetime. If you're lucky, you may also see humpbacks lunge to the surface with open mouths as they feast on schools of sardines or krill. In some cases, they corral bait fish by blowing bubbles around them and then swim through the mass of confused fish to feed.

Even if they fail to demonstrate their more specialized behavior, humpbacks are always fun to watch. Many individuals appear openly curious and are seldom alarmed by boats. Any competent skipper making a living conducting whale-watch excursions will allow the whale to approach

Big Blues

When you think about blue whales, think big. These endangered giants, the largest animal ever to have lived on Earth, do nothing in a small way.

With mottled blue-gray bodies typically 80 or more feet long and weighing more than 110 tons, they out-measure a Boeing 737. What's more, blues have big babies. After a gestation of 12 months, calves are born 23 feet long and weighing 2.5 tons. They guzzle more than 50 gallons of fat-rich milk a day, putting on 200 pounds per day. When weaned eight months later, they can weigh up to 50,000 pounds and be 50 feet long.

Like other rorqual whales, blues have throats with pleated skin. Running from beneath the lower jaw to behind the flippers, the throat expands like an accordion during feeding. The mouth cavity balloons so large that a 100-foot whale can take in about 1,000 tons of food and water in a single mouthful.

Blues travel vast distances to chilly high latitudes to feed in spring and summer and then head to wintering grounds around the Equator. There are distinct populations in the North Pacific, North Atlantic, and Southern Hemisphere. But after being overhunted worldwide, their total population is small, between 6,000 and 14,000. The good news is that if a blue whale is in the vicinity, you'll see it: The whale's distinctive blow sprays water 20 to 40 feet high in a slender upright column – conspicuous enough to alert curious whale watchers. – *Beth Livermore*

Blue whales (left) are fast for their size, reaching speeds of 19 mph. Their mottled backs reflect blue sea and sky, hence their name.

Pelagic tuna crabs (left, middle) and other tiny creatures make up much of a blue whale's diet.

Sailors spot a dolphin off Catalina Island (bottom), the most developed of the Channel Islands.

A gray whale (opposite, above) gazes into a photographer's lens. "Like time," observes nature writer Sherry Simpson, "whales mostly appear in fragments … rarely do you glimpse the immensity of the whole."

Sunset illuminates Santa Barbara Harbor (opposite, bottom), home to several whale-watching companies.

the craft rather than the other way around for the best experience. A pod of feeding or playing humpbacks will often loll around a boat for an hour or more and almost seem to enjoy posing for the cameras.

Blue whales, the largest creatures on the planet, are more diffident than humpbacks;

their exhibitions tend to be minimal, though you may sometimes see them lunge-feeding in venues where the krill is especially thick. Perhaps one out of ten blues will display its gigantic flukes as it dives. More often, you will witness a robust spout as a blue surfaces. Blue whales typically float on the surface for five minutes or so after a dive, but they are somewhat like icebergs in this mode: The portion that is visible above the surface is only a fraction of the vast bulk that lies below. The largest blue whales, after all, may attain 100 feet in length and weights of 200 tons.

Don't expect to see a blue whale immediately after it sounds. They usually stay submerged for 10 minutes or more before resurfacing, and they'll travel in excess of a half-mile, seining the depths for krill and small fish. Experienced whale watchers will scan the horizon for a blue once it sounds rather than look around in the immediate vicinity of the boat. The next time you see the animal – or, rather, *if* you see the animal – it will be far away.

Blues appear to have increased in the Santa Barbara Channel in recent years; in each of the last few seasons, about 100 of the leviathans have shown up. This may be due at least in part to particularly rich concentrations of krill and sardines. Another theory is that with more people out whale watching, more whales are being seen. The international whaling ban appears to be successful, but it's too soon to say whether the global population of this beleaguered species is starting to recover from decades of overhunting. The blue whale season and fall gray whale season run from June though October. Trips are full-day affairs, with boats leaving about 8 A.M. and returning at 3 P.M.

The Lethal, the Fast, and the Rare

Orcas are also sighted with some regularity in the channel, particularly during the gray whale migration. These "transients" range widely and subsist almost exclusively on marine mammals, particularly baleen whales and pinnipeds. They travel in small family-based pods and are the most laconic of the orca races, possibly because orca chatter may alarm potential prey. Transient orcas appear particularly disposed to gray whale calves, and they will take them whenever possible. They do not, however, like to attack when the grays are among the kelp. Any sightings of an orca attack are apt

A gray whale calf approaches for a closer look (left). Its skin will eventually be covered with barnacles, scars, and tiny parasites known as whale lice.

Pacific white-sided dolphins (opposite, top) are distinguished from bottlenose dolphins by their short, thick snouts.

Ferries (opposite, bottom) shuttle visitors to the Channel Islands.

periods, particularly if the seas are calm. Two other whales that are turning up more regularly are minkes, which are small rorquals, and pilots – small, black-skinned, toothed whales that travel in large schools and live amid a complex social structure.

Very occasionally, beaked whales are seen. Little is known about these rare, strange-looking cetaceans, which look rather like over-sized dolphins with long snouts. They are pelagic by preference and are thus usually spotted only in the middle of the channel or windward of the Channel Islands. Though they spend much of their time plumbing the depths for squid, they sometimes loaf

to be made when the mother grays and their young are transiting open water. Due to local geography, this occurs less frequently in Santa Barbara than it does farther north in Monterey, but visitors may be lucky and glimpse the black, cleaverlike dorsal fins that indicate the presence of orcas.

Other whales sometimes seen in the channel include finbacks, second only to blues in size. Finbacks are among the world's fastest whales and can dive even longer and deeper than blues. If they are feeling skittish on a given day, you won't see much of them. But they often are blasé about boats and may hang around for prolonged

on the surface, swimming sluggishly in small pods. A sighting is a red-letter moment for any whale watcher.

These sightings of rarer cetaceans are encouraging, but conservationists caution against being overly optimistic. Past commercial whaling of large baleen whales may have reduced competition for food and allowed the numbers of smaller whales to increase even as the larger whales start to recover following the international ban on hunting. On the other hand, all cetaceans are facing so many other new oceanic threats – global pollution, overfishing, and incidental death in fishing

nets – that it can't be assumed that recovery is under way.

You won't have to look hard for other cetaceans – they'll come to you. A variety of porpoises and dolphins throngs these waters, and, typically, they'll accompany boats for the sheer pleasure of it, diving across the bow and leaping high into the air. Abundant dolphins include Pacific white-sided, Risso's, common, and Pacific bottlenose. You also may glimpse a Dall's porpoise. Sightings of harbor seals and California sea lions are commonplace, and northern elephant seals and Steller's sea lions are spotted with some regularity. Great numbers and varieties of marine birds are usually observed during mid-channel whale-watching trips, including the occasional black-footed albatross, which typically visits during the summer.

With special arrangements, whale watching may be combined with a hike on Santa Rosa or Santa Cruz Islands, which are part of **Channel Islands National Park**. Sometimes called America's Galapagos, these fascinating islands support several endemic species, most notably a small fox that is unusually

placid in temperament, which allows for easy observation, and a scrub jay that is much larger than its mainland counterpart. The park is also a good place to observe shorebirds and brown pelicans.

TRAVEL TIPS

DETAILS

When to Go

The best time to visit is March through May, during the northern gray-whale migration. The southern migration, when grays travel farther from shore, occurs from November to early February. Summer and early fall are prime seasons for blue, humpback, and finback whales. Chilly temperatures and high seas are common in winter, but rough water can strike the Santa Barbara Channel in any season. Summer mornings are usually foggy, clearing around midday, with temperatures in the 80s.

How to Get There

Santa Barbara County Airport, about six miles north of Santa Barbara, is served by commuter flights from Los Angeles, San Francisco, Oakland, and San Jose International Airports.

Getting Around

Car rentals are available at the airport. Highway 101, convenient for coastal exploration, passes through Santa Barbara. Areas immediately around the harbor and city center are best explored on foot or bicycle; bicycle rentals are available at the waterfront and in town. Santa Barbara Metropolitan Transit, 805-683-3702, provides bus service.

INFORMATION

Channel Islands National Park
1901 Spinnaker Drive, Ventura, CA 93001; tel: 805-658-5700.

Channel Islands National Marine Sanctuary
735 State Street, Santa Barbara, CA 93101; tel: 805-966-7107.

Santa Barbara Conference and Visitors Bureau
12 East Carrillo Street, Santa Barbara, CA 93101; tel: 800-676-1266.

Sea Landing (whale-watching tour information)
Santa Barbara Harbor, Santa Barbara, CA 93101; tel: 805-963-3564.

CAMPING

State and federal parks offer a huge network of campgrounds, with water, toilets, and other facilities. Reservations are essential in summer. Call 800-365-2267 for information and reservations.

LODGING

PRICE GUIDE – double occupancy

$ = up to $49 $$ = $50–$99
$$$ = $100–$149 $$$$ = $150+

Casa Del Mar Inn
18 Bath Street, Santa Barbara, CA 93101; tel: 800-433-3097 or 805-963-4418.
This small motel is one of the best buys near the beach. The inn has 21 one- or two-room units. Many rooms have kitchenettes, stoves, and refrigerators. A Jacuzzi and swimming pool are on the premises. Rates include a light breakfast. $$–$$$$

Eagle Inn
232 Natoma Avenue, Santa Barbara, CA 93101; tel: 800-767-0030 or 805-965-3586.
This former apartment house, a restored Spanish-Colonial from the 1930s, is now a 17-room inn. Guest rooms, many with kitchens, are furnished with period antiques. A bridal suite has a fireplace and private veranda. $$–$$$

La Mer European Bed-and-Breakfast
411 Poli Street, Ventura, CA 93001; tel: 805-643-3600.
This 1890 Cape Cod-style house has spectacular ocean views from the parlor and two of the five guest rooms, each decorated in a different style. The German-born owner serves Bavarian-style breakfasts and offers midweek packages that include gourmet candlelit dinners, cruises to Anacapa Island, massages, and other delights. $$$

Old Yacht Club Inn
431 Corona Del Mar Drive, Santa Barbara, CA 93103; tel: 800-549-1676 (California only), 800-676-1676 (outside California), or 805-962-1277.
One block from the beach, this inn's main building served as the Santa Barbara Yacht Club during the 1920s. The California Craftsman house, built in 1912 and restored in the 1980s, became the city's first bed-and-breakfast. Five cheerful guest rooms, one with a private deck, are available in the main house; the adjacent Hitchcock House offers seven guest rooms, a common room with a brick fireplace, and a rear patio and deck. All rooms have private baths. Gourmet breakfasts are served; five-course dinners are offered on Saturday. $$$–$$$$

Villa Rosa
15 Chapala Street, Santa Barbara, CA 93101-3507; tel: 805-966-0851.
This Spanish-style bed-and-breakfast has the casual sophistication for which Santa Barbara is known. One block from both the beach and Stearn's Wharf, the inn offers 18 guest rooms with private baths; four rooms have a fireplace. A walled courtyard encloses a swimming pool and spa. $$–$$$$

TOURS & OUTFITTERS

American Cetacean Society
Orange County Whale Watch, P.O. Box 18763, Irvine, CA

92623; tel: 714-675-9881.

Whale-watching excursions depart from Balboa Pavilion aboard boats carrying from 120 to 350 passengers. Sightings include gray, minke, and sperm whales, and Pacific white-sided dolphins. Trips are led by naturalists from the American Cetacean Society.

Captain Don's Coastal Cruises
P.O. Box 1134, Summerland, CA 93067; tel: 805-969-5217.

Daily half-day tours aboard 49-passenger boats view gray whales.

Island Packers
1867 Spinnaker Drive, Ventura, CA 93001; tel: 805-642-1393.

The concessionaire of Channel Islands National Park runs half-day trips to Santa Cruz and the Anacapa Islands.

Sea Landing Sportfishing
1321 Los Alamos Place, Santa Barbara, CA 93109; tel: 805-965-1985.

Whale- and dolphin-watching trips are made aboard the 88-foot *Condor*. Nine-hour trips to the Channel Islands are offered on weekends from December 15 to February 15, and daily from February 15 to April 30.

MUSEUMS

Sea Center
211 Stearn's Wharf, Santa Barbara, CA 93101; tel: 805-962-0885.

Highlights at this small, modern museum include a touch tank, a life-size model of a gray whale, aquariums, and other exhibits on the human and natural history of the Santa Barbara Channel.

Stephen Birch Aquarium
2300 Expedition Way, La Jolla, CA 92093; tel: 619-534-3474.

The aquarium is associated with the Scripps Institute of Oceanography and sponsors whale-watching cruises, scuba expeditions, and other educational activities.

Excursions

San Diego
San Diego Convention and Visitors Bureau, 11 Horton Plaza, San Diego, CA 92101; tel: 619-236-1212.

San Diego is a paradise for those who love marine life and history. Balboa Park is home to the unrivaled San Diego Zoo, an aquarium, and other natural and cultural delights; whale watchers have their pick of expeditions, from multiday trips to Baja Mexico to half-day offshore tours. Land-based whale watching is good, too, particularly at Cabrillo National Monument on Point Loma, which sponsors a Whale Watch Weekend in January. The Museum of Man documents the history of humankind with artifacts and physical remains.

Catalina Island
Catalina Island Visitors Bureau, P.O. Box 217, Avalon, CA 90704; tel: 310-510-1520.

Mediterranean-like in aspect and climate, Catalina Island, 22 miles west of mainland Los Angeles, quickly soothes the cares of harried Angelenos who come here to boat, snorkel, dive, and sea kayak in the crystal-clear water. William Wrigley, Jr., bought the 21-mile-long island in 1915. His mansion is now an opulent inn. Author Zane Grey, a fishing enthusiast, spent his last days here, writing books like *Tales of Swordfish and Tuna*. The Santa Catalina Island Interpretive Center offers exhibits on the area's rich marine life, flora and fauna, and history.

Ventura
Ventura Visitors Bureau, 89 South California Street, Number C, Ventura, CA 93001; tel: 800-333-2989 or 805-648-2075.

A seaside beauty, Ventura enjoys sweeping views of the Santa Barbara Channel, the Channel Islands, and, at night, the twinkling lights of oil rigs. Get information here about visiting the Channel Islands from the national park visitor center, then go next door to the concessionaire, Island Packers, to arrange a trip to the islands or a whale-watching tour. Anacapa is the most accessible island. The Nature Conservancy owns part of Santa Cruz Island and offers occasional trips to members.

Monterey Bay
National Marine Sanctuary
California

CHAPTER **18**

The sea here is that shade of deep cobalt that sailors call "blue water," and the voyager knows that a vast, abyssal canyon stretches beneath the hull. As the sun rises, the surface of the ocean is dappled with flecks of pink, gold, and salmon, and cries of gulls and shearwaters fill the air. Brown pelicans fly in formation off the bow; they veer sharply and, one by one, crash into the swells, emerging with pouches bulging with wriggling sardines. ◆ The captain suddenly shouts and steers north. Ahead, the water is churned to a froth by massive bodies, some patterned in black and white, at least one a dull gray. The captain cuts the throttle, and the boat drifts to within a hundred yards of the melee. It soon becomes apparent what's happening: A pod of orcas has attacked and killed a gray whale and is now feeding exuberantly. A bull orca grabs a chunk of blubber in its teeth and swims triumphantly about, brandishing the booty high in the air. Cow orcas bring their young to the gray's carcass and

Protected marine wilderness provides sanctuary for whales and dolphins, sharks and elephant seals, sea otters and seabirds.

demonstrate the tail slap that is used by killer whales to stun their prey. The youngsters mimic her clumsily. ◆ The sight is by no means charming, but it is awe-inspiring, magisterial – indeed, in its own way, beautiful. It is as emblematic of the wild as a wildebeest migration on the Serengeti or a grizzly fishing for salmon on Alaska's Copper River. And it all happened a mere hour from one of the country's toniest tourist spots. ◆ The **Monterey Peninsula** is renowned for its fine restaurants, inns, and shops. But civilization, with all its boons and drawbacks, stops at the beach. Just beyond lies **Monterey Bay National Marine Sanctuary**, a vast wilderness where

Humpbacks breed in warm, tropical or sub-tropical waters in summer and feed in cold, high-latitude waters in winter.

great beasts roam, mate, fight, and feed. The only rules here are the implacable laws of nature.

Primordial Life

This world is still primordial and pristine, and the daily dramas that are enacted have been playing since the Pleistocene epoch. Humpbacks breach, throwing the entire length of their massive bodies into the air before thunderously crashing back to the water. Great white sharks harry elephant seals and cull stragglers. Gulls

Gray whale calves like this newborn in Monterey Bay (above) are vulnerable to shark and orca attacks, despite the legendary ferocity of gray whale mothers in defense of their young.

Anemones (right) grow in profusion on the sea floor; the colorful creatures disable their prey with stinging tentacles.

scavenge the scraps. At night, schools of squid court and mate in amorous, multitentacled masses, and dawn breaks with great rafts of seabirds slashing the waves in search of even greater schools of anchovies and sardines. In the midafternoon, sea lions sun on the beaches and rocky headlands, and rare sea otters dive for abalone and mussels.

The sanctuary encompasses **Monterey Canyon**, a tremendous submarine gorge that reaches 25 miles offshore. Nutrient-rich cold water wells up along the canyon into relatively shallow areas near shore. Here, exposed to direct sunlight, it mixes with warmer water, stimulating an explosion of algae and plankton. This rich broth of microscopic life is the foundation for a remarkably complex food chain that supports everything from tiny copepods to salmon, seabirds, and gigantic blue whales. The great kelp forests that grow just offshore also comprise a separate ecosystem rich in rockfish, mollusks, crustaceans, and other sea life.

Although the sanctuary is one of the

best diving venues in the United States (particularly the Point Lobos peninsula, just south of Carmel), you don't have to be a diver to fully appreciate its wonders. A boat will do just fine, and is, in fact, the only way to explore the bay's pelagic regions where the great whales live. Several companies departing from colorful Fisherman's Wharf in **Monterey** do a brisk year-round trade shuttling passengers around the sanctuary to view whales and dolphins. Because different species of whales congregate in the sanctuary at different times of the year, the boats' daily schedules vary depending on the season. Trips last from three to six hours. Most boats have full galleys, though passengers can bring their own food. Dress warmly, and if you suffer from motion sickness take appropriate remedies, for the seas are sometimes rough.

Ocean Behemoths

An impressive array of cetaceans transits the sanctuary, including the Brobdingnagian blue whales and finback whales, which are almost as large. Both are usually seen traveling alone or in small groups of up to four animals as they rove ceaselessly in search of krill, bait fish, and zooplankton, which they strain from the water with their baleen, the feathery curtains of bone and cartilage in their maws. Though enormous, the whales are sometimes difficult to see; they typically surface only briefly before diving for 10 minutes or more. Finbacks, especially, are fast swimmers and can be hard to track after they sound.

From May through November, these two species wander between Monterey Bay and the **Farallon Islands**, several stony out-croppings located about 20 miles west of San Francisco. The Farallones form the heart of Monterey's sister refuge, **Farallon Islands National Marine Sanctuary**. For all practical purposes, the two contiguous sanctuaries form a single reserve. Like Monterey Bay, the Farallones are bathed in nutrient-rich upwelling currents, and plankton and forage fish are stunningly

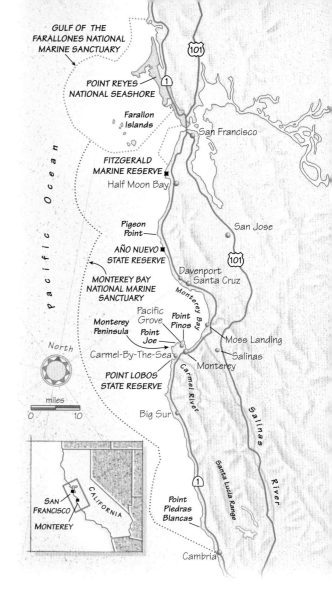

abundant. In some years, krill and anchovies are more prolific around the Farallones than in Monterey Bay; in other years, the reverse is true. Whale-watching tours depart **San Francisco's Fisherman's Wharf** for the Farallones, but check with the tour operators before deciding whether to leave from Monterey or San Francisco if blues and finbacks are your quarry: The whales will be found where the forage is thickest, and the whale-watching boats follow the krill just as reliably as the whales.

Humpbacks may also be seen in groups, although they are often spotted as pairs or solitaries. They employ more aggressive and

whale manages a couple of ponderous swallows before majestically sliding back into the sea.

While blues, finbacks, and humpbacks are often spotted by Monterey's whale-watching fleet, they play second fiddle in some ways to gray whales. Several hundred blue, finback, and humpback whales may frequent Monterey waters in a good year, but some 22,000 gray whales pass through annually on their seasonal migrations between the waters of Alaska and Baja California. The greatest numbers are seen during their southward journey in December and January. The whales, often traveling in large groups, range about five miles offshore at this time. They can be approached relatively closely, but they usually don't display the open curiosity and friendliness typical of their behavior in Baja lagoons. Instead, they seem determined to keep plowing southward, single-minded in their efforts to reach the warm, saline estuaries of Mexico where they can loll and give birth.

sophisticated feeding strategies than the phlegmatic blues and finbacks; humpbacks have been observed working cooperatively to corral small fish in "bubble-nets." Sanctuary visitors also sometimes see humpbacks lunge-feeding, a behavior that's stimulated when large schools of bait fish congregate close to the surface. The signs are easy to divine. The water suddenly explodes from the upward thrust of a humpback's huge gape-mouthed head. Anchovies and sardines fly through the air in a glittering curtain while the

Watching from Shore

Whale watchers with wobbly sea legs may want to skip boat tours altogether. The good news is that gray whales, harbor seals, sea lions, and other marine wildlife often can be seen from shore. Look for grays near points and headlands during the spring migration. In Northern California, the lighthouse at the tip of **Point Reyes**, just north of San Francisco, is a particularly good spot. South of San Francisco, try the **Pigeon Point Lighthouse** and **Davenport** near Santa Cruz. Reliable areas around Monterey include **Point Pinos, Point Lobos, Carmel Bay**, and **Point Joe**.

The Monterey Peninsula sits at the northern end of **Big Sur**, a breathtaking, 80-mile stretch of coastal wilderness with remote coves, craggy headlands, and redwood-cloaked gorges. Many overlooks on Highway 1, the serpentine coastal road, are fine vantage points for viewing the gray whale migration. South of Big Sur, promising places to see gray whales include **Point Arguello** and **Point Conception**.

A gray whale's skull (above) is displayed at Point Reyes National Seashore north of San Francisco. Point Reyes Light (right) is a fine whale-watching spot.

Common dolphins (opposite, top) are often spied schooling in the shallows off the California coast.

Cypress trees (opposite, bottom) cling to the rocky headlands of the Monterey coast.

This elephant seal pup (below) is a junior version of its four-ton father.

The Fearsome Orca

Whale fans get a second chance at the grays throughout the spring when they head back to Alaska. It is at this time when orcas are most likely to enter into the equation. Grays tend to travel in smaller groups on the way north; many of the bulls swim alone, and the cows typically travel with just their calves. They also often stay closer to shore at this time, sometimes traveling within the kelp beds a couple of hundred yards from shore. This may protect them from orca predation: The seaweed provides cover for grays, and orcas apparently are loath to enter the kelp forests. The gray females sometimes take the opportunity to rest and nurse their young.

On occasion, a gray whale cow and her calf will dash directly across the 30-mile-wide bay from **Pacific Grove** to **Santa Cruz** rather than hug the coast, the long way around. But when they opt for the shortcut, orcas are often there to ambush them. Here the grays have no chance of finding cover, and the orcas cut the calves from the mothers as easily as trained quarter horses perform the same maneuver on cattle. Occasionally the orcas will also attack the cows, but the calves are invariably the quarry of choice.

While orcas sometimes prey on blue whales and finbacks, they usually stay clear of humpbacks. These whales are far more aggressive than their larger kindred, and are quite adroit at buffeting inquisitive orcas with their powerful flukes and oversized pectoral fins.

An impressive variety of smaller cetaceans also lives in the sanctuary year-round. Several are likely to be seen on any trip. Dall's porpoises, which look like small orcas, often shadow the boats. Common longbeak dolphins and Pacific white-sided dolphins travel in gigantic schools sometimes comprised of thousands of animals. One of the sanctuary's most memorable sights is a large congregation of these animals porpoising joyously through the air, their excitement palpable and contagious. Other commonly seen dolphins include Risso's dolphins, Pacific bottlenose dolphins, and harbor porpoises. Two small whales, the minke and pilot, also frequent these waters, but sightings are apt to be a fleeting glimpse of a spout and a glistening patch of black skin.

Monterey whale watchers are also invariably bird-watchers, both by design and by circumstance. The sanctuary attracts vast flocks of migratory and resident marine birds. Extravagant numbers of storm petrels, pigeon guillemots, murres, and gulls prey on schooling krill and anchovies and scavenge bits of leftovers from orca and shark kills. Cassin's auklets – small, active gray birds that spend nights in their nests but days on the ocean to avoid predators – are also common sights.

Pelagic Wildlife Park

Versatile as they are for viewing wildlife, big motorboats aren't necessary for enjoying the sanctuary. Indeed, smaller, less obtrusive craft provide a more intimate experience. Kayaks, which can be rented at **Monterey**, **Pacific Grove**, and **Carmel**, are excellent vessels from which to view sea otters and coastal birds. Lucky kayakers will spot gray whales near the kelp beds during the spring as they warily thread their way north, trying to avoid orcas. The best spot for otters is the three-mile section of beaches and coves between the Monterey Bay Aquarium and Lover's Point in Pacific Grove. The waters here are relatively protected, and at least a few otters will be sighted during a typical paddle.

Sea otters are usually spotted feeding or lolling on their backs with their feet up. They often anchor themselves for a snooze by draping strands of kelp over their bellies. These big marine mustelids are true tool users; they are often seen floating on the surface cracking crabs or mollusks on large rocks that they balance on their chests. Otters display highly individual tastes when it comes to prey. Some will eat only fish, some only abalone, while others prefer crabs or mussels. Such idiosyncratic proclivities may prevent the otters from depleting particular food sources in any given territory.

The Monterey breakwater supports an exceptionally large colony of California sea lions, and visitors can get up close and personal with them (a wire fence prevents the interactions from getting too cozy). During the spring, the huge bulls fill the air

with sonorous roars as they contest with each other for territories and females. The biggest and boldest will gather the largest harems of sleek cows. Breeding extends well into summer.

Northern elephant seals, the world's largest pinniped, are also found here. One of their biggest rookeries is 20 miles north of Santa Cruz at **Año Nuevo State Reserve** (the waters directly offshore of Año Nuevo are part of the Monterey federal refuge). Here hundreds of four-ton "beachmasters" (dominant bulls) brawl fiercely for the attention of the cows, which, at one ton each, are comparatively svelte. Three other pinniped species breed here, and the island and its environs are consequently a prime hunting ground for great white sharks. An ongoing University of California study tracks shark predation on the seals, and attacks are sometimes seen by visitors.

In the words of a marine biologist who works in the sanctuary, Monterey Bay is "Pelagic Park," a place teeming with animals far larger and just as fascinating as any featured in the fictitious Jurassic Park.

And unlike Michael Crichton's dinosaurs, these creatures are real – they can be seen in their native habitats with minimum effort and time.

There is a final compelling advantage to the Monterey Peninsula as a whale-watching destination: A day of adventuring can be capped with a fine meal, a good bottle of California wine, and a comfortable bed in a pleasant inn. For whale watchers, it doesn't get much easier than that.

Squid (opposite, top) and other small invertebrates are a vital link in the food chain.

Boaters (opposite, bottom) greet a spyhopping humpback.

A gray whale (above) passes through a kelp bed. Kelp provides safe resting places away from marauding orcas.

Fisherman's Wharf, Monterey (left), offers several whale-watching tours and a superb aquarium.

TRAVEL TIPS

DETAILS

When to Go

The southern migration of gray whales, from November to February, offers the best chance of seeing a large number of whales; expect storms, chill winds, and rough seas during this period. Northern migration may be seen from March to early June. Blue, humpback, and fin-back whales are sighted from May to November, when the ocean is calmer and foggy mornings give way to tempera-tures in the 70s. Elephant seals give birth and mate from November to March.

How to Get There

Major airlines serve San Francisco, Los Angeles, San Jose, and Oakland International Airports. Commuter airlines fly into Monterey Peninsula Airport.

Getting Around

A car is useful for touring the peninsula and essential for driving California's dramatic coastal highway. Car rentals are available at airports. Much of the peninsula may be enjoyed by bicycle; rentals are available in Monterey. Monterey-Salinas Transit, 831-899-2555, provides bus service. Land-based whale watching at any time of year may be a better option for those susceptible to seasickness.

INFORMATION

California Whale Hotline
Tel: 415-474-0488.

Monterey County Visitors and Convention Bureau
380 Alvarado Street, Box 1770,

Monterey, CA 93942-1770; tel: 831-649-1770

Monterey Bay and Gulf of the Farallones National Marine Sanctuaries
National Oceanic and Atmospheric Administration, Golden Gate National Recreational Area, Fort Mason, San Francisco, CA 94123; tel: 415-556-3509

CAMPING

State and federal parks offer a huge network of campgrounds, with water, toilets, and other facilities. Call 800-365-2267 for information and reservations.

LODGING

PRICE GUIDE – double occupancy

$ = up to $49 $$ = $50–$99
$$$ = $100–$149 $$$$ = $150+

Jabberwock
598 Laine Street, Monterey, CA 93934; tel: 831-372-4777.

You are invited to fall down the rabbit hole at this gracious bed-and-breakfast, where Nuddy Nubble Abblestuffel is served at breakfast, clocks run backward, and guests stay in rooms such as the Mimsey and the Wabe. The 1911 Craftsman-style house, a convent from 1937 to 1972, has three guest rooms with private baths, four with shared baths; several rooms have expansive ocean views, Jacuzzis, and tiled fireplaces. The inn is furnished with Victorian furniture and decorated with William Morris wallpaper. $$$–$$$$

Monterey Hotel
406 Alvarado Street, Monterey, CA 93940; tel: 800-727-0960.

This downtown hotel, built in 1904, was reopened in 1987 and renovated in 1996. Victorian touches include oak paneling, ornate fireplaces, marble floors,

antique furnishings, and rose-colored fabrics. The hotel's 45 rooms have private baths; suites have sunken baths and fire-places. $$$–$$$$

Pacific Grove Lighthouse Lodge
1150 and 1249 Lighthouse Avenue, Pacific Grove, CA 93950; tel: 831-655-2111 or 800-858-1249.

One block from Point Pinos Lighthouse, the lodge is nestled among pine trees and a Cape Cod-style village. Suites have king-size beds, fireplaces, kitchenettes, and Jacuzzi tubs. A swimming pool is on the premises. $$$

Post Ranch Inn
Highway 1, Box 219, Big Sur, CA 93920; tel: 831-667-2200 or 800-527-2200.

The quintessential retreat for nature lovers with deep pockets, this lovely inn is built on 98 acres overlooking the Big Sur coastline. Choose from 29 dou-ble rooms and one suite housed in environmentally friendly structures – some with earth-covered roofs, others on stilts, still others made of redwood and steel. A spa, pool, and restaurant are on the premises. $$$$

Sandpiper Inn
2408 Bayview Avenue, Carmel, CA 93921; tel: 831-624-6433.

In operation since the 1930s, this inn lies 100 yards from white-sand beaches. The 16 guest rooms, overlooking either the ocean or gardens, have skylights, fireplaces, private baths, and king- or queen-size beds. Tea and sherry are offered in the common room, which has antiques and a fireplace of Carmel stone. $$–$$$$

TOURS & OUTFITTERS

Chris' Fishing and Whale-Watching Trips
48 Fisherman's Wharf, Monterey, CA 93940; tel: 831-375-5951.

Whale-watching trips aboard 50- to 75-passenger boats view gray whales between December and late March, and blues, minkes, and orcas in summer and fall.

Monterey Bay Kayaks

693 Del Monte Avenue, Monterey, CA 93940; tel: 800-649-5357 or 831-372-5357.

Natural-history kayak tours for expert and beginner paddlers explore Monterey Bay. Naturalists guide paddlers to views of sea otters, sea lions, and a variety of birds.

Monterey Sportfishing and Whale Watching

96 Old Fisherman's Wharf #1, Monterey, CA 93940; tel: 831-372-2203.

Naturalists from the American Cetacean Society narrate the trips. Boats accommodate 50 to 80 passengers.

Oceanic Society Expeditions

Fort Mason Center, Building E, San Francisco, CA 94123; tel: 415-474-3385.

This nonprofit educational organization offers several different whale-watching tours, including a nine-hour tour of the Farallon Islands. Boats accommodate 80 passengers.

MUSEUMS

Maritime Museum of Monterey

Stanton Center, Custom House Plaza, Monterey, CA; tel: 831-373-2469.

Ship models, whaling relics, and other artifacts chronicle Monterey's seafaring history.

Monterey Bay Aquarium

886 Cannery Row, Monterey, CA 93940; 831-648-4888.

Don't miss this superb aquarium on Fisherman's Wharf. More than 6,500 marine creatures are exhibited here in beautifully constructed habitats, including a three-story kelp forest.

Excursions

Año Nuevo State Reserve

New Year's Creek Road, Pescadero, CA 94060; tel: 650-879-2025.

Twenty-two miles north of Santa Cruz, this reserve is one of California's prime wildlife sites. Herds of northern elephant seals mate and give birth here each winter. Naturalists lead two-hour tours to view this spectacle from December 15 to March 31, giving visitors a chance to watch two-ton bulls vie with one another in bloody contests for females. Elephant seals may be viewed onshore all year, particularly during the April and August molts.

Fort Bragg/Mendocino

Fort Bragg/Mendocino Chamber of Commerce, 332 North Main Street, P.O. Box 1141, Fort Bragg, CA 95437; tel: 707-961-6300.

A different kind of whale-watching experience can be had at Fort Bragg, 176 miles north of San Francisco. Once a logging and fishing center, Fort Bragg is rapidly becoming a haven for galleries, boutiques, and restaurants, spilling out from trendy Mendocino. The annual Whale Festival in March celebrates the migration of gray whales, and a number of operators offer whale-watching tours. Kayak rentals are available at Van Damme State Park.

Point Reyes National Seashore

Point Reyes National Seashore, Point Reyes, CA 94956; tel: 415-663-1092.

Less than 50 miles north of San Francisco, this 86,000-acre park offers outstanding whale watching. One of the best locations is Point Reyes Lighthouse, which may be reached from Drakes Beach by free shuttle in January and February, peak season for gray whale migration. Lectures on whale watching are

presented at Bear Creek Visitor Center. The park's other wildlife include Tule elk, fallow deer, axis deer, and more than 430 bird species.

Oregon and Washington Coast

CHAPTER **19**

Swells are running eight to ten feet – calm as winter days go, but double summer's usual ride – as the captain steers the 65-foot whale-watching boat past the end of the rocky breakwater at the mouth of **Yaquina Bay** and over the bar into the open ocean. It's a little disconcerting to be maneuvering this mountain of swells, motoring up one gray slope and sliding down its back side, until you learn that the captain spent 20 years crabbing from Siberia to Santa Cruz before he and his wife gave up the itinerant fishing life to lead whale-watching tours out of **Newport, Oregon**. ◆ It's early in the southbound migration of gray whales, and the onboard naturalist has warned passengers that whale activity may be light. Three miles offshore, the captain points the boat north to begin cruising the coastline. He scans the swells. Suddenly, loudly, he reports the first sighting: a single blow off the port bow. It's nothing like the waterspouts of cartoons but more like a puff of gray smoke, as massive

Migrating gray whales – breaching, spouting, and spyhopping – are the star attractions off the storm-tossed Northwest coast.

lungs compress and expel a single huge, moist breath. A second blow to the west lets us know that he – or she – isn't alone. Soon the whales themselves appear, their mottled gray backs, encrusted with barnacles and speckled with whale lice, just breaking the surface in smooth arcs before disappearing beneath the dark, roiling sea. ◆ They move steadily, heading south. The boat follows at a judicious distance, keeping the whales company for a spell. Harbor porpoises briefly splash alongside the boat, keeping pace effortlessly. After a few false alarms, the passengers spot several genuine whale spouts, but they never see anything as dramatic

Heceta Head Lighthouse, Oregon, was built in 1893. The lighthouse keeper's home is now a bed-and-breakfast where guests can watch whales from their rooms.

as spyhopping or breaching. Winter's coming, and the gray whales are on a mission, bound for Mexico after a summer spent feeding in the bountiful, frigid waters of Alaska. After an hour, the captain turns back toward Yaquina Bay. He scoots aside to let kids take turns at the wheel. In the calm of the harbor, fat brown sea lions lounging on barges raise their heads to bark at one another, apparently savoring this unusually calm December day as much as the whale watchers are.

Seasonal Pulses

Boats aren't allowed to chase whales or even intentionally approach closer than 100 yards. On occasion, however, gray whales on the outer coast take an interest in those who motor out to see them and may approach the boats in order to investigate. It would be too much to suggest that they've timed their migrations to suit the winter vacation schedules of their human admirers, but the coincidence is certainly fortuitous. Southbound whales start showing up off the Washington coast at the end of November, off Oregon in early December, and the migration is well under way by the week

A pod of orcas (above) passes through the Strait of Juan de Fuca, Washington. Transient orcas prey on gray whales migrating along the outer coast.

A petroglyph (right) in the Wedding Rocks at Ozette, Washington, depicts an orca.

between Christmas and the new year. The peak of winter migration – some 28 whales passing per hour – generally falls in the first week of January.

The spring gray whale migration extends over a longer period and comes in waves. Males and noncalving females start to appear off Oregon in early March and peak in mid- to late March at about 12 to 15 whales per hour. They're followed by mothers with calves in late March. More than 22,000 gray whales make the annual round-trip from Mexico to Alaska – an impressive increase from the 11,000 whales that researchers estimate made the trip in 1969–70. The growth in population led to the removal of gray whales from the endangered species list in 1994.

Besides those whales that migrate through the region, some 200 grays have taken to summering off the Oregon and Washington coasts in recent years and have become familiar to residents. Little is known of their migratory habits. Researchers believe that they spend the winter off Baja and arrive at the tail end of the northbound migration in June. They spend the summer off Oregon and head south in November or December. Attempts to attach radio tags to track their movements have failed: Tags don't withstand the commotion of feeding and courting. But their presence off the Oregon and Washington coasts gives visitors a good chance of seeing whales throughout the year, except for mid-February and early- to mid-November.

Getting a Good View

Whale-watching tours start from **Westport, Washington**, and at least a half-dozen Oregon ports. They range from floating classrooms staffed with naturalists to charter fishing boats seeking new sources of income in the wake of dwindling salmon catches. Even the latter type of operation may be staffed with a naturalist, as well as an eagle-eyed captain knowledgeable about marine mammals. But boat tours aren't for everyone. These

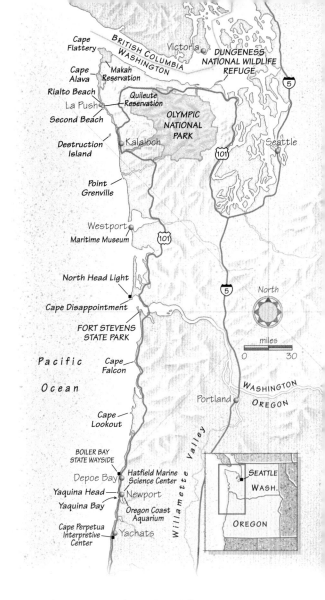

are rough waters, and motion sickness can take you by surprise (though it's possible to head off queasiness with various over-the-counter and prescription medications). Some small children are thrilled by boat trips, and some aren't. And it's tough to watch whales – especially when the signs, such as blows or brief surfacing, are subtle – when you're also trying to watch roving kids.

Fewer people take to the air to see whales (cost per hour is four to six times that of whale watching by boat), but it's an unforgettable experience. At last count, seven air charter outfits were offering whale-watching tours from runways along

the Oregon coast and in the **Willamette Valley**. Federal regulations require pilots to maintain an altitude of 1,000 feet or higher when they're within 100 surface yards of a whale. So you're not close. But from the air you don't need to wait for a whale to break the surface or expel a breath: Migrating whales tend to swim just beneath the surface, giving you extended views of their entire 50-foot length, from their V-shaped heads to their wide, center-notched flukes.

Watching from Shore

Most whale watchers in Oregon and Washington aren't in a boat or a plane. They're traveling Highway 101 along the coast and stopping at overlooks along the way. Whale watching in Washington is rather hit or miss, because the most accessible parts of the coast are also the flattest. Few points are high enough to allow you a good look at passing whales, even in spring when they may be a bit closer to land than they are in winter. Washington has more than 60 miles of wilderness coastline from Kalaloch to Cape Flattery, part of Olympic National Park, as well as several small but fascinating Indian reservations where the residents' lives once revolved around the migration of gray whales. There are a few bluffs where you can look down on the ocean: **Kalaloch** has a lodge, cozy cabins, and a campground; **Second Beach** and **Rialto Beach** are next to La Push, home to the Quileute tribe, which has its own resort and rooms facing the breakers. **Cape Flattery** can be reached by hiking and camping along the beach, or by driving inland, turning toward the Strait of Juan de Fuca, then following the coast road to the Makah Reservation at Neah

Orca, wolf, and thunderbird totems adorn a building at the Makah Reservation in Neah Bay, Washington (opposite, top).

Oregon's coastal road (opposite, bottom), shown here at the foot of Mount Humbug, has many superb pullouts from which to spy migrating whales.

Pacific white-sided dolphins (right) are seen swimming the Northwest coast in schools of up to 300 animals.

A large mural in Newport, Oregon (below), testifies to the town's affection for gray whales.

Bay. **Cape Alava** in Flattery Rocks National Refuge, **Destruction Island overlook**, **Point Grenville**, and **North Head Light/Cape Disappointment** are also good bets.

A wealth of accessible headlands and a nationally acclaimed whale-watching assistance program have made the Oregon coast a magnet for more casual cetacean sighters. Two weeks each year, between Christmas and New Year's Day and again in late March, some 300 volunteers array themselves at 30 overlooks from **Harris Beach State Park** just north of the California line to **Fort Stevens State Park** at the Columbia River's south jetty (plus a couple of spots just inside Washington and California). They're on duty from 10 A.M. to 1 P.M. daily, rain or shine, giving tips to visitors and, at some sites, offering a peek through a spotting scope. Trained by researchers at Mark O. Hatfield Marine Science Center in Newport, they know a thing or two about the gray whale's behavior and life cycle. But their real value is social, as they chat with visitors about whales and help pass the some-

times chilly minutes between sightings at breezy overlooks. They're easy to find: Just look for one of the dozens of signs that say "Whale Watching Spoken Here" along U.S. 101.

Not every spot where volunteers are stationed is a great viewpoint for whales; some locations are chosen more for the convenience of visitors than the bounty of whales. Other sites require a little more effort but can yield great rewards: The tips of **Cape Lookout** and **Cape Falcon**, for example, require a five- to six-mile,

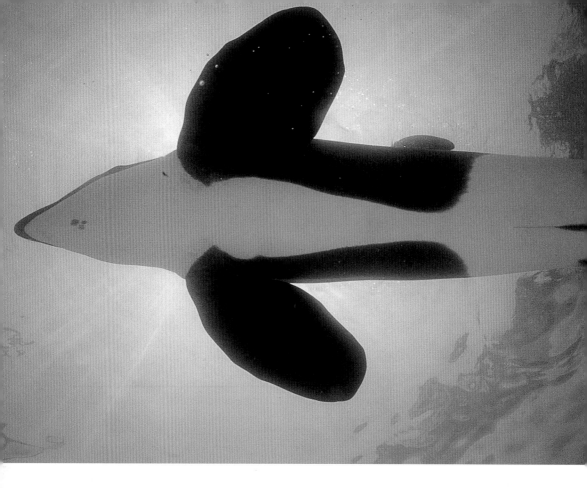

fairly level round-trip hike through the coastal forest.

Ironically, perhaps, the best spot for whale watching on the Oregon coast may be one of the most accessible: the seawall in lively, touristy **Depoe Bay** right on U.S. 101 north of **Newport**. No one knows exactly why whale watching here is so good. It could be the deep water and proximity to the bay (gray whales tend to concentrate at bay and river mouths). But it's not unusual for tour boats cruising offshore to look back toward a pod of whales breaching and spouting just off the sea-wall, closer, in fact, to those standing on dry land than those in the boats.

The second-best spot may be **Boiler Bay State Park**, not much more than a highway overlook, really, a few miles north of Depoe Bay. The compact bluff jutting into the Pacific offers no beach access, but the wildlife watching is so good here that state park officials use low-power radio broadcasts at the site so motorists can tune in a series of messages about the biology and behavior of gray whales and the other creatures they're likely to see.

Refuges in the Rain

Winter storms on the Oregon and Washington coasts tend to blow in from the south with short bursts of hard rain interspersed with stretches of brilliant sunshine and dramatic clouds. On days like that, get out of your car for a little whale watching along the beach. Then there are the days of unremitting rain or nonstop drizzle when even a few minutes at an ocean overlook can soak you to the skin. Days like this are more common in December than in March, but they can catch spring whale watchers as well. That's the time to snuggle into an ocean-view motel room, or to whale watch from someplace like **Cape Perpetua Interpretive Center** south of **Yachats, Oregon**, where wide picture windows might afford a view of a distant spout. If not, peruse the exhibits and watch the interpretive film.

In **Newport**, whale watchers stymied by storms can stop at three interpretive centers: **Yaquina Head**, where displays illustrate the gray whale's migratory patterns; **Hatfield Marine Science Center**, where an articulated whale skeleton is suspended overhead and there are exhibits on the studies conducted by the center's research staff; and the **Oregon Coast Aquarium**, which is no longer home to Keiko the celebrity killer whale but is still worth a visit for its exhibits of jellyfish, sharks, tufted puffins, and other marine life. (A walk-through deep-ocean exhibit is slated to open in Keiko's old tank.) The **Maritime Museum** in **Westport** also has whale and other marine mammal skeletons on display and offers weekend lectures on the natural history of gray whales during the spring migration.

Such exhibits can't really compete with even a glimpse of the real thing: a dark-gray back easing above the surface, a blow as transitory as a wave splashing on a submerged rock, a giant fluke slipping beneath the waves. Even at the height of the migration, there are no guarantees that you'll see a whale. Some days you get lucky, some days you don't. Then a day comes when you spot not one, not two, but three or more whales frolicking at the base of a steep cliff just off U.S Highway 101. They are not merely surfacing but breaching, even spyhopping, and not for a passing moment but for an hour or more. Those great dark animals at play in the cold Pacific – it's a sight you won't soon forget.

Distinct coloring (opposite, top) and large pectoral and dorsal fins make orcas easy to identify.

Bald eagles (opposite, bottom) nest in tall trees along the Northwest coast and, like orcas, are particularly fond of salmon.

A sea arch (right) frames the rocky headlands of Rialto Beach in Olympic National Park, Washington.

TRAVEL TIPS

DETAILS

When to Go

Prime whale watching lasts from November to March, a period marked by rain, cool temperatures, and winter storms. Large numbers of gray whales migrate along the coast between December and May; some grays linger from June to September – the most pleasant time to watch whales. Volunteers are available to assist visitors at lookout points along the Oregon coast during Whale Watch Weeks in December and March.

How to Get There

Major airlines serve the Portland and Seattle areas.

Getting Around

A car is necessary for travel along the coast; rentals are available at the airports.

INFORMATION

Olympic National Park

600 East Park Avenue, Port Angeles, WA 98362; tel: 360-452-4501.

Oregon Coast Visitors Association

P.O. Box 670, Newport, OR 97365; tel: 888-628-2101.

Oregon Tourism Commission

775 Summer Street NE, Salem, OR 97310; tel: 800-547-7842 or 503-986-0000.

Washington State Tourism

P.O. Box 42500, Olympia, WA 98504-2500; tel: 800-544-1800 or 360-586-2088.

CAMPING

Seventeen state campgrounds are available on the Oregon coast; 14 accept reservations at 800-452-5687. National forest campgrounds, clustered along the central coast, are more primitive and don't take reservations. Sixteen campgrounds, some coastal, are operated on a first-come, first-served basis in Olympic National Park; for information, call 360-452-0330.

LODGING

PRICE GUIDE – double occupancy

$ = up to $49 $$ = $50–$99

$$$ = $100–$149 $$$$ = $150+

Channel House Bed-and-Breakfast Inn

35 Ellingston Street, P.O. Box 56, Depoe Bay, OR 97341; tel: 800-447-2140 or 541-765-2140.

Perched at the mouth of Depoe Bay, a short walk from the center of town, this bed-and-breakfast affords breathtaking views of the Oregon coastline. Guest rooms and suites have private baths, queen-size beds, balconies, and whirlpools. Some rooms have fireplaces and kitchenettes. Breakfast is served on a seaside deck or in a room filled with nautical antiques. $$–$$$$

Heceta House

92072 Highway 101, Yachats, OR 97498; tel: 541-547-3696.

Guests stay in the former home of the lighthouse keeper next to Heceta Head Lighthouse, erected in 1893. Three second-floor rooms, each filled with antiques, are available; one has a private bath. Rates include an eight-course breakfast. $$–$$$

Inn at Otter Crest

301 Otter Crest Loop, P.O. Box 50, Otter Rock, OR 97369; tel: 800-452-2101 or 541-765-2111.

The resort sits on 35 acres overlooking the ocean at Cape Foulweather. Whale sightings occur regularly. Many of the inn's 200-plus guest units have fireplaces, full kitchens, and great ocean views; all have private decks. Amenities include a heated swimming pool, sauna, and tennis courts. An isolated beach is footsteps away. $$$–$$$$

Inn at Spanish Head

4009 Highway 101, Lincoln City, OR 97367; tel: 800-452-8127 or 541-996-2161.

This 10-story hotel is an excellent stop for whale watchers. A record-breaking 225 whale sightings were made here during Whale Watch Week 1998. The inn has 120 rooms, including suites and studios. Standard rooms have private baths and a king- or queen-size bed. Suites and studios have kitchens. Most rooms have ocean views. A restaurant, heated swimming pool, Jacuzzi, and exercise room are on the premises. $$$–$$$$

Kalaloch Lodge

157151 Highway 101, Forks, WA 98331; tel: 360-962-2271.

Olympic National Park's only lodge is perched on a seaside bluff. The rustic lodge has 58 units, including 18 ocean-view cabins and a secluded 10-room motel. Cabins have kitchenettes and fireplaces and can sleep four to nine people in basic comfort. A restaurant and gift shop are also on the premises. $$–$$$

Sea Quest Bed-and-Breakfast

95354 Highway 101, Yachats, OR 97498; tel: 800-341-4878 or 541-547-3782.

This cedar-and-glass inn is set on a bluff above the sea. The five guest rooms have private baths, Jacuzzis, and ocean views. A wraparound deck has telescopes and binoculars for whale watching. $$$–$$$$

TOURS & OUTFITTERS

Deep Sea Charters/Whale-Watching Headquarters

P.O. Box 1115, Westport, WA 98595; tel: 360-268-9300.

Several two-hour trips depart daily from March to May. An educational talk about whales is given prior to departure.

Marine Discovery Tours

345 Southwest Bay Boulevard, Newport, OR 97365; tel: 800-903-2628 or 541-265-6200.

One- to two-hour whale-watching tours are led by naturalists.

Ocean Research and Conservation Association

720 Olive Way, Suite 900, Seattle, WA 98101; tel: 206-382-6722.

The association conducts daily trips from Westport, Washington, aboard six 25-passenger boats. Passengers receive their money back if no whales are sighted. Open March and April.

Oregon Museum of Science and Industry

4015 S.W. Canyon Road, Portland, OR 97221; tel: 503-222-2828.

Museum naturalists lead two-hour whale-watching tours from Depoe Bay.

Seattle Aquarium

Pier 59, Waterfront Park, Seattle, WA 98101; tel: 206-386-4300.

The aquarium leads three-hour whale-watching trips out of Westport, Washington, on weekends in March and April.

Sunset Scenic Flights

P.O. Box 427, Depoe Bay, OR 97341; tel: 541-764-3304.

Observe whales from the air aboard a Cessna 172. Flights last from 30 minutes to two hours.

Tradewinds Charters

P.O. Box 123; Depoe Bay, OR 97341; tel: 541-765-2345.

Naturalist-led tours depart daily from Depoe Bay aboard 12 boats, accommodating up to 180 passengers.

Excursions

Dungeness National Wildlife Refuge

Washington Coastal Refuges Office, 33 South Barr Road, Port Angeles, WA 98362; tel: 360-457-8451.

Fronting the Strait of Juan de Fuca, seven-mile-long Dungeness Spit is one of the most idyllic spots on the Olympic Peninsula. Visitors may walk out to the lighthouse for a tour and watch for porpoises, orcas, and harbor seals, which breed and give birth here. Other regulars in this 631-acre refuge include gulls, migratory brant, and cormorants. Bald eagles nest on the bluff trees of nearby Dungeness Recreation Area, popular among crabbers, campers, kayakers, and picnickers.

Neah Bay

North Olympic Peninsula Visitors and Convention Bureau, P.O. Box 670, Port Angeles, WA 98362; tel: 360-452-8552.

Neah Bay is set on the Makah Indian Reservation near Cape Flattery, the northwesternmost point in the contiguous United States. It's remote but worth the journey. One of the country's most significant archeological finds was uncovered near here in the 1970s, from a 500-year-old mud slide that buried a traditional Makah longhouse village. Some of the half-million artifacts – many associated with the traditional whaling culture of the Makah – are displayed in the superb Makah Cultural Resource Center, which offers Indian perspectives on the exhibits.

La Push

Forks Chamber of Commerce, P.O. Box 1249, Forks, WA 98331; tel: 800-443-6757 or 360-374-2531.

La Push, a few miles west of Forks, offers the best access to the wild coast of Olympic National Park, via Second and First Beaches and nearby Rialto Beach. Watch whales from your room at an oceanfront resort, or camp on the beach or in the park's Mora Campground, where you can explore tide pools and observe harbor seals, bald eagles, and seabirds. The area's Quileute Indians are reviving traditional crafts such as basketry and carved tribal canoes.

British Columbia and Northern Washington

CHAPTER **20**

iller whales burst from the sea like locomotives from a tunnel. Plumes of mist erupt from their blowholes, but it's the harshness of their breathing – those explosive chuffs – that startles you most.   ◆   At first glance you see only traces: clouds exhaled from warm-blooded lungs, bubbles, and surface swirls. But within seconds the frigid waters of **Haro Strait** split open and leathery black fins, some taller than a human, slice through the waves like those of sharks. Even in a 20-foot inflatable vessel with a dozen whale watchers and in the company of 30 other boats, there's a sense of vulnerability. Kayaks have been bumped by surfacing orcas; researchers have been sprayed by whale spouts. Yet no one has ever been attacked. The whales that patrol the Pacific Northwest coast have learned to tolerate the thousands of curious people who come each year for some of the best whale watching on the continent.   ◆   These orcas have likely followed migrating salmon in from

With their year-round orca populations, quiet islands, and inlets, the waterways at the U.S.–Canada border make ideal whale-watching venues.

the open Pacific through the **Strait of Juan de Fuca**, the wide and windy channel between Washington's **Olympic Peninsula** and the southern tip of **Vancouver Island**, in British Columbia. As they move toward the inner coast, they often congregate in Haro Strait, an international passage that divides the United States' **San Juan Islands** from Canada's **Gulf Islands**.   ◆   Today, spotters on surrounding hills have pinpointed these whales in Haro Strait chasing fish against the cliffs on San Juan Island. Word has swept through the whale-watching network of a guaranteed sighting, and boatloads of ecotourists have raced out from

Killer whales leap gracefully in Puget Sound. Pod members often swim and dive in unison.

Friday Harbor, Bellingham, and Anacortes, and from the Vancouver Island ports of Victoria, Sooke, and Sidney. On San Juan, hundreds of shore-based observers peer through binoculars from Lime Kiln State Park, one of the world's most reliable orca-watching sites. Many of them had been studying the exhibits at the island's Whale Museum in Friday Harbor when they received the alert about the whales' arrival.

Orca Ahoy!

Twenty or thirty whales are just offshore, blowing and porpoising through the surface in twos and threes. One torpedoes up from the ocean and splashes down beside a flotilla of drifting sea kayakers, who holler with excitement at the spectacle. Another whale hoists up its ponderous flukes and slaps the water with a crack like a gunshot as it dives out of sight.

With more than 50 nature-cruise companies running the waters of Puget Sound, northwest Washington, and southern British Columbia, whale sightings rarely remain secret longer than half an hour. At peak times, more than 100 boats – Zodiacs, cabin cruisers, a variety of private craft, even inter-island ferries – may mingle with the whales. By simply flipping through local yellow pages, tourists can easily choose the kind of boat that suits them. Some operators provide pagers to

An exuberant orca breaches close to shore (above). Northern and southern orca communities reside in Puget Sound and can be seen best in summer.

A kayaker (left) encounters orcas in the tranquil waters of Puget Sound.

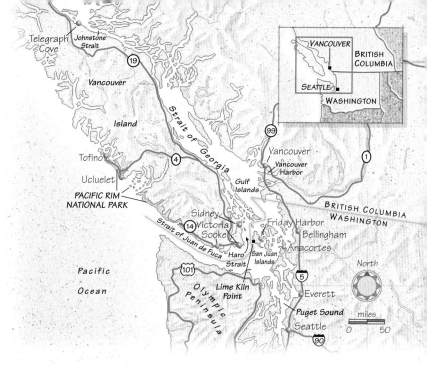

alert customers when whales are found. But even in the halcyon days of summer, there are times when the whereabouts of whales is known but blustery weather forces the whale-watch fleet ashore. Rain may be heavy at any time of year, reducing visibility and comfort.

Out in Haro Strait, the orcas are oblivious to the scenery around them: the wintry peak of Mount Baker in the Cascade Range to the east, the steel-blue ridges of the Olympic Mountains on the Olympic Peninsula to the south, and the maze of wooded islands and channels between Vancouver Island and the mainland. Gulls wheel expectantly overhead, hoping for scraps left by the whales. Cormorants and other diving birds pop through the surface with bills full of minnows.

Vessels jostle for position while keeping a respectable distance from the whales. Controversy over disturbance by boats has prompted commercial operators to follow self-imposed whale-watching guidelines. A hundred yards is close enough, they agree, but occasionally a whale decides to surface alongside a boat to everyone's good fortune.

Hello, Old Friend

The skipper of a 12-passenger inflatable checks the radar, eases in closer to **Lime Kiln Point**, and cuts the motor. As the naturalist lowers a hydrophone over the gunwale, a full-grown bull – 30 feet, maybe longer – appears a boat-length off the starboard bow. People spring up off their seats, clicking cameras and craning for a better look before it slips beneath the hull.

"That's J18," the naturalist tells the passengers, looking in her orca catalogue for confirmation. "Nineteen years old. They call him Everett." Everyone's adrenaline is still pumping when K11, a 64-year-old grandmother also known as Georgia, appears off the stern, verifying that two pods totaling more than 40 animals are swimming amid the whale-watch fleet.

Since the advent of photo-identification in the 1970s, about 700 individual killer whales have been catalogued in the Pacific Northwest. Through thousands of photographs, researchers have found that one orca can be distinguished from another by color variations on their saddle patches and by nicks and scratches on their backs and dorsal fins. Each is assigned an individual number and a letter denoting its pod. By matching animals in one picture with those in another, researchers along the coast have learned which orcas are always seen together and where they travel. Through long-term observation, they have deciphered the complexities of pod society and documented the development or demise of newborn calves and old-timers. Seasoned whale watchers can glance at almost any orca and tell you its alphanumeric name.

Resident Communities

By the late 1970s, photographs had helped determine that at least two distinct races of orcas were cruising this coast: residents and transients. They have subtle differences in

boundary near the north end of **Georgia Strait** between Vancouver Island and mainland Canada. These whales off San Juan Island are members of the southern community, made up of J, K, and L pods. Numbering about 100 whales, they forage Georgia and Juan de Fuca Straits, Puget Sound, and the outer coasts of Washington and southwest Vancouver Island. The northern community of about 200 whales in 16 pods fish the waters off northern Vancouver Island and up the coast to southeastern Alaska.

Southern residents en route to Washington are known to swim through northern territory, but they don't linger or mingle with the northern residents. "Superpods," seen only by the luckiest whale watchers, invariably are meetings of pods from the same community. The occasion could be mating bouts, where bulls from one pod impregnate cows from another and thereby avoid inbreeding. Although residents are the most familiar of all orcas, no one knows where they go in winter. Occasionally they appear near shore, but it's likely they feed over the continental shelf. It's possible that northern and southern communities mix there in winter storms that force human observers ashore.

dorsal fins and major differences in lifestyles. Residents form pods, extended families that stay together for generations. Mothers and offspring, grandmothers, uncles, aunts, and cousins exist within a matriarchal society. Who the fathers are is still unknown, but it's possible the mothers breed with whales from other pods. Residents are the mainstay of the whale-watching industry: As fish eaters, they are predictably seen from spring until autumn, when they follow migrating salmon through near-shore waters.

Resident orcas are territorial. Pods are grouped into southern and northern communities that seem to respect an invisible

Wolves of the Sea

Transients, the other race of Pacific Northwest killer whales, are the notorious wolves of the sea. They thrive on the warm-blooded flesh of seals, dolphins, and other seagoing mammals, including large whales. Hunting alone or in small packs, they silently approach and surprise their prey. Whale

Killer Reputation

"In whatever quarter of the world the orcas are found, they seem always intent upon seeking something to destroy or devour," wrote 19th-century whaler Charles Scammon, who coined the phrase "wolves of the sea." A century later, the U.S. Navy warned that orcas, commonly called killer whales, "will attack human beings at every opportunity."

In fact, unprovoked attacks by wild orcas were virtually unheard of until 1972, when a California surfer was bitten by a whale that may have mistaken the unfortunate fellow for a seal or other prey. Ten years earlier a pair of killer whales off Bellingham, Washington, had charged a boat manned by whale catchers who had lassoed one in the hope of taking it to an aquarium.

Ironically, it was captive orcas that dispelled many myths about the whale's supposed perniciousness. And it was controversy over capturing wild orcas in the Pacific Northwest that prompted a coast-wide study of whales in their own domain. Researchers discovered that orcas would rather avoid people than eat them. They learned that orcas, the largest member of the family of oceanic dolphins, live about as long as humans and mature and bear offspring from their late teens through their thirties. They are social creatures. Many live their entire lives in close, extended families. The bond between mother and son is so strong that it's common for a bull to die shortly after the death of its mother.

These findings led to a ban on orca captures in the Pacific Northwest, where more than 50 had been taken by the mid-1970s. Now, orca populations there are finally showing signs of recovery.

Scientists (opposite, top) monitor orcas from an observation station on Johnstone Strait, British Columbia.

Whale watching (opposite, bottom) is big business in Puget Sound. Scientists are studying the impact of increased boat traffic on orca populations.

An orca's conical teeth (above) are designed for predation.

watchers sometimes see transients battering a hapless seal or sea lion for as long as two hours before devouring it. They frequently change traveling companions and are unpredictable and nomadic: A transient orca in Washington could show up a month later in Alaska.

Scientists had been studying West Coast orcas for two decades when a boatload of whale watchers encountered a huge pod of mystery whales – 60 or 70 orcas – charging though the Strait of Juan de Fuca. The tourists watched in awe as researchers from both sides of the border dashed out and photo-identified 55 whales, none of which matched those from other pictures. This third race of orcas has been dubbed "off-shores" because that's where they're probably from. More than 200 have been photo-identified since 1992, but sightings are rare, and little is known of their feeding habits or migrations.

Like residents, offshore orcas are particularly vocal, emitting sounds like those that can be heard through a hydrophone by the whale watchers off San Juan Island. Though these orcas are hunting fish, no echolocation clicks are audible, but behind the cacophony of motorboats are the faint calls of J and K pods, the eerie squeals and whistles that keep them in touch as they travel.

Research on vocalizations, pioneered by Dr. John Ford, marine mammal scientist at the Vancouver Aquarium, shows that each resident pod has its own language, or unique repertoire of calls, that can be heard underwater 10 miles away. The dialects are

Indigenous Whalers

For indigenous whaling societies from the Inuit of Alaska to the Makah of northwest Washington, hunting whales is a sacred undertaking. Traditions and techniques vary, but the ethic remains the same: to be worthy of taking the animal's life. This often requires a year-round preparation cycle of prayer, fasting, and clan rituals accompanied by intense physical conditioning.

Historically, Makah whalers paddled cedar canoes to the open ocean to harpoon whales. The injured whale towed the crew until it tired and died, then a crew member would dive underwater and sew the mouth shut to keep the whale afloat. Similarly, the Inuit hunted bowhead whales in sealskin boats, using harpoons but not divers. Back onshore, the people prepared the whale meat, carved the bones into tools, rendered the blubber into oil, and carried out ceremonies for the whale's soul, allowing it to return to the spirit world.

Over the past century, whaling societies have had to adapt to many changes. Today's native hunters continue to perform traditional preparations and ceremonies, but now they use guns, motorized boats, and other modern equipment. The devastation of whale populations by commercial forces nearly drove the bowhead and gray whale to extinction. Some native communities halted whaling, while others, such as some Inuit communities, were able to continue hunting without interruption.

In 1999, Makah tribal leaders resumed traditional whaling, a right guaranteed by the tribe's 1855 treaty with the U.S. government. The move sparked controversy even within the 2,000-member tribe, with some elders joining both animal-rights groups and other concerned citizens worldwide to oppose it. In 1997, the International Whaling Commission set a quota of 56 bowhead whales to be taken by the Inuit and up to five gray whales to be taken by the Makah. – *Beth Hege Piatote*

A Makah whaler (above), photographed in the early 1900s by Edward Curtis, holds two sealskin floats used to keep a harpoon afloat.

Indians of the Northwest coast lead lives tied to the sea. Carvings of totem animals like this orca (left) honor the qualities of an animal's spirit.

Pacific white-sided dolphins (opposite, top) prefer deep water but sometimes come close to shore.

A breaching orca (opposite, bottom) off Washington's San Juan Islands splashes down in view of boaters.

learned by youngsters and passed down through generations. Old recordings of orcas reveal that changes in their calls are slow and subtle, occurring over hundreds, maybe thousands of years. J pod, recorded by the Canadian Navy in 1958, makes the same sounds today. Transient orcas speak an entirely different language than residents. It consists of about half a dozen calls that are shared, with some minor differences, by transients that roam throughout the Pacific Northwest. Acoustically, the offshores are quite different from both other races,

but there have been few opportunities to record them.

An Industry Is Born

Orcamania in the Pacific Northwest is a fairly recent phenomenon. It wasn't until 1987 that an enterprising boatman determined that orca sightings were frequent enough to offer tours off the Vancouver Island city of **Victoria**, a well-established vacation destination known for its manicured gardens and Olde English charm. Ferries from Victoria and Washington had been shuttling tourists between the two countries for decades, and whale watching soon became

a significant component in the international travel industry.

The birthplace of Pacific Northwest whale watching, however, was farther up the coast, off northeast Vancouver Island. In 1980 the first whale watchers motored out of **Telegraph Cove**, an isolated cluster of wharves and cottages stretched along a seaside boardwalk at the edge of Johnstone Strait. These waters are a warren of islands, reefs, and passes squeezed between the Vancouver Island Mountains and the Coast Range of the British Columbia mainland. They have become a mecca for summer whale watchers and kayakers: Tens of thousands make the seven-hour drive from Victoria to paddle and cruise an area much wilder than the populated south coast. Eagles, black bears, even grizzlies are sometimes seen foraging the beaches.

It was here in the late 1980s that mariners were surprised by the arrival of a cetacean species previously thought to inhabit only offshore waters – Pacific white-sided dolphins. Now these oceanic acrobats are seen year-round, sometimes in herds of 200 or 300, swimming the bays,

inlets, and channels throughout the Pacific Northwest. They appear on the horizon as a moving wall of froth, zeroing in on boats to ride in the bow and stern wakes and delighting whale watchers with their somer-saults, half-gainers, flips, and other amazing feats. Like Dall's and harbor porpoises, they show up literally out of the blue and vanish just as quickly.

Sometimes Pacific white-sided dolphins pester humpback whales by leaping and scooting around them, prompting the sluggish leviathans to bellow like elephants in protest. Since they were internationally protected in 1966, humpbacks have been rediscovering traditional feeding sites and are still a rare treat for whale watchers.

Spyhopping orcas (right) in Puget Sound may be orienting themselves to their surroundings.

The lighthouse at Limekiln State Park (below) overlooks Haro Strait and is a fine spot for viewing orcas.

Loud, misty huffs announce the presence of orcas near a sailboat off British Columbia (opposite).

Each year a few gray whales wander off the main migration route into the Strait of Juan de Fuca and the inside passage between Vancouver Island and the mainland. They occasionally surface amid the shipping traffic and bustle of Vancouver Harbour, or off the Puget Sound cities of Tacoma, Seattle, or Everett.

Cetacean experts are optimistic that their recovery will be as successful as that of Pacific gray whales.

Hunted to the brink of extinction, gray whales – protected 30 years earlier than humpbacks – now number 22,000 or more. Their annual migration from subtropical breeding lagoons to Alaskan feeding waters takes them past the outer shores of Vancouver Island, where they're the backbone of a whale-watching season that runs from late February through summer. Dressed in winter woolies and rain suits, naturalists gather on the headlands of **Pacific Rim National Park** to scan beyond the surf line for the telltale spouts of surfacing whales. Others board boats in the nearby villages of **Tofino** and **Ucluelet** and head for the open Pacific.

Migration Time

By autumn, the grays and humpbacks are on their southbound migrations. And with seasonal salmon runs dwindling, so too are orca sightings. For marine-mammal aficionados, orcas are replaced by wintering sea lions. Every fall about 3,000 California sea lions migrate up from southern climes to join about 8,000 Steller's sea lions that disperse from northern breeding rookeries. They congregate, often with harbor seals and eagles, on reefs, islets, beaches, and log booms where they feast on herring and other small fish. It's a noisy, chaotic scene with hungry gulls swirling overhead, seabirds diving, and sea lions barking incessantly.

These blubbery beasts are a bonus for birders who arrive with hundreds of thousands of wintering waterfowl that come to feed in the ice-free waters of the Pacific Northwest. The huge flocks, along with big schools of herring, are food for bald eagles that migrate to the coast when inland feeding areas freeze. In the dead of winter, about 30,000 eagles, three times the summer population, are spread along the Pacific Northwest coast.

A growing number of nature-cruise companies in both Washington and Canada are capitalizing on the Pacific Northwest's abundant wintering wildlife. But orcas remain the prime quarry, and sightings, fortunately, are most frequent in the calmer, drier months from May to October. As with all wildlife viewing, there are rarely guarantees, but ecotourism here is no longer a fledgling industry. The expertise of whale-watching operators is growing with the wildlife populations that sustain them.

TRAVEL TIPS

DETAILS

When to Go

July, August, and September are the warmest and driest months and the best time to see orcas, Dall's porpoises, harbor porpoises, and gray whales. Migrating grays are also seen off Vancouver Island in March and April. Mornings are foggy in summer, but weather can be variable, cool, and wet year-round.

How to Get There

Major airlines fly into SeaTac and Vancouver Airports; commuter airlines serve Victoria in British Columbia, and Everett, Port Angeles, and Bellingham in Washington. Washington State Ferries, 800-843-3779 or 250-381-1551, run from Seattle, Everett, Mukilteo, and Anacortes to the Kitsap and Olympic Peninsulas, Bainbridge and Whidbey Islands, the San Juan Islands, and Sidney. Black Ball Transport, 360-457-4491, provides ferry service between Port Angeles and Victoria. British Columbia Ferries, 250-386-3431, operates between Vancouver Island and the Gulf Islands; Victoria Clipper, 800-888-2535 or 206-448-5000, sails between Seattle and Victoria.

Getting Around

Cars are necessary on Vancouver Island and mainland Washington and British Columbia. Automobile ferries are available. Buses and taxi service are available on San Juan Island.

INFORMATION

Tourism British Columbia

Parliament Buildings, Victoria, BC V8V 1X4, Canada; tel: 800-663-6000 or 250-387-1642.

Tourism Vancouver Island

302-45 Bastion Square, Victoria, BC V8W 1J1, Canada; tel: 250-382-3551.

Washington State Tourism

P.O. Box 42500, Olympia, WA 98504-2500; tel: 800-544-1800 or 360-586-2088.

CAMPING

Bella Pacifica Campground

Tofino, BC, Canada; tel: 250-725-3400.

The campground is on McKenzie Beach and has protected tent sites, full RV hookups, showers, and laundry facilities.

Lakedale Campground

2627 Roche Harbor Road, Friday Harbor, WA 98250; tel: 800-617-2267.

This 82-acre property, four miles north of Friday Harbor, has lakes, tent sites, and a few rental cabins.

San Juan County Park

380 West Side Road North, Friday Harbor, WA 98250; tel: 360-378-2992.

This lovely waterfront park on Smallpox Bay has 11 campsites with clear views of Haro Strait, Vancouver Island, passing orcas and other marine life.

LODGING

PRICE GUIDE – double occupancy

$ = up to $49 $$ = $50–$99
$$$ = $100–$149 $$$$ = $150+

Best Western Tin Wis Resort

1119 Pacific Rim Highway, P.O. Box 389, Tofino, BC V0R 2Z0, Canada; tel: 800-661-9995 or 800-528-1234 (reservations).

This Native-owned lodge has 86 oceanfront guest rooms with private baths, patios or balconies, and queen- or king-size beds. Some rooms have kitchenettes, fireplaces, Jacuzzis, and separate bedrooms. Kayaks and bikes are available for rent. $$–$$$$

Empress Hotel

721 Government Street, Victoria, BC V8N 2T2, Canada; tel: 800-441-1414 or 250-384-8111.

Designed for the Canadian Pacific Railroad in 1908, this Scottish Gothic grande dame has pride of place on Victoria's Inner Harbour. Rooms are decorated with Victorian antiques, but the big draw is the traditional British afternoon tea. Whale-watching tours leave from the dock in front of the hotel. $$$–$$$$

Friday Harbor House

130 West Street, P.O. Box 1385, Friday Harbor, WA 98250; tel: 360-378-8455.

This luxurious little inn on a bluff overlooking Friday Harbor has contemporary decor, fireplaces, whirlpool tubs, private balconies, and great views of the harbor and Orcas Island. $$$$

Lonesome Cove Resort

5810A Lonesome Cove Road, Friday Harbor, WA 98250; tel: 360-378-4477.

This quiet six-acre property has six rustic waterfront cabins, each with a deck, stone fireplace, and kitchen. A beach and trout pond are on the premises. $$

Wickaninnish Inn

P.O. Box 250, Tofino, BC V0R 2Z0, Canada; tel: 800-333-4604 or 250-725-3100.

Situated on the north end of Vancouver Island, this 46-room rustic lodge has sweeping views of passing gray whales and a restaurant serving gourmet Northwest Coast fare. $$$

TOURS & OUTFITTERS

San Juan Kayak Expeditions

3090 Roche Harbor Road, Friday Harbor, WA 98250; tel: 360-378-4436.

Multiday kayak trips explore the San Juan Islands from May through September. Participants view orcas, harbor porpoises, and minke whales.

Seacoast Expeditions

1655 Ash Road, Victoria, BC V8N 2T2, Canada; tel: 250-383-2254.

The operator offers three-hour whale-watching trips aboard 12-passenger, inflatable rafts from May 1 to September 30. Customized trips are available.

Sea Quest Expeditions

P.O. Box 2424, Friday Harbor, WA 98250; tel: 360-378-5767.

Five-hour cruises view harbor porpoises, orcas, and minkes. Naturalists also lead multiday kayaking trips from the Whale Museum in Friday Harbor.

MUSEUMS

Seattle Aquarium

1483 Alaskan Way, Pier 59, Waterfront Park, Seattle, WA 98101; tel: 206-386-4320.

The aquarium specializes in the marine life of Puget Sound and sponsors Orca Search Cruises on weekends from mid-July to August 31.

Vancouver Aquarium

P.O. Box 3232, Vancouver, BC, V6B 3X8, Canada; tel: 604-685-3364.

North America's third-largest aquarium displays more than 8,000 aquatic animals, including orcas, belugas, sea lions, and seals. A rehabilitation center holds rescued marine mammals.

Whale Centre

411 Campbell Street, Tofino, BC VOR 2ZO, Canada; tel: 250-725-2132.

The museum is devoted to the natural history of gray whales.

Whale Museum

62 First Street North, Friday Harbor, WA 98250; tel: 360-378-4710.

Skeletons, models, and other exhibits explore the local whale population. Workshops and orca-watching tours are available.

Excursions

Pacific Rim National Park

P.O. Box 280, Ucluelet, BC V0R 3A0, Canada; tel: 250-762-7721.

The park protects coastal rain forest, beaches, and offshore islands along the west side of Vancouver Island. Hikers will enjoy Long Beach and the West Coast Trail, a rugged path constructed for the rescue of shipwrecked sailors. Take a water taxi from Port Alberni to visit abandoned Indian villages, trading posts, and a whaling station on the Broken Group Islands. Orcas are a familiar sight around the islands.

Telegraph Cove

Tourism British Columbia, Parliament Buildings, Victoria, BC V8V 1X4, Canada; tel: 800-663-6000 or 250-387-1642.

This remote spot is prime orca-watching territory, with daily cruises to view killer whales and explore the north island's Native culture. Built on 19th-century boardwalks, this was the northern terminus of a telegraph line along Vancouver Island's coast. Now a wilderness lover's haven, Johnstone Strait accesses Robson Bight Provincial Park, an ecological reserve established in 1982 to protect the mouth of the Tsitika River, where orcas come every summer to rub themselves on the gravel beaches.

Victoria

Greater Victoria Visitors and Convention Bureau, 812 Wharf Street, Victoria, BC V8W 1T3, Canada; tel: 250-953-2033.

Grand stone edifices, afternoon teas, fish 'n' chips, pubs, double-decker buses, the formal Butchart Gardens – this is British Columbia's capital, Victoria, an England recalled through rose-tinted glasses. Blessed with a mild climate, Victoria is easy to walk or bicycle; the winding Saanich Peninsula coast is great for kayaking or boating. The Royal British Columbia Museum interprets Canada's coastal Indians with totem poles, masks, and recreated long-houses. Whale-watching tours depart from the Inner Harbour.

Southeast
Alaska

CHAPTER 21

t's mid-morning on a sun-splashed July day. A converted, 40-foot salmon-fishing boat, departing on a week-long whale-watching cruise, motors south out of a secluded bay on the east coast of **Admiralty Island** in Southeast Alaska. Two separate whale spouts have been seen, and the captain says that the breaching may have been a humpback cow and calf signaling to one another, or simply a playful calf. Just then there's a giant splash in the boat's wake. All heads turn just in time to see a whale slam into the sea and disappear. The captain cuts the power and spins the wheel hard to port. Everyone waits.   ◆   There's an eruption of water just a hundred yards away, and a humpback calf rockets straight out of the water, spinning as it clears the surface. Silver spray flies in all directions and cascades from

Humpback and gray whales and a host of other cetaceans ply the frigid waters of North America's last frontier.

the whale's winglike fins and body. The calf clears the water before crashing back on its side. A spontaneous cheer rends the silence. The reaction is always the same: This is whale watching's game-winning touchdown.   ◆   Commercial whale watching is a relatively new and growing industry in Alaska. With twice the shoreline of the contiguous 48 states and 17 types of cetaceans plying its waters, this is one of the most spectacular places in the United States to see whales. Because most whales roam stormy and remote seas, areas too dangerous for whale-watching boats, fewer than a half-dozen species are easy to view. But three areas – **Southeast Alaska's panhandle**, **Prince William Sound**, and the waters adjacent to **Kenai Fjords National Park** – offer prime whale-watching opportunities and a variety of different tours.

Humpbacks are the showstoppers in Southeast Alaska. They perform an array of spyhops, lobtails, flipper and tail slaps, and breach up to 100 times in a row.

Ports of Call

Harbors in **Petersburg**, **Juneau**, **Valdez**, **Seward**, **Sitka**, and other small towns are host to ever-increasing numbers of whale watchers who board boats for anything from half-day to week-long excursions. In recent years, boats built for whale watching have taken to the sea along with myriad other styles of craft, from inflatables to cruise ships. Some whale-watching boats are converted fishing vessels in the 40- to 50-foot range and usually accommodate no more than six passengers and two crew. Larger boats handle up to 100 passengers, generally for day trips. Many boats give visitors the chance to sample salmon, king crab, and other fresh Alaskan seafood. Shore-based lodges and tent camps also offer whale-watching adventures.

Whale watching in Alaska takes place in summer for good reason. Spring and fall bring frequent, often harsh storms, and though summer along the coast is typically cool and rainy, inclement weather often gives way to clearing skies that reveal spectacular surroundings in sharp contrast to the usual moody but beautiful mists. Summer is also good for the whales: The humpbacks that winter off the Hawaiian Islands and

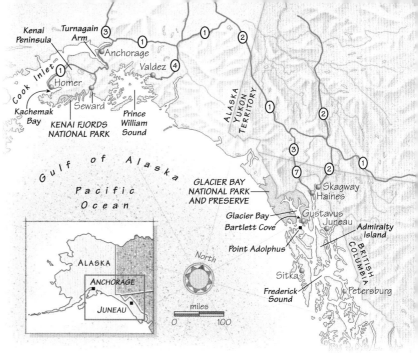

Baja California migrate in summer to Alaska waters, where they feed on vast schools of herring and candlefish. Well over half the world's 10,000 to 12,500 endangered humpbacks summer here. Each year females migrate north with their calves to these important feeding areas. It is not uncommon to see humpbacks feeding within a few feet of the shoreline.

Inside Passage Waterways

For sightings, Southeast Alaska's **Inside Passage** is the best bet. This marine route is protected by numerous islands stretching nearly 375 miles from the Alaska-British Columbia border north to **Skagway**, with coves and bays that shelter boats from severe storms. The waters around mountainous, 100-mile-long, 25-mile-wide Admiralty Island, west of Juneau and north of Petersburg, are the premier location for humpbacks.

Whales can be encountered on any cruise covering the length of the Inside Passage, but it's a common misconception that the best way to see them is from a cruise ship. While large cruise ships sometimes deviate from course for whale sightings, they rarely linger or move far from the marked sea lanes through the maze of islands and passages. For the fit and adventurous, some areas offer kayak trips and an unparalleled opportunity to view whales at sea level. The downside to kayaking for the casual tourist is the exposure to weather and the limited area that can be explored. Tent camping on uninhabited islands is another way not only to see whales but to explore Alaska and other wildlife within their own environment.

Glacier Bay National Park and Preserve has been touted as *the* place to see whales in Alaska. But some years witness few humpbacks in the bay, and even at peak numbers the population does not approach that of **Frederick Sound**, south of Admiralty Island. Because of the park's protected status, travel inside the bay is highly controlled. Private boats are limited by permit, and vessel speed and approach distances are rigid. Cruise-ship passengers often see whales in the confines of the bay and its inlets. Though serious whale watchers may want to go elsewhere, Glacier offers budget whale-watching opportunities. The concessionaire's tour boat, *Spirit of*

A breaching orca (opposite, top) splashes down on its side. Breaching may be a form of communication, perhaps a warning to intruders.

Mist enshrouds a small whale-watching vessel (opposite, bottom) cruising slowly through Alaska's Inside Passage.

The unmistakable dorsal fin of a bull orca (left), which can reach six feet tall, slices through the waters of Frederick Sound.

Comeback of the Humpback

For encouraging proof that international wildlife conservation can be successful, consider the annual return of humpback whales to the North Pacific. Once believed to be the most plentiful of the North Pacific's great whales, the species numbered only 1,000 when protected in 1966. Today there may be more than 6,000 in the North Pacific, and sightings are increasing. Humpbacks appear each spring off the coasts of Alaska, British Columbia, and Washington, where they sift krill, herring, and other small fish through baleen plates that hang 30 inches from their upper jaws.

Anyone who sees a humpback is impressed by its enormity and grace. The size of a city bus, it rises from the sea firing vaporous plumes from its blowholes, then slowly rolls headlong into the depths, exposing a tiny dorsal fin on top of a small hump. A parting view may be a pair of 15-foot-wide flukes raised over the water like the outstretched wings of an eagle.

The most acrobatic of the big baleen whales, humpbacks may breach 40 times in succession – 100 times isn't unknown. As they hoist their 30- to 40-ton bodies up from the sea, they're easily identified by long, narrow pectoral fins with scalloped edges. The tops of their heads are spotted with sensitive tubercles, or wartlike bumps, each embellished by a single hair. Their skin is scarred, and barnacles cling to their chins, throats, and flippers. Deep throat grooves stretch to their navels. – *Bruce Obee*

A breaching humpback (above) reveals its long, knobby pectoral fins. Breaching is "contagious." Once one whale does it, others often join in.

Kayaking in Kenai Fjords (bottom) is a fine way to view whales but may be chilly even in summer.

Bubble-net feeding (right) was first observed in Alaska. Humpbacks corral fish by blowing bubbles around them, then lunge through the "net" and feed.

Adventure, takes passengers to view glaciers, bears, and whales and drops off kayakers and campers. Day-trips are also available from **Gustavus**, the park's gateway community, to **Point Adolphus**, a prime whale-watching location outside the park. One of the best-kept secrets of this national park is the tent campground at **Bartlett Cove**, the site of park headquarters. Here campers, without a charter-boat fee, can see whales close to shore – and fall asleep to

nearby whale sounds and the footfalls of bears passing in the night.

Step Right Up

Whether you are watching from a boat or from shore, you'll see that when humpbacks play, there's no show like it on earth. Tail lobbing, fin flopping, chin slapping, and breaching are all part of the repertoire. The trumpetlike sounds made by humpbacks in summer are different from those made in winter off Hawaii. There, males sing complex songs that can last a half-hour and be repeated all day. Some researchers believe the females choose mates by song; others believe the males sing to attract females and establish dominance over other males. Humpback calves are born in winter and by the time they reach Alaskan waters they may weigh 10 or more tons. Using their distinctive tail markings, seasoned observers delight in recognizing individual whales as they arrive year after year in traditional feeding zones.

The unique strategy of bubble-net feeding used by humpbacks was first witnessed off Southeast Alaska's Admiralty Island less than three decades ago. Usually five to seven animals work together, although one observer counted more than 20 whales in one bubble net. This display of intelligence and cooperation is awesome to observe up close, and only in Alaska can it be easily seen. But getting a good look at bubble-net feeders can be a challenge. Once a group is spotted, there's no predicting when or where they'll come up. Boats must stay back the requisite 100 yards from feeders and take care not to disturb or interrupt the feeding pattern. Rising bubbles are an indication of where to look, but even a slight chop may render them invisible.

Humpbacks, despite their visibility off Alaska in summer, are an endangered species. The slow-moving humpback's habits of remaining close to coasts during migration and clustering near prime island feeding areas made the species vulnerable to commercial whalers. Shore-based fleets took a large toll, and floating processing factories killed large numbers of humpbacks around the eastern Aleutians and Alaska Peninsula as late as the 1960s. The International Whaling Commission did not give protected status to the North Pacific humpbacks until 1966. They have not been hunted commercially here since then.

Cetacean Paradise

Because of their shore-hugging feeding strategies and spectacular acrobatic behavior, humpbacks are, not surprisingly, Alaska's big whale-watching attraction. Other cetaceans swim these waters, too. Gray whales migrate in spring from Baja California's sheltered lagoons north along the Pacific coast to feeding grounds in Alaska's Arctic Ocean and Bering Sea, a swim of 5,000 miles or more. Rarely are they seen in Prince William Sound or the Inside Passage, but in 1998 observers were shocked to see a small gray swimming by the dock in Glacier Bay's **Bartlett Cove**. Viewing gray whales in Alaska is limited to spring and fall migration times, which often coincide with storm seasons. A limited number of tour operators are developing spring gray whale cruises. The beluga is a high-arctic species rarely seen without considerable expense.

Orcas, minke whales, harbor, and Dall's porpoises are commonly observed in inshore waters. On a weeklong cruise for humpbacks, orcas may be sighted once or twice. Shy minkes and harbor porpoises may approach quiet, stationary boats, whereas exuberant

Dall's porpoises play in a boat's wake. These small, speedy porpoises, colored like miniature orcas, swim in huge schools (an estimated 3,000 were once observed in a single group). The more acrobatic Pacific white-sided dolphins are rarely seen inshore, but again in 1998, amid other unusual marine sightings, a white-sided dolphin spent time around Haines, swimming with people and playing around boats.

If you want to stay on dry land and you are

traveling on a tight budget, three locations offer good roadside viewing. Belugas may be seen in **Kachemak Bay** on the northwest **Kenai Peninsula** in late April. Sometimes they cruise quite close to the shoreline and along **Homer Spit**. The pods there seldom linger very long before heading north. Belugas are observed nearly all summer in **Turnagain Arm** near **Anchorage**. **Beluga Point**, another favored viewing site, is next to the **Seward Highway**, just a 20-minute drive from Anchorage. The main drawback is that the water is muddy, and the whales are difficult to see as they roll and rise in the channels where they feed on migrating salmon and smaller fish.

The Alaskan backdrop is as much a draw as the whales themselves. Dense conifer forests skirt mountains rising to glacial summits. Numerous islands and fjords punctuate wild coastlines thick with grizzlies and eagles. Massive tidewater glaciers tower over inlets choked with icebergs calved from their faces. When whales are inactive, there are seals, sea lions, eagles, and bears to spot, puffins and marbled murrelets to count. Sea otters, once threatened with extinction because of overhunting by early Russian fur hunters, are now abundant and delight visitors. A crow calling from silent, mist-draped woods reminds you that this land once was solely the home of Native Alaskans, the Tlingit and Haida, the clans of the bear, eagle, raven, and whale. It takes very little imagination to conjure visions of warriors heading out in cedar dugout canoes to hunt whales or fish for salmon. Here in Alaska, the word wilderness takes on its full and complete meaning.

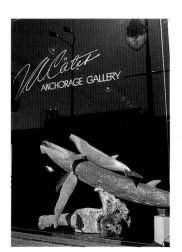

Orcas (opposite) patrol island passages in pods of 10 or more. They feed primarily on salmon, although transients also eat marine mammals.

Seals (above) haul out on ice floes in John Hopkins Inlet, Glacier Bay National Park.

A sculpture of a humpback cow and calf (left) is displayed in an Anchorage art gallery.

TRAVEL TIPS

DETAILS

When to Go

The best time to visit is in summer, when the average daytime temperature is 55°F. July is the peak season for humpbacks, porpoises, and dolphins. Belugas summer in Turnagain Arm, and are seen briefly in late April in Kachemak Bay and off Homer Spit. Even sunny days can be quite cold on the water, and rain is always a possibility. Spring and fall are the best times to see migrating grays, September to January the finest time for migrating humpbacks around Sitka. Expect cold, wet, stormy weather during the off-season.

How to Get There

Airlines serve Anchorage, Juneau, Ketchikan, Petersburg, Wrangell, and Sitka in Southeast Alaska; Cordova, Valdez, and Whittier in Prince William Sound; Seward and Homer on the Kenai Peninsula. Coastal towns are small, strung out, and unconnected by roads, except for Haines and Skagway. The Alaska Railroad, 907-265-2494, links Anchorage, Whittier, and Seward.

Getting Around

Ferries offer practical and economical transportation on the Alaska Marine Highway, 800-642-0066. Air taxis are convenient but expensive.

INFORMATION

Alaska Public Lands Information Center

605 West Fourth Avenue, Suite 105, Anchorage, AK 99501; tel: 907-271-2737.

Alaska Tourism

P.O. Box 110801, Juneau, AK 99811-0801; tel: 907-465-2010.

Glacier Bay National Park

P.O. Box 140, Gustavus, AK 99826; tel: 907-697-2231.

Kenai Fjords National Park

P.O. Box 1727, Seward, AK 99664; tel: 907-224-3175.

Prince William Sound Tourism Coalition

P.O. Box 1477, Valdez, AK 99686; tel: 907-835-2984.

CAMPING

Campsites and public-use cabins are available in national parks and forests throughout the region. Contact individual parks or the Forest Service Information Center, 907-586-8751.

LODGING

PRICE GUIDE – double occupancy

$ = up to $49 $$ = $50–$99

$$$ = $100–$149 $$$$ = $150+

Crescent Harbor Hideaway

709 Lincoln Street, Sitka, AK 99835; tel: 907-747-4900.

This historic home has two guest units with private baths and entrances. The inn's proprietors – marine-mammal researchers – lead small-boat charters for guests. Open year-round. $$–$$$

Glacier Bay Country Inn

P.O. Box 5, Gustavus, AK 99826; tel: 800-628-0912 or 907-697-2288.

This attractive log inn, set in the woods four miles from Glacier Bay National Park, has eight rooms and a suite. Fishing, whale-watching, kayaking, flightseeing, and glacier trips can be arranged. Open May to September. $$$$

Gustavus Inn

P.O. Box 60, Gustavus, AK 99826

(May to September) or 7920 Outlook, Prairie Village, KS 66208 (October to April); tel: 800-649-5220 or 907-697-2254.

Overlooking Icy Strait about eight miles from Glacier Bay, this cedar-sided inn offers 13 guest rooms, each with a private bath, and queen-size and twin beds. Included in the price are three daily meals featuring fresh vegetable and seafood dishes. Fishing charters, whale watching, and sea kayaking are availabe. Open May to September. $$$

Kachemak Bay Wilderness Lodge

P.O. Box 956, Homer, AK 99603; tel: 907-235-8910

The lodge, perfect for those seeking luxurious accommodations in a rugged setting, is constructed of lumber salvaged from wrecked ships. Modern cabins are cozy, with private, tile-and-cedar baths, homemade quilts, and picture windows. Gourmet meals, guide services, sea kayaks, canoes, hiking trails, and a hot tub are available. A three-day minimum is required. Open June to September. $$$$

Westmark Shee Atika Lodge

330 Seward Street, Sitka, AK 99835; tel: 907-747-6241.

This downtown Sitka hotel on Crescent Harbor is owned by an Alaska Native corporation and is dominated by tribal motifs and artwork. The best rooms for viewing whales are on the fourth and fifth floors of the East Wing. A restaurant overlooks Sitka Sound. $$–$$$

TOURS & OUTFITTERS

Alaska Discovery

5449 Shaune Drive, Suite 4, Juneau, AK 99801; tel: 800-586-1911 or 907-697-2411.

Day and extended sea-kayak tours explore Bartlett Cove and the Beardslee Islands.

Glacier Bay Lodge

523 Pine Street, Suite 203, Seattle, WA 98101; tel: 800-622-2042 or 206-623-7110.

The official concessionaire for Glacier Bay National Park runs whale-watching trips from Bartlett Cove. A variety of packages can be had, some of which include air transportation, lodging, and multiday cruises.

Kenai Fjords Tours

P.O. Box 1889, Seward, AK 99664; tel: 800-478-8068 or 907-276-6249.

Day cruises to Resurrection Bay depart from Seward and offer chances to see calving icebergs, whales, and other natural wonders.

Northgate Tours and Cruises

P.O. Box 20613, Juneau, AK 99802; tel: 888-463-5321 or 907-463-5321.

Three- to five-night cruises aboard the 86-passenger MV *Wilderness Discoverer* explore Glacier Bay and the Inside Passage. Passengers sleep on board and spend each day sea-kayaking or hiking ashore.

Oceanic Society Expeditions

Fort Mason Center, Building E; San Francisco, CA 94123; tel: 415-441-1106.

The society conducts a 10-day trip each July to study humpbacks in Southeast Alaska. The 14-passenger, 126-foot vessel departs from Juneau.

MUSEUMS

Alaska SeaLife Center

301 Railway Ave., P.O. Box 1329, Seward, AK 99664; 907-224-6300 or 800-224-2525

This new museum should be on every whale lover's itinerary. The $52-million facility combines research, wildlife rehabilitation, and public education, and houses birds, fish, and marine mammals. Humpback whales can be seen through the museum's viewing scopes in late spring and early summer.

Excursions

Kenai Peninsula

Kenai Visitors and Convention Bureau, 11471 Kenai Spur Highway, Kenai, AK 99611; tel: 907-283-1991.

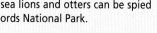

About three hours from Anchorage, beautiful Kenai Peninsula is home to massive icefields, glaciers, fjords, and lakes. Some of the world's best fishing is enjoyed on the Kenai River, and hiking trails meander through Kachemak Bay State Park and Kenai National Wildlife Refuge. Summer visitors watch belugas in Turnagain Arm and Cook Inlet. Orcas, humpbacks, and numerous sea lions and otters can be spied in the icy waters of Kenai Fjords National Park.

Prince William Sound

Prince William Sound Tourism Coalition, P.O. Box 1477, Valdez, AK 99686; tel: 907-835-2984.

Most of Prince William Sound – 3,500 miles of coastline and 150 glaciers – lies within Chugach National Forest, the country's second largest forest. Paddlers glide across sheltered waters, occasionally joined by sea otters and orca, minke, humpback, and fin whales. Whittier and Valdez make convenient bases for whale-watching trips. For a more peaceful experience, head to the small fishing village of Cordova, home of famous Copper River Delta salmon and excellent bird-watching.

Sitka

Sitka Convention and Visitors Bureau, P.O. Box 1226, Sitka, AK 99835; tel: 907-747-5940.

Hailed as the "Paris of the Pacific," Sitka once welcomed ships from all over the world. The two-harbor town, one of Alaska's most enchanting, was the stomping ground of Tlingit Indians before the arrival of Russians in the 18th century. Both

cultures are interpreted at Sitka National Historical Park. St. Michael's Cathedral, built by the Russian Orthodox Church in the 1840s, is well worth a visit. Humpbacks visit the area during the off-season to bulk up on herring.

Maui
Hawaii

C H A P T E R
22

As faithfully as old friends, Hawaii's most famous visitors, more than 3,000 humpback whales, return every winter for much the same reasons other visitors come – rest, recreation, and romance. Although whales can be spotted from the shores of every island from November until April, and each major island mounts whale-watching expeditions, they are most abundant in the deep, sheltered waters of the Au'au channel between Maui and Molokai, and **Maui** claims the largest whale-watching fleet in its two harbors, **Lahaina** and **Maalaea.** ◆ Maui is rich in whaling history. On October 1, 1819, the *Belena*, out of New Bedford, Massachusetts, was the first American whaler to sail into Lahaina. The crew thought it had gone to heaven. Word of the safe anchorage and Hawaiian hospitality spread quickly and soon the whole Yankee Pacific whaling fleet, storm-battered and wave-lashed, came limping into port to rest before heading back out into the fray. ◆ Today's whale watchers, gathered in bright

Home of the first American whale sanctuary, this tropical mecca offers sun, sand, sea, and humpbacks galore.

touristy clusters on the waterfront, can practically still hear echoes of the yells, swagger, and oaths of the salt-crusted sailors who caroused along Front Street in the days when the harbor was a forest of masts. Armed with diet sodas and credit cards, the modern whalers wait good-naturedly in the maw of the old black cannon, which was installed by a Hawaiian queen determined to exact a measure of civility from the rowdy crews. She had her work cut out. As many as 1,500 sailors at a time, high on demon rum, attempted to ravage the town's beauties. Whaling ships even fired on the parsonage, blaming missionaries for their deprivations. The riots are legendary.

"Humpbacks are the most gamesome and lighthearted of all whales," wrote Herman Melville, who observed them in their winter grounds off Lahaina, Maui.

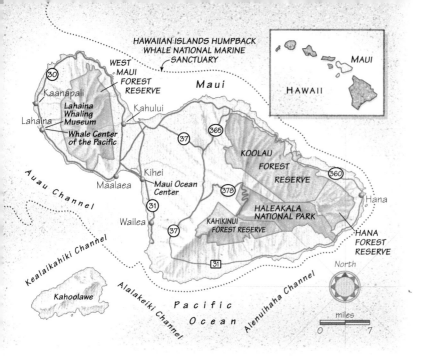

HAWAIIAN ISLANDS HUMPBACK WHALE NATIONAL MARINE SANCTUARY

WEST MAUI FOREST RESERVE

Maui

HAWAII

MAUI

30

Kaanapali

Lahaina Whaling Museum

Lahaina

Whale Center of the Pacific

Kahului

Auau Channel

Maalaea

Kihei

Maui Ocean Center

365

37

KOOLAU FOREST RESERVE

360

378

31

Wailea

KAHIKINUI FOREST RESERVE

HALEAKALA NATIONAL PARK

Hana

37

HANA FOREST RESERVE

31

North

miles

0   7

Kealaikahiki Channel

Kahoolawe

Alalakeiki Channel

Pacific Ocean

Alenuihaha Channel

a whale-watching expedition. They may be fishing boats, catamarans, junks, power cruisers, yachts, even a pleasure submarine, but they go seeking humpback whales in the briny deep. Their weapons are no longer harpoons but cameras. Some boats go out for an hour, others a half-day or more. Some include snorkeling and diving adventures or lunch. There are sunset whale watches with cocktails and taro chips. We've come a long way from the weevily biscuits of *Moby Dick*, Herman Melville's classic

In one of history's satisfying ironies, this lusty port of call for the Yankee whalers is now the center of a new whaling industry. Instead of hunting the great whales to the brink of extinction, business now depends on saving and celebrating them.

Whale-watching Fleet

During whale season, roughly from November to April, practically every commercial boat bobbing in the snug harbor at the foot of the West Maui Mountains offers

whaling saga. Melville, incidentally, once roamed the streets of Lahaina gathering grist for his tall tale of the great white whale.

The whaler, this bright sunny February day, is a sleek, white, 50-foot fiberglass sloop, and the captain is a research scientist with the Pacific Whale Foundation, which mainly studies humpback whales. The best whale-watching expeditions have at least one marine biologist on board.

The view, as the boat chugs from the harbor, looks much the same as it did in Melville's time, except that the old wooden waterfront buildings that once housed grog shops and ship chandlers have morphed into art galleries, seafood restaurants, and bikini boutiques. Time has gentled even demon rum into mai tais with paper umbrellas. Most of Lahaina has been declared a national historic preservation district, but it still has a delightful bit of the tar's twang.

Hawaiian waters sustain a great profusion of life. Moray eels (right, top) and green sea turtles (right, bottom) are just two of the colorful creatures divers are likely to encounter beneath the surface.

Researchers record humpbacks (opposite, top) with video cameras and hydrophones in Hawaii's Humpback Whale National Marine Sanctuary.

Returning humpbacks (opposite, bottom) swim past whale watchers off the west coast of Maui.

Lured by Humpback Songs

As soon as the sloop clears the breakwater, the captain winches up the main sail. The crew unbags the jib. It snaps out smartly, and the engine is cut. In the sudden silence, water whooshes along the hull, and wind sings in the wire rigging. The heavy

melancholy fragrance of flowers drifts off the land, mixing with the quickening smell of tides. In the boat's wake, Lahaina grows smaller, dwarfed by the green mountains behind it.

Then the captain gives a talk on humpback whales, toothless whales, or Mysticeti, a name that means "moustached whales," referring to the baleen that toothless whales use for filter feeding. Humpbacks are the most commonly encountered whale species in Hawaiian waters. Of all the fascinating things about humpbacks – their easily recognized knobby heads, enormous flukes with individual markings, their lack of hostility toward humans, and their marine acrobatics – the most remarkable is their song. They hang suspended, motionless, while they sing, and the sound carries for miles. Human swimmers can hear it. On still Maui mornings, even people on shore claim to have heard the haunting melodic cries and moans.

The song is like a bird's but much more complex. Each song contains a group of notes repeated to form a phrase, and these phrases form a theme. A whale's song may have eight or ten themes, and the animal often sings for hours at a time.

Researchers now say that only males sing and only in their warm wintering grounds, leading scientists to conclude that the songs are related to mating. Each whale sings the same song, which changes slowly but dramatically over the course of a season. Every year the whales compose a new song, improvising on the old, another indication of their uncanny intelligence. These almost mystic melodies add immeasurably to the

into the blue of sea and sky.

"Two spouts!" someone shouts.

"Whale and calf," the captain confirms. He scans for an escort whale – and there it is, dead ahead at noon. "We're being mugged by whales!" he shouts joyously. Three dark, shining shapes, little islets in themselves, move through the water under their umbrellas of mist. Camera shutters click; camcorders whir. And then the huge mother whale flips her enormous wing-shaped flukes into the air, noses down, and dives, taking her big baby with her. The escort male is still spouting. Suddenly he breaches, heaving 40 tons gracefully into the air. Rivers of white water stream from the great dark body as he lifts and arches in his elephantine ballet, pectoral fins stretched like wings, then he crashes down, displacing tidal waves of water.

enchantment of the humpback whale.

To local people, the humpbacks are faithful old friends, returning every year from their summer feeding grounds in polar waters. Here they mate and give birth. A baby humpback weighs in at two tons and gains an astonishing 200 pounds a day. Immediately after birth, it swims to the surface to take its first breath.

Suddenly the captain stops his whale talk. He lifts his binoculars. A plume of water, white and glistening, barely noticeable in the ultraviolet haze of day, spouts up high as a house from the cobalt ocean. Only the green mountains of Maui in the background render the geyser visible. "There, over there, starboard at two o'clock," he calls out, one hand on the helm, the other pointing. The passengers squint

The thrill can almost be tasted. The passengers are all energized by the one simple fact: "We have seen a whale."

Before the cruise ends, they'll see a dozen more, each inspiring awe. A whale is never commonplace, even in crowds.

Cetacean Domain

Because humpbacks are an endangered species, and Hawaiian waters have been

Hawaiians and the Whale

Traditional Hawaiians revered the whale as one of the forms of Kanaloa, the Sustaining God, who appears in the Hawaiian chant of creation, the Kumulipo. Kanaloa was born of the night, nurtured by the oceans, and formed himself into his true nature, 'o ka palaoa, the ivory-toothed whale – specifically, the sperm whale. Whales appear in at least four Hawaiian legends, each telling of a young man being taken to sea on the back or in the belly of a whale on a journey to the land of the gods to acquire greater knowledge.

Endangered sperm whales (above) are found around Hawaii but are seldom seen, because they prefer deeper offshore waters.

A melon-headed whale calf (top left), just two months old, has become separated from its pod and approaches a diver.

Hawaii's volcanic origins (bottom) can be seen in the black sand beach at Maui's Waianapanapa State Park, pictured here at sunrise.

In everyday Hawaiian society, beached whales were considered the property of the paramount chief, or ali'i. Only the highest ali'i could possess or wear the lei niho-palaoa, a distinctive tongue-shaped ornament carved from whale ivory; women and commoners were barred from eating whale meat.

With the arrival of Western whalers, Hawaiians replaced many men who jumped ship in the islands, and by the 1860s, the crews were half Hawaiian. This became such a drain on the population that the monarchy required a deposit of $200 for every Hawaiian signed aboard a ship. The money was returned when the native son came home. A whale station was briefly established on the island of Kaho'olawe in 1858. It failed for several reasons: depletion of stock, the discovery of petroleum, the American Civil War, the great loss of ships in arctic waters. But one reason stood out. Whalers didn't come to Hawaii to hunt. They came, like everyone else, to refresh themselves in a climate of eternal June. Whaling in Hawaii was like working on a Sunday.

officially declared the **Hawaiian Island Humpback Whale National Marine Sanctuary**, boats must approach no closer than 100 yards. The whales, however, acknowledge no sovereignty but their own and surface wherever they wish, sometimes quite close to passing boats. One surfaces

close to the sloop and seems to shoot a pitying look at the passengers, confined as they are to the decks, penned in by railings. The voyeur whale smells fishy and tidal – a surprise because one would imagine such magnificent wild creatures wholly pure and sweet smelling.

Although humpbacks are the stars of Hawaii's aquatic show, island waters are home to substantial populations of other cetaceans. False killer whales, pygmy killer whales, melon-headed whales, beaked whales, and pilot whales are here in abundance. The most common is the black pilot whale, with its round bulbous head. Pilot whales travel in pods of 20 to 40 individuals and are most often seen off the **Kona Coast** of the **Big Island** and in the **Alenuihaha Channel** between the Big Island and **Maui**.

The sperm whale is also plentiful but rarely seen because it prefers deep waters far from land. This largest of the toothed whales was the target of the 19th-century

of speed and utter freedom play in the waves.

Later, big sea turtles swim languorously just beneath the waves, occasionally raising their gentle brutish heads like snorkelers getting their bearings. Schools of flying fish zoom from the water in a flurry of beating fins and flashing silver, gone so fast they seem unreal, until someone else says, "Wow, did you see that?"

Explorations on Land

The whale experience doesn't quit when the cruise is over. Maui is whale immersion. The **Carthaginian**, an impressive old brig berthed in front of the suitably tawdry Pioneer Inn, is the icon of Lahaina's seagoing heritage. Almost a century old, this fully rigged 97-foot-long ship with its 87-foot-high main mast groans and strains against its mooring lines as if remembering the open ocean. In exhibits and films aboard ship, it documents the history of whaling in Hawaii and celebrates the life of whales. Belowdecks, visitors can dial a whale and hear a recording of its eerily haunting song.

whaling industry. As a result, it is also on the endangered species list.

Four species of dolphin, a small variety of toothed whale, inhabit island waters: bottlenose, rough-toothed, spotted, and spinner. And, as if on cue, while the captain is talking about them, a school of bottlenose dolphins begins to race with the sloop, leaping, diving under the hull, riding the bow waves, grins on their faces the whole time, easy winners. Everyone rushes from side to side to watch these sleek shining emblems

There are no less than four excellent museums dedicated to the whale at Lahaina. The **Lahaina Whaling Museum** on Front Street features antique miniature ships, handcrafted nautical tools, and three rooms of whaling displays. The **Whale Center of the Pacific**, located in the Whalers

Cuvier's Beaked Whale

Officially named for French anatomist Georges Cuvier, who in 1823 described the new species, Cuvier's beaked whales are also known as goosebeak whales because of their somewhat avian profile. Like a bird, this whale has a relatively small head that occupies only about 10 percent of its 21-foot body length. Its forehead slopes gradually toward a stubby beak. The lower jaw extends just beyond the upper beak to create an under bite. But here the comparison ends.

An adult male's two large teeth, sometimes crusted with barnacles, protrude from the tip of the lower jaw. It has broad flukes, long, double-tracked scars, white- or cream-colored blotches on its belly and sides, and a dorsal fin that may be tall and falcate, like a shark's, or low and triangular. The color of the whales varies from sienna, tan, and cream to gray, smoke blue, and dark purple. The head and undersides are generally lighter, especially in old males, but some whales are dark all over.

Living in deep waters worldwide, with the exception of polar seas, Cuvier's beaked whales are one of the most plentiful whale species. They can be elusive as they travel in pods of 10 or fewer and stay below the surface for up to 40 minutes. Eagle-eyed whale watchers should be on the lookout for them off the coast of Hawaii. – *Beth Livermore*

Bottlenose dolphins
(opposite, top) are easily
spotted in shallow, sun-
dappled water.

Cuvier's beaked whales
(opposite, bottom) travel
alone or in small groups
and feed on deep-sea fish
and squid.

Lahaina Harbor (right) is
home to the vintage
Carthaginian, now a
whale museum.

**Short-finned pilot
whales** (below) are often
found between the Big
Island and Maui.

Village shopping complex in nearby Ka'anapali Resort, consists of two unique museums that have been telling the whale's tale for 12 years. The **Whaler's Village Museum** combines exhibits and educational displays about Lahaina's role in whaling history. It also houses Hawaii's most extensive collection of scrimshaw and marine antiques.

The other museum, **Hale Kohola** (House of the Whale), takes an in-depth look at the biology and physiology of the whale, focusing primarily on the humpback. Highlights are a baby humpback skeleton and the skull of one of the largest humpbacks ever recorded. Each museum has its own theater airing critically acclaimed whaling films throughout the day. Guided tours by marine naturalists are free.

At the new multimillion-dollar **Maui Ocean Center** in **Kihei**, the **Whale Discovery Center** takes visitors on a 7,000-mile journey from the humpback's polar feeding grounds to Maui. The exhibits are interactive with a dazzling mix of Hollywood special effects and computer modules. Whales are often seen cavorting in the ocean just outside the center. There are no captive marine mammals here. Who needs them?

Two major Maui festivals take place

during whaling season. For the past 20 Februarys, the Pacific Whale Foundation has organized "Whale Day Celebration," a weeklong event at the Wailea Resort. It features a children's carnival, a Run for the Whales marathon, and a fund-raising Wild and Wonderful Whale Regatta, all with Hawaiian music and hula. Another weeklong whale party happens every March in Lahaina and Kaanapali. Marine experts give lectures, conduct special whale-watching excursions, and offer snorkel and dive adventures. Films and dinners are part of the program.

Guests of honor are those great hump-backs, the gentle giants of the deep, who obligingly come every year and show off their fantastic gymnastics, while everyone cheers them on, praying for their future.

TRAVEL TIPS

DETAILS

When to Go

Humpback season lasts from late November to April, peaking in February and March. A variety of dolphins and false killer and short-finned pilot whales may be seen in any season. Temperatures average 71° to 80°F year-round. Strong Kona winds occasionally deliver rain and high seas.

How to Get There

Major airlines serve Kahului Airport in Maui. Interisland flights arrive daily. Boat transportation between Lahaina, Maui, and Manele is operated by Expeditions, 808-661-3756, whose one-hour trips offer whale watching en route.

Getting Around

Automobiles are the principal conveyance. Rental cars, available at airports, should be reserved well in advance.

INFORMATION

Hawaii Visitors and Convention Bureau

2270 Kalakaua Avenue, Suite 801, Honolulu, HI 96813; tel: 800-464-2924 or 808-923-1811.

Hawaiian Islands Humpback Whale National Marine Sanctuary

726 South Kihei Road, Kihei, HI 96753; tel: 808-879-2818.

Maui Visitors Bureau

1727 Wili Pa Loop, P.O. Box 580, Wailuku, HI 96793; tel: 800-525-6284 or 808-244-3530.

CAMPING

Camping is available at Kanaha Beach Park near Kahului Airport, and at Waianapanapa State Park, on the black-sand beach of Hana. For information, call the State Parks Division, 808-984-8100, or Maui County Parks and Recreation, 808-243-7380.

LODGING

PRICE GUIDE – double occupancy

$ = up to $49 $$ = $50–$99
$$$ = $100–$149 $$$$ = $150+

Aston Wailea Resort

3700 Wailea Alanui Drive, Wailea, HI 96753; tel: 800-922-7866 or 808-879-1922.

The resort has eight low-rise buildings, an eight-story tower, gardens, and a private half-mile oceanfront. Each of the 566 units has a lanai and private bath. The hotel is located near the Maui Ocean Center, site of the annual Whale Days Celebration. $$$$

Best Western Pioneer Inn

658 Wharf Street, Lahaina, HI 97761; tel: 800-457-5457 or 808-661-3636.

Whale-watching tours depart from in front of this 19th-century whaler's saloon and inn. The 50 rooms have been fully restored. Three restaurants and a pool are on the premises. $$–$$$$

Garden Gate Bed-and-Breakfast

67 Kaniau Road, P.O. Box 12321, Maui, HI 96760; tel: 808-661-8800.

This bed-and-breakfast, just north of Lahaina, is owned by artists, and it shows. The inn has three attractive units with private baths, including a 500-square-foot studio that overlooks a garden. $$–$$$$

Lahaina Shores Beach Resort

475 Front Street, Lahaina, HI 96761; tel: 800-321-6284 or 808-661-4496.

Situated beyond the busy tourist section of Lahaina, this condo complex is the town's only beachfront resort. The 151 units have breezy rooms, kitchens, and whale-watching views. A pool and spa are available. $$$–$$$$

Ritz-Carlton Kapalua

1 Ritz-Carlton Drive, Kapalua, HI 96761; tel: 800-262-8440 or 808-669-6200.

The hotel has 598 guest rooms and suites. All have marble bathrooms and spacious patios. The hotel overlooks Kapalua Beach and offers spectacular views of Molokai and a chance to see humpbacks swimming close to shore. Golf courses, tennis courts, scuba diving, restaurants, and a pool are available. $$$$

Whaler on Kaanapali Beach

2481 Kaanapali Parkway, Lahaina, HI 96761; tel: 800-367-7052 or 808-661-4861.

This luxury condo complex occupies a peaceful setting next to Whaler's Village. The complex's 360 units have marble bathrooms, 10-foot-high beamed ceilings, full kitchens, and lanais overlooking the ocean. $$$$

TOURS & OUTFITTERS

Hanalei Sea Tours

P.O. Box 1437, Hanalei, Kaui, HI 96714; tel: 800-733-7997 or 808- 826-7254.

Eight boats, including catamarans and inflatable rafts, depart from Mawiwili Harbor and encounter humpbacks and dolphins.

Nature Expeditions International

P.O. Box 11496, Eugene, OR 97440; tel: 503-484-6529.

Fifteen-day trips depart from Honolulu and explore Kauai, Oahu, Maui, and the Big Island. Led by a biologist, the expeditions concentrate on humpback calving grounds and whaling history.

Oceanic Society Expeditions

Fort Mason Center, Building E, San Francisco, CA 94123; tel: 415-441-1106.

Five-day research trips aboard

the 41-foot ketch *Pacific Pearl* are offered between January and April. Passengers collect data on humpbacks in an ongoing project for the Oceanic Society. Trips depart from Kailua-Kona and sail around the the Big Island.

Pacific Whale Foundation

101 North Kihei Road, Suite 25, Kihei, Maui, HI 96753; tel: 800-942-5311 or 808-879-8811.

This nonprofit group specializes in marine research and conservation and offers excellent whale-watching tours from Lahaina and Maalaea Bay.

Trilogy Excursions

P.O. Box 1121, Lahaina, Maui, HI 96761; tel: 800-874-2666 or 808-661-4743.

A family-operated business, Trilogy leads "Whale of a Sail" whale-watching tours aboard several sleek catamarans.

MUSEUMS

Whale Center of the Pacific

Whaler's Village, 2435 Kaanapali Parkway, Lahaina, Maui, HI 96761; tel: 808-661-5992

You'll find two museums here: The Whaler's Village Museum, chronicling the whaling industry in Hawaii and featuring exhibits on more than 70 whale species, and the Hale Kohola, celebrating humpback whales, their habits, migrations, and protection.

Whaling Museum

865 Front Street, Lahaina, Maui, HI 96761; tel: 808-661-4775.

The museum features art and artifacts from the golden age of whaling.

Maui Ocean Center

192 Ma'alaea Rd., Maui, HI; 808-270-7000

This new aquarium features a Whale Discovery Center and is host to the annual Whale Days Celebration.

Excursions

The Big Island of Hawaii

Big Island Visitors Bureau, 75-5719 West Alii Drive, Kailua-Kona, HI 96740; tel: 808-329-7787.

Double the size of its sister islands, the Big Island is still "under construction" – still, that is, being shaped by volcanic eruptions. In addition to its abundant historic and cultural destinations, the island offers wonderful hiking, biking, and ocean activities. The Kailua-Kona coast is best for whale-watching tours. North of Kona is Puukohola Heiau ("Hill of the Whale"), the main war temple of Hawaii's unifying ruler, Kamehameha, and a place of great spiritual power. Hawaii Volcanoes National Park is one of the best places in the world to view active volcanoes and lava flows.

Kauai

Hawaii Visitors and Convention Bureau, 3016 Umi Street, Suite 207, Lihue, HI 96766; tel: 808-245-3971.

The oldest of Hawaii's main volcanic islands, the "Garden Isle" of Kauai has been softened by rain and vegetation into a lush paradise. Helicopter rides venture along the spectacular Na Pali coast, with its surf-pounded and green-cloaked *pali* (cliffs), giving passengers a chance to gaze down into the volcanic mouth of the wettest place on earth. Whale-watching tours off the Na Pali coast leave from Poipu or Nawiliwili in the south, and from Hanalei Bay in the north. Passengers view humpback whales, dolphins, and sea turtles, and snorkel among sea caves, lava tubes, and coral reefs.

Oahu

Oahu Visitors Bureau, 737 Bishop Street, Suite 2860, Honolulu, HI 96813; tel: 808-523-8802.

There's more to Oahu than luaus. Visitors to the island can climb Diamond Head at dawn, wade among tropical fish in Hanamau Bay, and take a whale-watching tour from Honolulu Harbor or Kaneohe Bay. Motorists may wish to travel the scenic windward coastal highway to North Beach, returning through the pineapple plantations of Oahu's central section. The Bishop Museum communicates Hawaii's rich natural and cultural heritage, while the Maritime Museum examines the islands' seafaring history.

SECTION FOUR

◆

Resource Directory

FURTHER READING

History

Arctic Chase: A History of Whaling in Canada's North, Daniel Francis (Breakwater Books, 1984).

Arctic Whales and Whaling, Ken Faris and Bobbie D. Kalman (Crabtree Publishing, 1988).

Children of Light: The Rise and Fall of New Bedford Whaling and the Death of the Arctic Fleet, Everett S. Allen (Little, Brown and Company, 1973).

Harpooned: The Story of Whaling, Bill Spence (Crescent Books, 1980).

A History of World Whaling, Daniel Francis (Viking, 1990).

Men and Whales, Richard Ellis (Knopf, 1991).

Melville in the South Seas, C. R. Anderson (Columbia University Press, 1939).

Whaling in the North Atlantic from Earliest Times to the Mid-19th Century, J. P. Proulx (Canadian Printing Service, 1986).

Whales, Ice, and Men: The History of Whaling in the Western Arctic, John R. Bockstoce (University of Washington Press, 1995).

Whalesong: The Story of Hawaii and the Whales, MacKinnon Simpson (Beyond Words, 1986).

The Yankee Whaler, C. W. Ashley (Houghton Mifflin, 1938).

Natural History

Among Whales, Roger Payne (Delta, 1996).

Arctic Whales, Stefani Payne (Greystoke Books, 1995).

Behind the Dolphin Smile, Richard O'Barry and Keith Coulbourn (Algonquin Books, 1989).

Beluga: A Farewell to Whales, Pierre Beland (The Lyons Press, 1996).

Beluga Whales, Anthony Martin (Voyageur Press, 1996).

Blue Whales, John Calambokidis and Gretchen Seiger (Voyageur Press, 1997).

The Book of Dolphins, Mark Carwardine (Dragon's World, 1996).

The Book of Whales, Richard Ellis (Knopf, 1985).

The Bottlenose Dolphin, Stephen Leatherwood and Randall R. Reeves, eds. (Academic Press, Inc., 1990).

Bottlenose Dolphins, Paul Thompson and Ben Wilson (Voyageur Press, 1994).

Cetacean Behavior: Mechanisms and Functions, L. M. Herman, ed. (Wiley, 1980).

The Charged Border: Where Whales and Humans Meet, Jim Nollman (Henry Holt and Company, Inc., 1999).

The Conservation and Management of Whales, K. R. Allen (University of Washington Press, 1980).

The Delicate Art of Whale Watching, Joan McIntyre (Sierra Club Books, 1982).

Dolphin Days, Kenneth S. Norris (Norton, 1991).

Dolphins, Chris Cotton (Boxtree, 1995).

Dolphin Societies, Karen Pryor and Kenneth S. Norris (University of California Press, 1991).

The Dolphins Swim Free, Marianne Rogers (Kangaroo Press, 1994).

The Ecology of Whales and Dolphins, David E. Gaskin (Heinemann, 1982).

Giants of the Sea, Andrew Cleave (Todtri Publications, 1998).

Gray Whales: Wandering Giants, Robert H. Busch (Orca Book Publishers, 1998).

The Greenpeace Book of Dolphins, John May, ed. (Sterling, 1990).

Guardians of the Whales: The Quest to Study Whales in the Wild, Bruce Obee and Graeme Ellis (Whitecap Books, 1992).

A Guide to the Photographic Identification of Individual Whales, Jon Lien and Steven Katona (American Cetacean Society, 1990).

Humpback Whales, Phil Clapham (Voyageur Press, 1996).

Killer Whales, Dorothy Hinshaw Patent (Holiday House, 1993).

Killer Whales, Sara and James Heimlich-Boran (Voyageur Press, 1994).

Life Cycle of the Pacific Gray Whale, John Klobas (Heian International Publishing, 1993).

The Lives of Whales and Dolphins: From the American Museum of Natural History, Richard C. Connor, Dawn Micklewaite Peterson, et al. (Henry Holt, 1996).

Man and Dolphin, John Lilly (Doubleday and Company, 1961).

Masters of the Ocean Realm: Whales, Dolphins, and Porpoises, John E. Heyning (Natural History Museum of Los Angeles, 1995).

Mind in the Waters: A Book to Celebrate the Consciousness of Whales and Dolphins, Joan McIntyre (Scribner's/ Sierra Club, 1974).

Monsters of the Sea, Richard Ellis (Knopf, 1994).

The Moon by Whale Light and Other Adventures Among Bats, Penguins, Crocodilians, and Whales, Diane Ackerman (Random House, 1991).

A Natural History of Marine Mammals, Victor Scheffer (Scribner's and Sons, 1976).

The Natural History of the Whale, Matthew L. Harrison (Columbia University Press, 1978).

The Natural History of Whales and Dolphins, P. G. H. Evans (Christopher Helm, 1987).

On the Trail of the Whale, Mark Carwardine (Thunder Bay Publishing Company, 1994).

The Orca Project: A Meeting of Nations, Randall L. Eaton, ed. (Access Publishing Network, 1999).

Orca: The Whale Called Killer, Erich Hoyt (Firefly Books, 1990).

Orca: Visions of the Killer Whale, Peter Knudtson and David Suzuki (Sierra Club Books, 1996).

The Presence of Whales: Contemporary Writings on the Whale, Frank Stewart, ed. (Alaska Northwest Books, 1995).

The Provident Sea, D. H. Cushing (Cambridge University Press, 1988).

Research on Dolphins, M. M. Bryden and Richard Harrison (Oxford University Press, 1986).

Reflections of a Whale Watcher, Michelle A. Gilders (Indiana University Press, 1995).

Sea Shepherd: My Fight for Whales and Seals, Paul Watson (Norton, 1982).

Seasons of the Whale: Riding the Currents of the North Atlantic, Erich Hoyt (WDCS/Humane Society, 1998).

Sperm Whales, Jonathan Gordon (Voyageur Press, 1998).

Strandings: Ways to Save Whales, A Humane Conservationist's Guide, F. Robson (Science Press, 1984).

Under Northern Seas, Linda Pitkin (Raincoast Book Distributors, 1998).

Voyage to the Whales, Hal Whitehead (Robert Hale, 1989).

Whale: Giant of the Ocean, Eric S. Grace (Thunder Bay Press, 1997).

Whales, Jacques Cousteau and Yves Paccalet (Harry N. Abrams, 1988).

Whales, David Jones (Whitecap Books, 1998).

Whales and Dolphins, Anthony R. Martin (Salamander Books, 1990).

Whales, Seymour Simon (Demco Media, 1992).

Whales and Man, Tim Dietz (Yankee Publications, 1987).

Whales, Dolphins, and Porpoises, Mark Carwardine, Erich Hoyt, R. Ewan Fordyce, and Peter Gill (Nature Company/Time-Life Books, 1998).

The Whales of Hawaii, Kenneth C. Balcomb, III (Legacy, 1983).

Whales of the World, Phil Clapham (Voyageur Press, 1997).

The Whale's Wake, Harry Morton (University of Hawaii Press, 1982).

With the Whales, James Darling (North Word Press, 1990).

The World of Arctic Whales: Belugas, Bowheads, and Narwhals, Stefani Paine (Sierra Club Books, 1997).

Field Guides

Eyewitness Handbooks: Whales, Dolphins, and Porpoises, Mark Carwardine (Dorling Kindersley, 1995).

Familiar Marine Mammals of North America (Audubon Society Pocket Guide Series), Stephen H. Amos (Knopf, 1990).

Field Guide to the Humpback Whale, Michelle Morris and Hann Bernard (Sasquatch Books, 1993).

Field Guide to the Orca, Chuck Flaherty and David G. Gordon (Sasquatch Books, 1990).

A Field Guide to Whales, Porpoises, and Seals from Cape Cod to Newfoundland, Steven K.

Katona, Valerie Rough, and David T. Richardson (Smithsonian Institution Press, 1993).

National Audubon Society Field Guide to North American Fishes, Whales, and Dolphins, Daniel W. Gotshall, ed. (Knopf, 1983).

The Oceanic Society Field Guide to the Gray Whale, The Oceanic Society (Sasquatch Books, 1989).

Sealife: A Complete Guide to the Marine Environment, Geoffrey Waller, ed. (Pica Press, 1996).

Sierra Club Handbook of Whales and Dolphins, Stephen Leatherwood and Randall R. Reeves (Random House, 1983).

Whales and Dolphins: A Guide to the Biology and Behavior of Cetaceans, Maurizio Wurtz and Nadia Repetto (Thunder Bay Press, 1999).

Whales, Dolphins, and Porpoises, James D. Darling (National Geographic, 1995).

Whales, Dolphins, and Porpoises, Mark Carwardine (Dorling Kindersley, 1995).

Whales, Dolphins, and Porpoises of the Eastern North Pacific and Adjacent Arctic Waters:

A Guide to Their Identification, Stephen Leatherwood, Randall R. Reeves, and William F. Perrin (Dover Publications, 1988).

Whales, Dolphins, and Seals (Collins Watch Guide), Francois Mouton (Harper-Collins Publishers, 1999).

The Whale-Watcher's Handbook: A Field Guide to the Whales, Dolphins, and Porpoises of North America, David K. Bulloch (The Lyons Press, 1993).

Regional Titles

Alaska Whales and Whaling, Rolland Elwell Stevens (Alaska Geographic Society, 1978).

The Emerald Sea: Exploring the Underwater Wilderness of the Pacific Northwest and Alaska, Diane Swanson, et al. (Alaska Northwest Books, 1993).

From Cape Cod to the Bay of Fundy: An Environmental Atlas of the Gulf of Maine, Philip W. Conkling, ed. (MIT Press, 1995).

Gone Whaling: A Search for Orcas in Northwest Waters, Douglas Hand (Sasquatch Books, 1996).

Guide to the Marine Life of the Caribbean, Bahamas and Florida,

Marty Snyderman and Clay Wiseman (Aqua Quest Publications, 1996).

A Guide to Whale Watching in the Maritimes, David Lawley (Nimbus Publishing, 1998).

Inside Passage: Living with Killer Whales, Bald Eagles and Kwakiutl Indians, Michael Modzelewski (Adventures Unlimited Press, 1997).

Killer Whales: The Natural History and Genealogy of Orcinus Orca in British Columbia and Washington State, John K. B. Ford, Graeme M. Ellis, and Kenneth C. Balcomb (University of British Columbia Press, 1992).

Marine Mammals of California, Robert T. Orr, Roger Helm, and Jacqueline Schoehnwald, eds. (University of California Press, 1989).

Marine Wildlife: From Puget Sound through the Inside Passage, Steve Yates (Sasquatch Books, 1998).

Monterey Bay Shoreline Guide, Jerry Emory (University of California Press, 1999).

New York and New Jersey Coastal Adventures: Whales, Beaches, Packets, Tugs, Tall Ships, Lighthouses, and More, Betsy Frawley Haggerty (Country Roads Press, 1995).

Marine Life of Puget Sound, the San Juans, and the Strait of Georgia, by Steve Yates (Globe Pequot Press, 1988).

New England Whales, Howard Garrett and Candice Keays (Cape Ann Publishing Company, 1985).

A Practical Guide to the Marine Animals of Northeastern North America, Leland W. Pollock (Rutgers University Press, 1997).

Stellwagen Bank: A Guide to the Whales, Sea Birds, and Marine Life of the Stellwagen Bank National Marine Sanctuary, Nathalie Ward (Down East Books, 1995).

Transients: Mammal-Hunting Killer Whales of British Columbia, Washington and Southeastern Alaska, John K. B. Ford and Graeme M. Ellis (University of British Columbia Press, 1999).

The Whales of Canada: The Equinox Wildlife Handbook, Erich Hoyt (Camden House Publishing, 1988).

The Whale Watcher's Guide: Whale-Watching Trips in North America, Patricia Corrigan and Roger Payne (North Word Press, 1999).

Fiction

Agviq: The Whale,
Michael Armstrong
(Questar, 1990).

Aka, Tristan Jones,
(Macmillan, 1981).

The Blue Dolphin, Robert
Barnes (H. J. Kramer, Inc.,
1994).

Falling for a Dolphin,
Heathcote Williams
(Little, Brown and
Company, 1990).

The Last Blue Whale,
Vincent Smith (Harper &
Row, 1979).

The Last Whales, Lloyd
Abbey (Ballantine/Ivy
Books, 1991).

Moby Dick, Herman
Melville (Penguin USA,
1992).

Night of the Whale, Jerry
Spinelli (Little, Brown and
Company, 1985).

Riding the Dolphin,
Amanda Thomas
(Beaufort Books, 1987).

*Songs of the Humpback
Whale: A Novel in Five
Voices*, Jodi Picoult (Faber
and Faber, 1992).

Sounding, Hank Searls
(Ballantine, 1982).

Whalesong, Robert Siegel
(Harper San Francisco,
1991).

*Whale Sound: An
Anthology of Poems
about Whales and
Dolphins*, Greg Gatenby,
ed. (J. J. Douglas, Ltd.,
1977).

Whales: A Celebration,
Greg Gatenby, ed. (Little,
Brown and Company,
1983).

The Year of the Whale,
Victor Scheffer
(Scribner's, 1969).

Magazines and Journals

Audubon
National Audubon Society,
950 Third Avenue, New
York, NY 10022.

Marine Mammal Science
Society for Marine
Mammalogy, Southwest
Fisheries Science Center,
P.O. Box 271, La Jolla, CA
92038.

National Wildlife
National Wildlife
Federation, 1400 16th
Street, N.W., Washington,
DC 20036.

Natural History
American Museum of
Natural History, Central
Park West at 79th, New
York, NY 10024.

Nature Conservancy
The Nature Conservancy,
1815 North Lynn Street,
Arlington, VA 22209.

Outdoor Photographer
12121 Wilshire Boulevard,

Suite 1220, Los Angeles,
CA 90025-1175.

Sierra
The Sierra Club, 730 Polk
Street, San Francisco, CA
94109.

Sonar
Whale and Dolphin
Conservation Society, Unit
2, Bumpers Way,
Chippenham, Wiltshire
SN14 6NG, U.K.

The Whale Watcher
American Cetacean
Society, P.O. Box 1391,
San Pedro, CA 90731.

NATIONAL MARINE SANCTUARIES AND SEASHORES

Cape Cod National Seashore
99 Marconi Site Road,
Wellfleet, MA 02667;
tel: 508-349-3785.

Channel Islands National Marine Sanctuary
113 Harbor Way, Santa
Barbara, CA 93109;
tel: 805-966-7107.

Cordell Bank National Marine Sanctuary
Fort Mason, Building 201,
San Francisco, CA 94123;
tel: 415-561-6622.

Florida Keys National Marine Sanctuary
P.O. Box 500368,
Marathon, FL 33050;
tel: 305-743-2437.

Gulf of the Farallones National Marine Sanctuary
Fort Mason, Building 201, San Francisco, CA 94123; tel: 415-561-6622.

Hawaiian Islands Humpback Whale National Marine Sanctuary
726 South Kihei Road, Kihei, HI 96753; tel: 808-879-2818.

Monterery Bay National Marine Sanctuary
299 Foam Street, Monterey, CA 93940; tel: 831-647-4201.

Olympic Coast National Marine Sanctuary
138 West 1st Street, Port Angeles, WA 98362; tel: 360-457-6622.

Point Reyes National Seashore
Point Reyes Station, CA 94956; tel: 415-663-1092.

Stellwagen Bank National Marine Sanctuary
175 Edward Foster Road, Scituate, MA 02066-4342; tel: 781-545-8026.

AQUARIUMS AND MUSEUMS

Alaska SeaLife Center
301 Railway Avenue, P.O. Box 1329, Seward, AK 99664; tel: 907-224-6300 or 800-224-2525.

Bar Harbor Whale Museum
52 West Street, Bar Harbor, ME 04609; tel: 207-288-2339.

Cabrillo Marine Museum
3720 Stephen White Drive, San Pedro, CA 90731; tel: 310-548-7562.

Le Centre d'Interprétation des Mammifères Marins
108 rue de la Cale-Sèche, Tadoussac, QB G0T 2A0, Canada; tel: 418-235-4701.

Dallas World Aquarium and Zoological Garden
1801 North Griffin Street, Dallas, TX 75202-1503; tel: 214-720-2224.

Florida Aquarium
701 Channelside Drive, Tampa, FL 33602-5600; tel: 813-273-4020.

Kendall Whaling Museum
27 Everett Street, Sharon, MA 02067; tel: 781-784-5642.

Maritime Museum of Monterey
Stanton Center, Custom House Plaza, Monterey, CA; tel: 831-373-2469.

Maui Ocean Center
192 Maalaea Road, Maui, HI; tel: 808-270-7000.

Monterey Bay Aquarium
886 Cannery Row, Monterey, CA 93940-1085; tel: 831-648-4800.

Mystic Aquarium
55 Coogan Boulevard, Mystic, CT 06355-1997; tel: 860-572-5955.

New Bedford Whaling Museum
18 Johnny Cake Hill, New Bedford, MA 02740; tel: 508-997-0046.

New England Aquarium
Central Wharf, Boston, MA 02110; tel: 617-973-5260.

New York Aquarium
Boardwalk and West 8th Street, Brooklyn, NY 11224-2899; tel: 718-265-3400.

Point Defiance Zoo and Aquarium
5400 North Pearl Street, Tacoma, WA 98407-3218; tel: 253-591-5337.

Sea Center
211 Stearn's Wharf, Santa Barbara, CA 93101; tel: 805-962-0885.

Seattle Aquarium
1483 Alaskan Way, Pier 59, Seattle, WA 98101-2059; tel: 206-386-4300.

Sidney Museum
9801 Seaport Place; Sidney, BC V8L 4X3, Canada; tel: 250-656-2140.

Steinhart Aquarium
California Academy of Science, Golden Gate Park, San Francisco, CA 94118-4599; tel: 415-750-7247.

Stephen Birch Aquarium
2300 Expedition Way, La Jolla, CA 92093; tel: 619-534-3474.

Texas State Aquarium
2710 North Shoreline
Boulevard, Corpus Christi,
TX 78402-1097; tel: 361-
881-1200.

Vancouver Aquarium
P.O. Box 3232, Vancouver,
BC V6B 3X8, Canada;
tel: 604-659-3474.

Waikiki Aquarium
2777 Kalakaua Avenue,
Honolulu, HI 96815;
tel: 808-923-9741.

**Whale Center of the
Pacific**
Whaler's Village, 2435
Kaanapali Parkway,
Lahaina, Maui, HI 96761;
tel: 808-661-5992.

Whale Centre
411 Campbell Street,
Tofino, BC V0R 2Z0,
Canada; tel: 250-725-2132.

Whale Museum
62 First Street North, P.O.
Box 945, Friday Harbor,
WA 98250; tel: 360-378-
4710.

Whaling Museum
15 Broad Street,
Nantucket, MA 02554;
tel: 508-228-1736.

Whaling Museum
865 Front Street, Lahaina,
Maui, HI 96761; tel: 808-
661-4775.

ORGANIZATIONS

**Alaska Geographic
Society**
Box 4, Anchorage, AK
99509.

Allied Whale
College of the Atlantic,
Bar Harbor, ME 04609;
tel: 207-288-5015.

**American Cetacean
Society**
P.O. Box 1391, San Pedro,
CA 90731; tel: 310-548-
6279.

**Audubon Ecology Camps
and Workshops**
National Audubon
Society, 613 Riversville
Road; Greenwich, CT
06831; tel: 203-869-2071.

**Center for Coastal
Studies**
P.O. Box 1036,
Provincetown, MA 02657;
tel: 508-487-3622.

**Center for Marine
Conservation**
1725 DeSales Street, N.W.,
Washington, DC 20036;
tel: 202-429-5609.

**Center for Whale
Research**
1359 Smugglers Cove, P.O.
Box 1577, Friday Harbor,
WA 98250-0157; tel: 360-
378-5835.

**Cetacean Society
International**
P.O. Box 953, Georgetown,
CT 08239; tel: 203-544-8617.

Cousteau Society
870 Greenbrier Circle,
Suite 402, Chesapeake,
VA 23320-2641; tel: 757-
523-9335.

Delta Society
P.O. Box 1080, Renton,

WA 98057; tel: 425-226-
7357.

Dolphin Project
P.O. Box 8436, Jupiter, FL
33468; tel: 561-575-5660.

Earthtrust
25 Kaneohe Bay Drive,
Suite 205, Kailua, HI
96734; tel: 808-254-2866.

Earthwatch Institute
680 Mount Auburn Street,
P.O. Box 403, Watertown,
MA 02272; tel: 617-926-
8200.

**Eastern Caribbean
Cetacean Network**
Box 5, Bequia Street, St.
Vincent and the
Grenadines, W.I.; tel: 809-
458-3223; or P.O. Box 573;
Woods Hole, MA 02543;
tel: 508-548-3313.

Great Whales Foundation
Box 6847, Malibu, CA
90264; tel: 415-458-3262.

Greenpeace USA
1436 U Street, N.W.,
Washington, DC 20009;
tel: 202-462-1177.

**International Dolphin
Watch**
Parklands, North Feriby,
Humberside HU14 3ET,
England; tel: 44-1482-
643-403.

**International Whaling
Commission**
The Red House, Histon,
Cambridge CB4 4NP,
England; tel: 44-1223-
233-971.

Marine Mammal Center
Marin Headlands Ranger
Station, Golden Gate
National Recreation Area,
Sausalito, CA 94965;
tel: 415-289-7325.

Marine Mammal Fund
Fort Mason Center,
Building E, San Francisco,
CA 94123; tel: 415-775-
4636.

**Marine Mammal
Stranding Center**
P.O. Box 773, 3625
Brigantine Boulevard,
Brigantine, NJ 08203;
tel: 609-266-0538.

**Marine Mammal
Stranding Network**
Office of Protected
Resources, Marine
Mammal Conservation
Division, P.R. 2, 1315
East-West Highway, Silver
Spring, MD 20910;
tel: 301-713-2322 (ext. 178
or 156) or 800-494-2989.

**Mingan Island
Cetacean Study**
124 boulevard de la Mer,
Longue-Pointe-de-Mingan,
QB G0G 1V0, Canada;
tel: 418-949-2845 (sum-
mer); or 285 Green Street;
Lambert, QB J4P 1T3,
Canada; tel: 514-465-9176
(winter).

**National Wildlife
Federation**
1412 16th Street, N.W.,
Washington, DC 20036;
tel: 202-797-6800.

**Ocean Research and
Conservation Society**
720 Olive Way, Suite 900,

Seattle, WA 98101;
tel: 425-774-6824.

**Oceanic Society
Expeditions**
Fort Mason Center,
Building E, Room 230,
San Francisco, CA 94123-
1394; tel: 415-474-3385.

Pacific Cetacean Group
UC MBEST Center, 3239
Imjin Road, Marina, CA
93933; tel: 408-582-1030.

**Pacific Whale
Foundation**
Kealia Beach Plaza, 101
North Kihei Road, Suite
25, Kihei, HI 96753;
tel: 808-879-8811.

**Sea Shepherd
Conservation Society**
1314 Second Street, Santa
Monica, CA 90401-1133;
tel: 310-394-3198.

Sierra Club
730 Polk Street, San
Francisco, CA 94109;
tel: 415-923-5630.

**Whale and Dolphin
Conservation Society**
Unit 2, Bumpers Way,
Chippenham, Wiltshire
SN14 6NG, U.K.; tel: 44-
1249-653-222.

Whale Fund
The Bronx Zoo, 185th
Street and South
Boulevard, Bronx, NY
10460; tel: 718-220-5197.

WhaleNet
200 The Riverway,
Boston, MA 02215; tel: 617-
734-5200.

World Wildlife Fund
1250 24th Street, N.W.,
Suite 500, Washington,
DC 20037-1175; tel: 202-
293-4800.

TOURISM
INFORMATION

Alaska Tourism
P.O. Box 110801, Juneau,
AK 99811-0801; tel: 907-
465-2010.

**Association Touristique
du Saguenay Lac-Saint-
Jean**
198 rue Racine est,
Bureau 210, Chicoutimi,
QB G7H 1R9, Canada;
tel: 418-543-9778.

Bahamas Tourist Office
19495 Biscayne
Boulevard, Aventura, FL
33180; tel: 800-224-3681
or 305-932-0051.

Baja Information
7860 Mission Center
Court No. 2, San Diego,
CA 92108; tel: 800-225-
2786 or 800-522-1516
(from California).

**California State Division
of Tourism**
801 K Street, Suite 1600,
Sacramento, CA 95814;
tel: 800-462-2543 or 916-
322-2881.

**Cape Cod Chamber of
Commerce**
307 Main Street, Hyannis,
MA 02601; tel: 888-332-
2732 or 508-362-3225.

Caribbean Tourism Organization
80 Broad Street, 32nd Floor, New York, NY 10004; tel: 212-682-0435.

Dominica Tourist Office
10 East 21st Street, Suite 600, New York, NY 10010; tel: 212-475-7542.

Florida Division of Tourism
126 Van Buren Street, Tallahasse, FL 32301; tel: 904-487-1462.

Gobierno del Estado de Baja California Sur
Coordinacion Estatal de Turismo, Apartado Postal 419, La Paz, Baja California Sur, Mexico; tel: 52-112-31702.

Grand Manan Tourism Association
P.O. Box 193, North Head, Grand Manan, NB E0G 2M0, Canada; tel: 506-662-3442.

Hawaii Visitors and Convention Bureau
2270 Kalakaua Avenue, Suite 801, Honolulu, HI 96813; tel: 800-464-2924 or 808-923-1811.

Kodiak Visitors Information Center
100 Marine Way, Kodiak, AK 99615; tel: 907-486-4782.

Maine Tourism
P.O. Box 2300, Hallowell, ME 04347; tel: 800-533-9595 or 207-623-0363.

Massachusetts Office of Travel and Tourism
100 Cambridge Street, 13th Floor, Boston, MA 02202; tel: 800-447-6277 or 617-727-3201.

Maui Visitors Bureau
1727 Wili Pa Loop, P.O. Box 580, Wailuku, HI 96793; tel: 800-525-6284 or 808-244-3530.

Monterey County Visitors and Convention Bureau
380 Alvarado Street, Box 17701, Monterey, CA 93942-1770; tel: 831-649-1770.

Newfoundland and Labrador Department of Tourism
P.O. Box 8730, St. John's, NF A1B 4K2, Canada; tel: 800-563-6353 or 709-729-2830.

Nova Scotia Department of Tourism
Box 130, Halifax, NS B3J 2M7, Canada; tel: 800-341-6096 or 902-424-5000.

Oregon Tourism Commission
775 Summer Street, N.E., Salem, OR 97310; tel: 800-547-7842 or 503-986-0000.

Prince William Sound Tourism Coalition
P.O. Box 1477, Valdez, AK 99686; tel: 907-835-2984.

Santa Barbara Conference and Visitors Bureau
12 East Carrillo Street, Santa Barbara, CA 93101; tel: 800-676-1266.

Tourism British Columbia
Parliament Buildings, Victoria, BC V8V 1X4, Canada; tel: 800-663-6000 or 250-387-1642.

Tourism Vancouver Island
302-45 Bastion Square, Victoria, BC V8W 1J1, Canada; tel: 250-382-3551.

Washington State Tourism
P.O. Box 42500, Olympia, WA 98504-2500; tel: 800-544-1800 or 360-586-2088.

PHOTO AND ILLUSTRATION CREDITS

Mike Bacon/Tom Stack & Associates 2-3, 101T, 181B

B. & C. Alexander/Innerspace Visions 37T, 82

Carl Bento/Nature Focus, The Australian Museum 32T

Werner J. Bertsch/Bruce Coleman, Inc. 111B

Walter Bibikow/The Picture Cube, Inc. 108, 149B

Walter Bibikow/The Viesti Collection, Inc. 185B

James Blank/Photophile 153T

Robin Brandt 5B, 8L, 189

Mark Carwardine/Innerspace Visions 58T, 93B, 111T

Maxine Cass 168T

Jim Cazel/Photo Resource Hawaii 203T

Luigi Ciuffetelli 8R, 43T, 43B

Kindra Clineff/The Picture Cube, Inc. 112, 113B, 114

Brandon D. Cole 9B, 16-17, 20B, 65, 77, 123B, 166B, 178T, 178B, 191, 195B

Melissa S. Cole 53T

Phillip Colla/Innerspace Visions 148T, 148M, 156T, 169T, 199T

Monte Costa/Photo Resource Hawaii 198B

Bob Cranston/Innerspace Visions 146T, 150, 161T

Richard Cummins/Photophile 117T

Renee DeMartin 181T

Tui De Roy/Bruce Coleman, Inc. 39

Cynthia D'Vincent 45T, 70T

John Elk 164, 168B, 169B, 182B

Richard Ellis/Innerspace Visions 31B, 132

Graeme Ellis/Ursus Photography 72

Thomas R. Fletcher 107T

Peter Folkens 21

Jeff Foott/Tom Stack & Associates 97M, 163T

John K. B. Ford/Ursus Photography 174

Bob Glasheen/Photophile 47B

Jon Gnass/Gnass Photo Images 205T

Carolyn Gohier 45B

Francois Gohier 4, 9T, 37B, 40, 68, 85, 86T, 86B, 93T, 98, 102, 104T, 123T, 131, 136, 143M, 158T, 166T, 170B, 185M, 190T, 192

Jeff Greenberg/Photophile 104B

Howard Hall/Innerspace Visions 149T

Christian Heeb/Gnass Photo Images 153M

Kenneth J. Howard 159T

Peter Howorth/Mo Yung Productions 46B

George H. H. Huey 128, 133B, 144, 146B, 151B, 200-201

Robert Jensen/Photo Resource Hawaii 198T

Greg Johnson 42

Darrell Jones 118

Wolfgang Kaehler 97T, 97B, 135B, 163M, 173M, 185T

Marilyn Kazmers/Innerspace Visions 53BL, 53BR, 183

Kendall Whaling Museum 26B, 27T, 28, 32B, 33T, 33B,

Thomas Kitchin/Tom Stack & Associates 89B, 179

Lee Kline 62B

Brian Kosoff 52, 103B

D. Larsen/Bruce Coleman, Inc. 141B

Tom and Pat Leeson 80-81, 94, 127B, 176B

Library of Congress 27B, 31T, 180T

Craig Lovell 5T, 105, 107B, 193T

Alan Majchrowicz/Alan Majchrowicz Exhibit Images 173B

Michael Philip Manheim 110

Buddy Mays/Travel Stock 140B, 188B

Hiroya Minakuchi/ Innerspace Visions 46T, 76B, 206–207

Randy Morse/Tom Stack & Associates 151T, 158M, 159B

Steve Mulligan Photography 138, 141T

Amos Nachoum/ Innerspace Visions 50

New Bedford Whaling Museum 30T, 30B

Paul Nicklen/Ursus Photography 44

Michael Nolan/ Innerspace Visions 62T, 64T, 139, 154, 173T, 182T

Leslie O'Shaughnessy 107M

Brian Parker/Tom Stack & Associates 124T, 205M, 205B

Tammy Peluso/Tom Stack & Associates 121T

Doug Perrine/Innerspace Visions 6–7, 10–11, 14–15, 54, 57, 60, 64B, 70B, 71T, 71B, 73, 120, 121B, 122B, 127M, 133T, 188T, 196, 200T, 202T

Don Pitcher 195M

Robert Pitman/ Innerspace Visions 34

Chuck Place 20T, 148B, 159M, 180B

Paul Rezendes 117M, 117B

George Robbins 163B

Joel W. Rogers 190B

Jasmine Rossi/Innerspace Visions 63T, 63M, 63B

Jeff Rotman 79

Kevin Schafer 36, 87, 143B

Fred Sears 115T

Roland Seitre/Innerspace Visions 67, 115B, 124B

Bill Silliker, Jr. 100

Marshall Smith 103T

Marty Snyderman/ Innerspace Visions 74, 135M, 170T

Stock Montage, Inc. 24

Tom Till 92, 101B, 135T, 171

Tom Vezo 89M, 90, 95T, 95B

Ingrid Visser/Innerspace Visions 38, 56

Tom Walker 140T

James D. Watt/ Innerspace Visions 47T
James D. Watt 18, 122T, 176T, 199B, 201T, 203B

Dave Watts/Tom Stack & Associates 66

Stuart Westmorland 78T, 113T

Whale Watch Azores/ Innerspace Visions 202B

Nik Wheeler 153B, 161B, 193B

Doc White/Innerspace Visions 12–13, 160B

Art Wolfe 1, 48–49, 84, 89T, 186, 195T

Nobert Wu 58B, 59, 76T, 78B, 125, 127T, 143T, 147, 156M, 156B, 160T

Marilyn "Angel" Wynn 26T

Maps by Karen Minot

Design by Mary Kay Garttmeier

Layout by Ingrid Hansen-Lynch

Index by Elizabeth Cook

T–top, B–bottom, M–middle, R–right, L–left

INDEX

Note: page numbers in italics refer to illustrations

A

Acadia National Park, ME 99, 101–2, 106, 107
acoustic tracking 71
Admiralty Island, AK 187, 189
Alaska *16–17*, 180, 186–95
algal blooms 39
Amazing Grace 78
ambergris *32*
Anacortes, WA 176
anemones *156*
Año Nuevo State Reserve, CA 160, 163
aquariums 36, 72, 127, 160, 171, 179–80
Archaeoceti 52
Argentina *63*, *65*, 105
art *5*, *20*, *26*, 117, *141*, *180*, *169*, *193*; *see also* **scrimshaw**
Atlantic Provinces 90–7
attention-seeking 75–9
Australia *76*, 105
Avalon Peninsula, Nfld 94–5

B

Baffin Island *44*
Bahamas *14–15*, *60*, 118–27, *124*
Bahia Magdalena, Baja California 138, 143
Baie Sainte-Marguerite, QC 86
Baird's beaked whales 53
Baja California *21*, *40*, 77–8, 136–43, *138*
baleen *52*, 157, 190; *see also* **Mysticeti**
Bar Harbor, ME 105
Bartlett Cove, AK 190, 192
bat stars *146*

Bay Bulls, Nfld 95
Bay of Fundy *37*, 77, 91–4
beaked whales 52, 53, 129, 150, *202*
bears 181, 193
behavior 61–7
Bellingham, WA 176, 178
Beluga Point, AK 193
belugas *48–9*, 53, *82*, *84*, *85–6*, *85*, *86*, *87*, 89, 95, 192–3
Big Island, HI 201, 205
Big Sur, CA 159
Bimini Islands 118–27, *124*
binoculars 41–2
birding 89, *90*, 95, 109, 151, 160, 173, 182, 195
Blacks Harbour, New Brunswick 92
blowholes *52*
blubber 91, 111, 115
blue whales 36, 52, 112, 148
  Atlantic Provinces 94, 95
  calves 65, 148
  Cape Cod 109
  feeding 148, 149, 157
  migration 58, 71, 148, 149
  Monterey Bay 156
  Québec 86–7, *86*, 89
  sounds 69, 71, 148–9
  spout 148
boat tours 44–6; *see also Travel Tips sections*
Boiler Bay State Park, OR 170
Boothbay Harbor, ME *100*, 101
bottlenose dolphins 53, *59*, *73*, *76*, *120*, *121*, *202*
  Bimini Islands 119, 123–4
  breeding 66
  feeding 63
  "Flipper" 27, 77
  Honduras *59*, *73*, *78*
  hunting behavior 124
  mass die-offs 35
  midwifery 124
  Pacific 151, 160, 202
  social behavior 124

  sounds 55–6, 72
  swimming with 75–6
bottlenose whales 53, 58
Bowman, Bob 71
bow riding *42*, *47*, 76
Boy on a Dolphin 77
brain 55–8, 122
breaching 43, 67, 141; *see also* **humpbacks**; **orcas**
breathing 51
breeding 64–6, 146, 167, 178; *see also* **humpbacks**
British Columbia *46*, 175–85
Bryde's whales 52, 129

C

Cabot Trail 97
Cabrillo National Monument, CA 153
callosities 91, *93*, 105, 114–15
calves *10–11*, *50*, 65–6, 129, 148, *200*; *see also* **gray whales**
cameras 43, 47
Campobello Island, New Brunswick 93, 107
Canada 82–97, 174–85
Cap de Bon-Désir, QC 86
Cape Ann, MA *110*, 117
Cape Breton Island, NS 94, 97
Cape Cod, MA 108–17, *110*
Cape Flattery, WA 169, 173
captivity 36, *59*, *73*, 78
Caribbean 128–35
Catalina Island, CA *148*, 153
Cather, Willa 92
Cetacean species 51–3
Channel Islands, CA 144–53, *144*, *147*, *148*, *151*
chemical pollution 38–9, 87
clothing 43–4
Colorado River Delta Biosphere Reserve 143
communication 55–8, 67, 70, 72–3
conservation *37*, 39, 46
Cook Inlet, AK 195

coral reefs 205
Cordova, AK 195
courtship 63–5
Cousteau, Jacques 27
curiosity *46*, 76–9
Cuvier's beaked whales *202*
cypress trees *158*

D

Deer Islands, New Brunswick 93
Deer Isle, ME 107
Delphi (Greece) 25
delphinese 56
Delphinidae 53
Depoe Bay, OR 170
devilfish 26, 138
Digby Neck, NS 93–4
disorders 39, 87
diving *18*, 127, *200; see also* **swimming with dolphins**
Doak, Wade 79
Dobbs, Horace 79
Dolphin Research Center, FL 126–7
dolphins 53, *54, 57, 118, 124*, 143, 151, *158*, 160
  Bahamas *42*, 118–27
  Cape Cod 109
  Dominica 129, 132–3
  echolocation 57, 73
  evolution 52
  Fraser's 129, 135
  Hawaii 202, 205
  hunting 36–8
  intelligence 56, 122
  long-beaked *34*
  manmade dangers 123–4
  mass die-offs 35, 39
  myths 25–7
  Risso's 129, 151, 160
  rough-toothed 202
  social behavior 62, 63, 66, 67
  sounds 55–6, 72
  spinner 38, *47, 62*, 129, 133, 135, 202
  spotted *60, 76*, 119, 121–3, *122*, 127, 132, *133*, 135, 202
  striped 35, 37, 39
  swimming with *14–15, 18,* 75–6, *79*, 121–3, *125*, 127
  therapy *79*, 123
  white-sided 89, 109, *151*, 160, *169, 181*, 192
  see also **bottlenose dolphins**
Dominica 128–35, *128, 133*
Dominican Republic *71*, 129–30, 134
Dorias, Charles 26
drift-netting 38
Dungeness National Wildlife Refuge, WA 173

E

eagles *170*, 173, 181, 182, 193
Earthwatch 39, 46, 127
Eastport, ME 93, 101
echolocation 57, 66, 73
Edgartown, MA 117
Ellis, Richard *31*, 112
embryo 52
Encounters with Whales and Dolphins 79
environmental conservation 39
equipment 41–7
evolution 52

F

false killer whales 66, 129, 201
Farallon Islands National Marine Sanctuary, CA 157
feeding 52, 62–3
  blue whales 148, 149, 157
  bottlenose dolphins 63
  finbacks 157
  gray whales 167
  see also **humpbacks**
  orcas 149–50
  sperm whales 130–1
field guides 42
films/TV 36, 67, 77, 112
finbacks 52, 77, *102*
  Alaska 195
  Atlantic Provinces 93, 95
  Cape Cod 109
  feeding 157
  Gulf of Maine 101, 104
  Mexico 143
  migration 58
  Monterey Bay 156
  Quebec 86
  Santa Barbara 150
fin profiles 42
fin slapping 67
flightseeing 95, 167–8
Flipper 27, 77
Florida 123–7
flying fish 202
Ford, John 73, 179–80
Fort Bragg, CA 163
Fort Pierce, FL 123
Fort Stevens State Park, OR 169
fossil whales 52
Frederick Sound, AK *189*
Free Willy 36, 67, 171
Friday Harbor, WA 175–6
fulmars 109
Fundy Isles 92–3

G

gannets *95*, 109
Georgia Strait, BC 178
Glacier Bay, AK 189–90, *193*
goosebeak whales 202
Grand Bahama Island 127
Grand Manan, New Brunswick 92–3
gray whales *22–3*, 36, *58, 62*, 65, 139, *146, 149, 161*
  Atlantic 36
  breaching 141, 170
  breeding 146, 167
  British Columbia 182
  feeding 167
  interaction with humans *21*, 77–8, 137–41
  Mexico *12–13*
  migration 58, 137, 145–9, 149, 158–71, 182, 192
  Monterey Bay 155, 158, 159, 160
  mothers and calves 79, 138–41, *140*, 145–7, 149, *150, 156*

Oregon 164–73
predated by orcas 146, 149–50, 155, 159
San Ignacio Lagoon 77–8, *78*, 137–43
Santa Barbara 145–7, 149
skull *159*
sounds *68*
spout 165, 170
spyhopping *136*, *141*
Washington State 164–73
Greenpeace 38
Grenadines 135
Grey, Zane 153
Gros Morne National Park, Nfld 97
Guadeloupe 134
Guerrero Negro, Baja California 138
Gulf of California Biosphere Reserve, Baja California 143
Gulf Islands, BC 175
Gulf of Maine 90–2, 98–107
Gulf Stream 100, 119, 120
Gustavus, AK 190

H

Halifax, NS *92*, 97
Haro Strait 175, 177, *182*
Harris Beach State Park, OR 169
Hawaii *64*, 190–1, 196–205, *198*, *199*, *200*, *203*
Hawaii Volcanoes National Park, HI 205
herding behavior 62–3
historical beliefs 25–7
Homer Spit, AK 193
Honduras *59*, *73*, *78*
Honolulu, HI 205
humpbacks 10–11, *20*, *37*, *50*, 52, *71*, 112–14, 187–92, *193*, *196*
acrobatics 186, 190
Alaska *16–17*, 187–92, 195
Atlantic Provinces 93, 95
breaching *16–17*, 67, *113*, 147, *186*, *190*, 200

breeding *64*, 65, 71, 114, 135, 200
British Columbia 181–2
Cape Cod 109, 112–14
curiosity *46*, 77, 113, 147–8
Dominica 129
feeding *62*, *101*, *103*, 105, 147–8, 158, *191*, 192
flippers *4*
Gulf of Maine 101, 105
Hawaii *64*, 197–205
Mexico 143
migration 58, 114, 189
Monterey Bay 156, 158
photographing 43
Puerto Rico 130, 135
St. Lawrence River 84, 89
Santa Barbara 146–7
skeletons 112, 203
social behavior 62, 63–4, 65, 67, 114
song 63–4, 70, 105, 135, 190–2, 198–9
sounds 72, 73, 190
spout 42, 190
spyhopping *98*, *160*
tail 43, *80–1*, *93*, *111*, 112, 113–14, 190
tubercles *94*
hunting behavior 62–3, 73, 124
hunting by man *see also* **whaling**
hydrophones *68*, 69, *70*, 72–3

I

identification 42, *93*, 177–9
Inside Passage, AK 189
intelligence 55–8, 67, 122
interaction with humans 75–9, 137–41; *see also* **swimming with dolphins**
International Dolphin Watch 79
International Whaling Commission 36, 53, 180, 192
Inuit 180

Isle au Haut, ME 107
Israel *79*

J

Japanese whaling 36–8
John Pennekamp Coral Reef State Park, FL 127
Johnstone Strait, BC *178*, 181
Jonah and the Whale 26, *27*
Juan de Fuca, Strait of, WA *166*, 175, 179, 182
Juneau, AK *5*, 188, 189

K

Kachemak Bay, AK 193, 195
Kalaloch, WA 169
Kauai, HI 205
kayaking *44*, 45–6, 160, 163, 175, *176*, 181, 185, 189, 195
Keiko *36*, 67, *170*, 171
Kenai Fjords National Park, AK 187, *190*
Kenai Peninsula, AK 193, 195
Kennebunkport, ME 101
killer whales *see also* **orcas**
krill *148*

L

Labrador Current 92
Lahaina, HI 197, *203*
language 55–8
laptop computers 47
La Push, WA 173
Larsen, Dotte 79
legends 25–7, 76–7, 123, 201
L'île-Bonaventure-et-du-Rocher-Percé Provincial Park, QC 89
Lilly, John 27, 55–6, 57
Lime Kiln State Park, WA 176, *182*
Linnaeus, Carl 51–2
lobtailing 43, 67
Long Island whaling 29
loons 109
Lunenburg, NS 97

M

Maalaea, HI 197
Magdalena Bay, Baja California 138, 143
magnetic field 58, 66
mahi-mahi 53
Maine, Gulf of 90–2, 98–107
Makah Indians 20, 79, *166, 168,* 173, *180*
Mammalodon 52
manatees *123*
Marine Mammal Stranding Network 39, 66
Martha's Vineyard, MA *114,* 117
Martinique 134
Massachusetts 29, 32, *108, 109–17*
mating 63–5
matriarchal society 65–6
Maui, HI 196–205, *199, 200, 203*
melon-headed whales 129, 133, *200,* 201
Melville, Herman 6–7, 30, *31,* 51, 113, 197, 198
Mendocino, CA 163
Mexico 36, 77–8, 136–43
migration 58, 92, 114, 127, 189; *see also* **gray whales**
Mingan Archipelago National Park Reserve, QC 89
minke whales 52, *70, 115*
Alaska 192, 195
Atlantic Provinces 93, 95
Cape Cod 109
Gulf of Maine 104–5
Monterey Bay 160
Quebec 84, 89
Moby Dick 30, *31,* 198
monsters *24,* 25–7
Monterey Bay, CA 154–63, *158, 161*
moray eels *198*
motherhood 65–6, 124, 148; *see also* **gray whales**
Mount Desert Island, ME 99, 101–5, *101*

museums 36, 97, 117, 153, 171, 176, 185
Dominica 135
Hawaii 202–3, 205
whaling 29, 32, *112,* 202–3
Mysticeti 52–3, 62, 63–4, 72
myths 25–7, 76–7, 123, 201

N

Nantucket, MA 19, 32, 33, 110, *113,* 117
narwhals 53, 95
Native Alaskans 193, 195
Native Americans 20, *26,* 29, 79, 110, *141, 166, 168,* 173, *180*
Neah Bay, WA *168,* 173
netting *37,* 38, 150
New Age beliefs 27, 79
New Bedford, MA 30, 31, 33, *112,* 197
New Brunswick 91–3
New England 29–33, 109–15
Newfoundland *90,* 94–5, 97
Newport, OR *169, 170*
New Zealand *38, 77,* 115
Norway 36
Nova Scotia *92,* 93–4, 97

O

Oahu, HI *20,* 205
Oceanic Society 39, 135, 143, 163, 195, 204–5
Odontoceti *52,* 53, 57, 61–2, 66
Ogunquit, ME 101
Ojo de Liebre, Baja California 143
Olympic National Park, WA *168, 171,* 173
orcas *5, 26, 36,* 53, *56, 166, 174,* 177–9, *178, 183*
Alaska *5,* 192, 195
breaching *176, 181*
breeding 178
British Columbia *46, 72,* 175–85
Cape Cod 109
Dominica 129

dorsal fin *189*
echolocation 73
feeding 149–50
hunting *63, 73,* 146, 149–50, 155, 159–60, 178–9, *179*
photographing 43
photo-identification 177–9
pods 62, 64–5, *166,* 177–9, *192*
pygmy 201
Santa Barbara 149–50
skull *52*
social behavior 61–2, 64–5, 177–9
sounds 72, 179–80
spout 42, 175
spyhopping *77, 182*
transient 149–50, 178–80
Washington State *20,* 175–85
Oregon *164,* 165–73, *168*
Oregon Coast Aquarium *36,* 171

P

Pacific Rim National Park, AK 182, 185
Pacific Whale Foundation 45, 198, 203
Passamaquoddy Bay, ME 92
Pelorus Jack 77
Penobscot Bay, ME *104,* 107
Percé, QC 89
Peru 37
pesticides 39, 87
Petersburg, AK 188, 189
petroglyphs *20, 166*
phalaropes 109
photography 43
photo-identification *93,* 177–9
pictographs *20, 141*
pilot whales 53, 111
Atlantic Provinces 95, 97
calves 65–6
Cape Cod 111, 115
Dominica 129
Hawaii 201
long-finned *38, 66, 115*
mass strandings 66, 115
Monterey Bay 160

St. Vincent 135
short-finned *203*
social behavior 61, 65–6, 67, 115
plankton 110
Pliny the Elder 25–6, 76–7, 123
Point Adolphus, AK 190
Pointe-Noir, QC 86
Point Reyes National Seashore, CA *159*, 163
pollution 38–9, 87, 123–4, 150
porpoises *37*, 52, 53, 72, 90, 109, 160, 165, 192
Dall's 37, 151, 160, 192
Mexico (vaquita) 143
Portland, ME 101
Prince William Sound, AK 187, 195
Provincetown, MA *108*, 109–11
Puerto Peñasco, Mexico 143
Puerto Rico 134, 135
puffins 89, *95*, 171, 193
Puget Sound, WA *174*, *176*, *178*, *182*

Q – R

Quebec 82–9
Quileute Indians 173
record-keeping 46–7
remoras 129
right whales 36, 38, 91–5, 115
Atlantic Provinces 91–5
Atlantic species 36, 38
callosities 91, 105, 114–15
Cape Cod 109, 114–15
feeding 92
Florida 127
Gulf of Maine 101, 105, 107
migration 58, 92, 127
northern *104*
Pacific species 114
social behavior 62
sounds 72
southern *65*
spout 105, 114
Rivière-du-Loup, QC 85

Robson Bight Provincial Park, BC 185
Roosevelt Campobello International Park 107
rorquals 52

S

Saanich Peninsula, BC 185
Saguenay River, QC *85*, 86
St. Andrews, New Brunswick 93
Saint Brendan 27
St. John's, Nfld 94–5
St. Lawrence River, QC 82–9, *82*
Saint-Siméon, QC 85
St. Vincent and the Grenadines 135
salmon 171, 182, 193, 195
Samana Bay, Dominican Republic *71*, 129
San Diego, CA 153
San Francisco, CA 157, 159
San Ignacio Lagoon, Baja California *40*, *68*, 77–8, 136–43, *137*
San Juan Islands, WA 175, 176, *181*
Santa Barbara, CA 144–53, *149*
Sarasota, FL 127
Scammon, Charles 143, 179
Scammon's Lagoon, Baja California 143
scrimshaw *103*, 112
sea cows *123*
sea lions *63*, 156, 166, 193, 195
California 151, 160–1, 182
Steller's 151, 182
seals 109, 151, 173, 182, *193*
elephant *140*, 151, *159*, 161, 163
sea otters 156, 160, 193, 195
seasickness 42–3, 167
sea turtles 109, *198*, 202, 205
sei whales 52, 58, 93, 95, 109, 129
Seward, AK 188

Seward Highway, AK 193
shows 36
Sidney, BC 176
sign language 56
Silver Bank Marine Sanctuary, Dominican Republic 129–30, 135
Sitka, AK 188, 195
Skagway, AK 189
skeletons 112, 171
social behavior 61–7, 114, 115, 124, 130–1, 177–9
song 63–4, 69–73, 105, 135, 190–2, 198–9
Sooke, BC 176
sounds 55–6, 69–73, 87, 148–9, 179–80, 190; *see also* **song**
South Africa 105
Southern Ocean 35–6
species 51–3
sperm whales *6–7*, *28*, 52, 53, *58*, *131*, *201*
Atlantic Provinces 95
breeding 66, 67
bulls 67, 131–2
Cape Cod 109, 111, 112
disorientation 66
diving 131, 132
Dominica 128–32
dwarf 53, 129
echolocation 66, 73
feeding 130–1
Hawaii 201–2, *201*
migration 58
oil 111
pygmy 53, 129, 135
St. Vincent 135
social behavior 61–2, 66, 130–1
spermaceti 29, 111, 132
spout *45*
tail *30*, *32*
spouts 42, *45*, 105, 114, 148, 165, 170, 175, 190
spyhopping 77, *98*, *141*, *160*, 171, *182*
squid 38, *132*, 156, *160*, 202
Stellwagen Bank, MA 108–17

storm petrels 95, 109, 160
strandings *26, 34, 38,* 39,
   66, 79, 201
sunburn 44
sunglasses 41
swimming with dolphins
   14–15, 18, 75–6, *77,* 79,
   121–3, *125,* 127

T

Tadoussac, QC 84
tails *30, 32,* 43, 67, *80–1,*
   111, 112, 113–14, *139,* 190
Tampa Bay, FL 123, 127
Telegraph Cove, BC 181, 185
therapy 79, 123
toothed whales *see also*
   Odontoceti
toothless whales *see also*
   Mysticeti
tours 44–6; *see also Travel*
   Tips sections
toxic chemicals 38–9, 87
tubercles *94*
tuna netting 38
Turnagain Arm, AK 193, 195

U – V

underwater recording 69,
   71, 72–3, 179–80
Valdez, AK 188, 195
Vancouver Aquarium, BC
   72, 179–80
Vancouver Island, BC 175,
   176, 178, 180–2, 185
vaquita 143
Ventura, CA 153
Victoria, BC 176, 180–1, 185
video recording 47
vocalization 56, 73, 179–80;
   see also **sounds**
volcanoes 205
volunteering 39, *45,* 46

W – Y

Wampanoag Indians 110
Washington State 164–85;
   see also **Makah Indians**
West Indies 128–35
Westport, WA 167, 171
whalebone 33, 52, 112
art 103, 112
Whale Link 73

whale oil *33,* 111
whale species 51–3
whale watching
equipment 41–7
flights 95, 167–8
land-based 153, 159, 163,
   168–71, 176, 182, 190,
   192
safety at sea 44–6
whale woman (Omorka)
   25
whaling 29–33, 36, 111,
   185, 197–8, 201, 202
art *28, 31, 32,* 112
European 36, 91–2, 101
modern 35–8, 192
museums 29, 32, *112,*
   202–3
subsistence 36, 79, 173,
   180
white whales *see also*
   belugas
Whittier, AK 195
Willamette Valley, OR 168
Witless Bay, Nfld 95
Yachats, OR 171